INTRODUCTION TO ACCOUNTING

Certificate in Accounting

including Award in Bookkeeping

Award in Computerised Accounting

Award in Accounting (AAT Access)

Qualifications and Credit Fra

AAT Level 1 Certificate in

British Library Cataloguing-in-Publication Data

A catalogue record for this book is available from the British Library.

Published by
Kaplan Publishing UK
Unit 2, The Business Centre
Molly Millars Lane
Wokingham
Berkshire
RG41 2QZ

ISBN 978 1 78415 639 8

Kaplan Publishing would like to thank Deborah Seed and Julie Hodgskin for their contributions towards the production of this publication.

CONTENTS

CERTIFICATE IN ACCOUNTING STUDY TEXT

Access Award in Accounting / Award in Bookkeeping / Award in Computerised Accounting

Access Award in Accounting

Award in Bookkeeping

Award in Computerised Accounting

This book has been designed for use across all of the AAT Level 1 qualifications. Therefore, you may not require content from the entire book to pass the assessments you will be sitting.

If you are studying the Level 1 Certificate in Accounting, all of this book will be relevant.

If you are studying one of the individual awards within the Certificate, we would advise the following chapters are utilised:

- Award in Accounting (AAT Access) – Chapters 1-8 plus Mock Assessment

- Award in Bookkeeping – Chapters 1-5, 9-13, 21-22 plus Mock Assessment

- Award in Computerised Accounting – Chapters 1-5 for background information but not directly assessed, 14-18, 21-22 plus Mock Assessment

INTRODUCTION

HOW TO USE THESE MATERIALS

These Kaplan Publishing learning materials have been carefully designed to make your learning experience as easy as possible and to give you the best chance of success in your AAT assessments.

They contain a number of features to help you in the study process.

The sections on the Unit Guide, the Assessment and Study Skills should be read before you commence your studies.

They are designed to familiarise you with the nature and content of the assessment and to give you tips on how best to approach your studies.

ICONS

The study chapters include the following icons throughout.

They are designed to assist you in your studies by identifying key definitions and the points at which you can test yourself on the knowledge gained.

 Definition

These sections explain important areas of Knowledge which must be understood and reproduced in an assessment

 Example

The illustrative examples can be used to help develop an understanding of topics before attempting the activity exercises

 Activity

These are exercises which give the opportunity to assess your understanding of all the assessment areas.

UNIT GUIDE

Level 1 Certificate in Accounting

Introduction

The Level 1 Certificate in Accounting consists of eleven units and five assessments.

The qualification has been designed to help target the issues of the lack of literacy, numeracy and employability skills in the UK and aims to increase the availability of employment-ready candidates amongst long-term unemployed young people.

Overview

Unit title	QCF Credit	Assessment Method	Assessment Name	Units in other qualifications
Creating business documents	3	Computer based test	Access	Level 1 Access Award in Accounting
Mathematics for accounting	1			Level 1 Access Award in Accounting
Essential Accounting Procedures	3			Level 1 Access Award in Accounting
Accounting in a Professional Environment	2			Level 1 Access Award in Accounting
Introduction to bookkeeping	1	Computer based test	Bookkeeping and accounts	Level 1 Award in Bookkeeping
Working within bookkeeping	2			Level 1 Award in Bookkeeping
Bookkeeping and accounts	3			Level 1 Award in Bookkeeping
Computerised Payroll Administration	4	Computer based project	Computerised payroll processing and administration	N/A
Payroll processing	2			N/A
Computerised Accounts	3	Computer based project	Computerised Accounts	Level 1 Award in Computerised Accounting
Spreadsheet Software	3	Computer based project	Spreadsheet software	Level 1 Award in Bookkeeping and Level 1 Award in Computerised Accounting

KAPLAN PUBLISHING

This qualification builds upon the Access qualification, introducing units covering bookkeeping, payroll and computerised accounts to provide an all-round introduction to accounting for students.

The Level 1 Certificate in Accounting can be divided into four sections:

- Level 1 Award in Accounting (AAT Access) units
- Level 1 Award in Bookkeeping units
- Level 1 Award in Computerised Accounting units
- Payroll units specific to the AAT Level 1 Certificate in Accounting

These qualifications can be studied separately as well as part of the Certificate in Accounting.

This book has been designed for use across all of the AAT Level 1 qualifications. Therefore, you may not require content from the entire book to pass the assessments you will be sitting.

If you are studying the Level 1 Certificate in Accounting, all of this book will be relevant.

If you are studying one of the individual awards within the Certificate, we would advise the following chapters are utilised:

- Award in Accounting (AAT Access) – Chapters 1-8 plus Mock Assessment
- Award in Bookkeeping – Chapters 1-5, 9-13 and 21 plus Mock Assessment
- Award in Computerised Accounting – Chapters 1-5 for background information but not directly assessed, 14-18 and 21 plus Mock Assessment

Learning Outcomes and Assessment Criteria – Level 1 Award in Accounting (AAT Access) units

Level 1 Award in Accounting Overview

The Access Award is designed to introduce students to the world of business and finance and enable them to become familiar with finance language and standard business practices.

The assessment allows learners to perform a series of short tasks that cover basic business Maths and English, communication skills and knowledge of the accounting environment and related procedures.

The assessment is a computer based test, one and a half hours (90 minutes) in duration. It consists of 22 tasks – 12 in section one and 10 in section two. The learner must prove competence in each section to be successful.

Assessment criteria for the four individual units in the AAT Access Award are as follows:

Essential accounting procedures (Chapters 1, 2, 3, 4 and 5)
Students will understand and apply basic accounting terminology and procedures.

1. Understand basic accounting terminology
1.1 Explain the terms assets, liabilities, income and expenditure
1.2 Identify examples of assets, liabilities, income and expenditure
1.3 Explain the terminology associated with the sale and purchase of goods for cash and on credit
1.4 Identify examples of cash transactions and credit transactions
1.5 Explain the terms profit and loss

2. Understand the use of business documents
2.1 Identify documents used in the process of buying and selling goods on credit and when they are used
2.2 Identify documents used to process cash sales and cash purchases

3. Prepare to record business transactions in the books of prime entry
3.1 Select appropriate documents to record transactions in the books of prime entry
3.2 Select the appropriate book of prime entry to record transactions relating to credit sales and credit purchases
3.3 Select the appropriate book of prime entry to record payments made and monies received

4. Understand types of coding and batch control
4.1 Identify types of codes used when recording financial transactions
4.2 Explain what is meant by a batch control system

5. Be able to prepare documents to process receipts and payments
5.1 Complete a bank paying-in slip for notes, coins and cheques
5.2 Complete a cheque

6. Be able to prepare a basic profit statement
6.1 Calculate gross profit
6.2 Calculate net profit

Accounting in a professional environment (Chapters 5 and 6)
Students will be able to understand the role of a finance professional in any organisation and apply ethical behaviour and professionalism within an accounting environment.

1. Understand basic organisations and how the finance professional contributes to the organisation
1.1 Identify different types of business organisation
1.2 Identify the "customers" of the accounting function
1.3 Explain how the accounting function can support an organisation

2. Understand the need to apply appropriate ethical behaviour and professionalism within an accounting environment
2.1 Explain how to maintain confidentiality of information
2.2 Explain the importance of ethical and professional behaviour to the role of those in the accounting function
2.3 Identify the importance of an organisation adopting environmentally and socially responsible policies

3. Understand that there is a legal framework within which organisations must operate

3.1 Identify the responsibility an organisation has to the health and safety of its employees and of visitors to its premises

3.2 Explain the role of an employee in the accounting function in maintaining safe and effective working practices

3.3 Identify how an employee in the accounting function can ensure that personal information is protected and not disclosed without authority

4. Understand how efficient working practices and personal development contribute to achievement

4.1 Identify efficient working practices which contribute to the achievement of own and team goals

4.2 Explain how communication within the team contributes to its overall efficiency

4.3 Identify the personal skills required to work in the accounting function

4.4 Identify ways in which new skills and knowledge can be acquired

4.5 Explain how the acquisition of new skills can be agreed and subsequently reviewed with the line manager

Creating business documents (Chapter 7)

Students will be able to use to a range of business documents used within the accounting function and other areas of a business.

1. Know that there are different types of business document

1.1 Identify different types of business document and when they might be used

1.2 State why templates are used for some business documents

2. Know why it is important to use the right communication style in business documents

2.1 State why some businesses adopt a 'house style' for certain documents

2.2 Give examples of when to use a formal or informal communication style

3. Be able to produce routine business documents

3.1 Produce routine business documents using the appropriate communication style

3.2 Check documents for accuracy

Mathematics for accounting (Chapter 8)

Students should be able to perform a range of basic mathematical functions using financial data.

1. Be able to apply basic mathematical concepts to financial data

1.1 Add and subtract whole numbers and numbers up to two decimal places

1.2 Multiply and divide whole numbers and numbers up to two decimal places

1.3 Calculate the ratio or proportion of two numbers

1.4 Calculate the percentage of one number in relation to another number

1.5 Find a percentage of a whole number

1.6 Apply a fraction to whole numbers

1.7 Calculate the average of a range of numbers

Learning Outcomes and Assessment Criteria - Level 1 Award in Bookkeeping units

Level 1 Award in Bookkeeping

Bookkeeping and accounts (BKAC) enables students to understand the role of a bookkeeper and accounting terminology and to be able to process transactions through the accounting system and produce a simple trial balance.

This two hour assessment consists of 13 tasks in one section. Students will normally be assessed by computer-based assessment and will be required to respond to CBT tasks in a variety of ways, for example using multiple choice, true/false, drag and drop, pick lists, text select, linking boxes, gap fill tools and AAT purpose built question types to reflect real workplace activities.

The assessment criteria for the three individual units are as follows:

Introduction to bookkeeping (Chapters 1, 2, 5 and 9)

The aim of this unit is to enable students' understanding of the basic role of bookkeeping within different types of organisations, and to know and understand the basic terminology used in bookkeeping.

1.   Understand the job role and career path for a bookkeeper

1.1   Outline the job role of a bookkeeper

1.2   Outline how the role of the bookkeeper fits within the business organisation

1.3   Outline how bookkeeping can become a career pathway

2.   Understand different types of business organisations

2.1   Give examples of different types of business organisation

2.2   Define the organisations known as:

- sole trader
- partnership

3.   Know the terminology used in bookkeeping

3.1   Identify the difference between a bookkeeper and an accountant

3.2   Explain the correct use of two of the following (minimum) bookkeeping terms: petty cash imprest system; sales; purchase; customer; supplier; receipt; payment; income; expenditure

3.3   State how two (minimum) of the following bookkeeping documents are used: petty cash voucher; purchase order; invoice; credit note; statement of account

Working within bookkeeping (Chapters 1, 2, 3, 5 and 9)

The aim of this unit is to provide the student with knowledge of the general principles of single entry bookkeeping, VAT, cash and credit transactions, different systems and processing information, and in general the roles and responsibilities of individuals working in bookkeeping.

1.   Understand single-entry bookkeeping

1.1   Explain single entry bookkeeping

1.2   Outline the books used in single entry bookkeeping

2.   Know the general principles of VAT

2.1   State when a business must register for VAT

2.2   State the various rates of VAT in general use:

- reduced rate
- standard rate
- exempt
- zero rate

3.   Understand what is meant by both cash and credit transactions

3.1   Explain what is meant by cash sales

3.2   Explain what is meant by cash purchase

3.3   Explain what is meant by trading on credit

3.4   Identify the various documents needed to record a credit sale or purchase

4.   Understand the principles of coding and batch control

4.1   Explain why a coding system is used for financial transactions

4.2   Outline the use of batch control

5.   Understand how to process information in the books of prime entry (excluding the Journal)

5.1   State where to find financial information for entry into the bookkeeping system

5.2   State where to enter relevant information in the books of prime entry (excluding the journal)

5.3   Outline the need to cross check totals for accuracy

6.   Understand responsibilities when working in a bookkeeping environment

6.1   Outline the responsibilities relating to security of data when dealing with customers, suppliers and other external agencies

6.2   Identify where to gain authorisation for expenditure and when dealing with queries related to various financial transactions

Bookkeeping and accounts (Chapters 1, 3, 9, 10, 11, 12 and 13)

The aim of this unit is to test the student's ability to undertake basic bookkeeping practices and to process source documents that underpin accurate record keeping.

1.   Know how to complete financial documents.

1.1   State the purpose and identify the content of financial documents

1.2   Calculate sales tax, trade discount, settlement (cash) discount, price, price extension on invoices and credit notes

1.3   Complete financial documents

1.4   Check the accuracy of financial documents

2. Be able to record cash and credit transactions in books of original entry.

2.1 Enter invoices and credit notes into the appropriate day books

2.2 Transfer the total(s) of the day book(s) to the respective ledger account(s)

2.3 Post individual transactions from the day books to personal ledger accounts

2.4 Record cash book transactions and credit transactions using double-entry bookkeeping

3. Be able to prepare bank reconciliation.

3.1 Update a cash book (bank balance) using details from a bank statement

3.2 Recalculate the closing bank balance

3.3 Prepare a bank reconciliation statement using appropriate information

4. Be able to understand the petty cash imprest system.

4.1 Enter the opening balance in the petty cash book

4.2 Analyse petty cash vouchers to appropriate analysis columns

4.3 Balance and cross tally the petty cash book totals and analysis columns

4.4 Transfer totals to ledger accounts as appropriate

4.5 Restore the imprest

5. Be able to extract a trial balance from ledger accounts.

5.1 Balance ledger accounts

5.2 Bring down account balances to the following accounting period

5.3 Extract the trial balance from the ledger and cash book

Learning Outcomes and Assessment Criteria - Level 1 Award in Computerised Accounting units

Level 1 Award in Computerised Accounting

Computerised accounting systems are widely used in business and other organisations. This unit introduces students to the fundamental principles required to use a computerised accounting system.

Assessment of this unit is via a computer based project. The assessment The assessment will be one and a half hours (90 minutes) and will be based on a business organisation. It will be comprised of a series of tasks that ask the student to input data into a computerised accounting system and produce reports, allowing the student to demonstrate the skills and knowledge necessary to use computerised accounting software at Level 1. The assessment has not been designed for use with any one particular accounting software package. Assessment criteria for this unit is as follows:

Computerised accounts (Chapters 14, 15, 16, 17 and 18)

The aim of this unit is to enable students to operate computerised accounts software to carry out routine accounting tasks. These tasks include being able to create accounts, process accounting information in respect of the sales and purchase ledger, understanding how to use batch control sheets and being able to produce accounting reports such as trial balance, customer activity reports and supplier details reports.

1. Create accounts using computerised accounts software

1.1 Add new accounts to the purchase ledger

1.2 Add new accounts to the sales ledger

1.3 Create new accounts in the nominal ledger

2. Process accounting information using computerised software

2.1 Process information in respect of the sales ledger

2.2 Process information in respect of the purchase ledger

2.3 Enter initial capital

2.4 Process information involving transactions using different tax rates

2.5 Process information in respect of cash and cheque payments and receipts

3. Understand how to use batch control sheets

3.1 Calculate batch totals as required

3.2 Reconcile batch totals as required

4. Produce reports using computerised software

4.1 Produce a trial balance

4.2 Produce supplier activity reports

4.3 Produce customer activity reports

4.4 Produce supplier details reports

4.5 Produce customer details reports

4.6 Produce nominal ledger account reports

Learning Outcomes and Assessment Criteria - Level 1 Computerised payroll processing and administration units

Level 1 Certificate in Accounting – Payroll units

Accurately processing payroll is important for business organisations.

The aim of the **Computerised Payroll Administration and Payroll Processing (CPYA)** units is to enable students to know how to set up and use a computerised payroll system, provide the student with knowledge on calculating income tax and national insurance contributions and use tax codes and HMRC approved tools.

The units cover the fundamental skills required to accurately record and process basic payroll information in to a computerised payroll system for any business.

The practical nature of these units will help students develop skills that are valued in the workplace and will make students attractive to employers.

The two payroll units are assessed through a two hour computer based project that will consist of processing a payroll using HMRC approved software. The assessment criteria are as follows:

Computerised payroll administration (Chapter 19)

The aim of this unit is for students to set up and use a computerised payroll system by entering and processing various types of employee data, using various data sources, in a timely and accurate manner and within the requirements of specific company policy and statutory legislation.

1. Be able to set up a computerised payroll system

1.1 Enter company data and legislative parameters into commercial payroll software in accordance with company policy

1.2 Maintain the company data and legislative parameters in accordance with company policy

2. Be able to set up employee records and payroll data in a computerised payroll system

2.1 Create employee records within the payroll software from given information for example, HR information, contract of employment, P45

2.2 Maintain up to date employees' payroll records ensuring that all changes have been correctly authorised by the employee, employer or statutory body, including income tax codes changes, rates of pay etc.

2.3 Produce a range of reports relating to the employee's personal details, pay and deductions

3. Be able to enter details of gross pay into the computerised payroll system

3.1 Enter elements of basic gross pay for weekly and monthly paid employees from given information for example, timesheets, summaries, salary information, hourly rates

3.2 Enter overtime details from given information

3.3 Enter basic holiday pay as a separate gross pay element

4. Be able to process the payroll

4.1 Process gross pay in accordance with company policy and legislative requirements

4.2 Process the final pay period for a leaver

4.3 Produce internal period end reports including payslips and payroll summaries

4.4 Complete the processing of the payroll for the period

4.5 Prepare payroll data in a format suitable for submission to the relevant tax authority

4.6 Produce Form P45 or equivalent leaving statement, for a leaver

5. Be able to back up and/or restore payroll data

5.1 Understand the importance and need for backing up the payroll data at regular intervals

5.2 Back-up and restore payroll data

6. Understand statutory requirements for submitting information

6.1 Explain the importance of the processing date in relation to preparing and submitting the payroll data

6.2 Identify the minimum employee data required in order to process the payroll

6.3 Outline the procedure for submitting the payroll data at each pay period

Payroll processing (Chapter 20)

This unit aims to provide the student with knowledge on calculating income tax and national insurance contributions, use tax codes and HMRC approved tools, understand and provide information on the basic components of payroll and the methods of making payments to employees.

1.   Be able to determine Income tax to be deducted from gross pay

1.1   Calculate income tax using HMRC approved tools:

- standard suffix codes operated on a cumulative or non-cumulative basis
- BR code operated on a cumulative basis

1.2   Process changes to employees tax codes

2.   Be able to determine National Insurance Contributions to be deducted from gross pay

2.1   Calculate NIC using HMRC approved Tools for Categories A and C

- employee NI contributions
- employer NI Contributions

3.   Be able to reconcile the payroll and make payments to employees

3.1   Produce a payroll summary to itemise payments and deductions, including Income Tax, employee's NIC and employer's NIC, in accordance with the tax authority and organisational requirements

3.2   Produce payslips to detail statutory and organisational information regarding employees' individual pay.

3.3   Prepare payments to employees using cash analysis, cheque preparation or BACs payments

Learning Outcomes and Assessment Criteria – Level 1 Spreadsheet Software unit

Spreadsheet software (Chapters 21 and 22)

The aim of this unit is to enable students to understand the uses of a spreadsheet and populate a spreadsheet with a variety of different data. It also focuses on the use of formulas to provide information in a variety of formats, knowing how to use various approaches to present spreadsheet information accurately and effectively.

The time allowed for the computer based project assessment is 1 hour and 45 minutes. Learners should be able to construct a spreadsheet containing a minimum of five columns and seven rows of data and text, including headings. As most organisations now use spreadsheets, the skills tested will give learners the ability to use functions to produce professional-looking and meaningful spreadsheets.

Assessment criteria are as follows:

1.   Use a spreadsheet to enter, edit and organise numerical and other data

1.1   Identify what numerical and other information is needed and how the spreadsheet should be structured to meet needs

1.2   Enter and edit numerical and other data accurately

1.3   Store and retrieve spreadsheet files effectively, in line with local guidelines and conventions where available

2.   Use appropriate formulas and tools to summarise and display spreadsheet information

2.1   Identify how to summarise and display the required information

2.2   Use functions and formulas to meet calculation requirements

2.3   Use spreadsheet tools and techniques to summarise and display information

3.   Select and use appropriate tools and techniques to present spreadsheet information effectively

3.1   Select and use appropriate tools and techniques to format spreadsheet cells, rows and columns

3.2   Identify which chart or graph type to use to display information

3.3   Select and use appropriate tools and techniques to generate, develop and format charts and graphs

3.4   Select and use appropriate page layout to present and print spreadsheet information

3.5   Check information meets needs, using spreadsheet tools and making corrections as necessary

Summary

Achievement at Level 1 reflects the ability to use relevant knowledge, skills and procedures to complete routine tasks. It includes responsibility for completing tasks and procedures subject to direction or guidance.

Knowledge and understanding

- Use knowledge of facts, procedures and ideas to complete well-defined, routine tasks.
- Be aware of information relevant to the area of study or work.

Application and action

- Complete well-defined routine tasks.
- Use relevant skills and procedures.
- Select and use relevant information.
- Identify whether actions have been effective.

Autonomy and accountability

Take responsibility for completing tasks and procedures subject to direction or guidance as needed.

STUDY SKILLS

Preparing to study

Devise a study plan

Determine which times of the week you will study.

Split these times into sessions of at least one hour for study of new material. Any shorter periods could be used for revision or practice.

Put the times you plan to study onto a study plan for the weeks from now until the assessment and set yourself targets for each period of study – in your sessions make sure you cover the whole course, activities and the associated questions with answers at the back of the Study Text.

When working through your course, compare your progress with your plan and, if necessary, re-plan your work (perhaps including extra sessions) or, if you are ahead, do some extra revision/practice questions.

Effective studying

Active reading

You are not expected to learn the text by rote, rather, you must understand what you are reading and be able to use it to pass the assessment and develop good practice.

A good technique is to use SQ3Rs – Survey, Question, Read, Recall, Review:

1 **Survey the chapter**

    Look at the headings and read the introduction, knowledge, skills and content, so as to get an overview of what the chapter deals with.

2 **Question**

    Whilst undertaking the survey ask yourself the questions you hope the chapter will answer for you.

3 **Read**

    Read through the chapter thoroughly working through the activities and, at the end, making sure that you can meet the learning objectives shown within the summary.

4 **Recall**

    At the end of each chapter, try to recall the main ideas of the section/chapter without referring to the text. This is best done after short break of a couple of minutes after the reading stage.

5 **Review**

    Check that your recall notes are correct.

You may also find it helpful to re-read the chapter to try and see the topic(s) it deals with as a whole.

Note taking

Taking notes is a useful way of learning, but do not simply copy out the text. The notes must:

- be in your own words
- be concise
- cover the key points
- be well organised
- be modified as you study further chapters in this text or in related ones.

Trying to summarise a chapter without referring to the text can be a useful way of determining which areas you know and which you don't.

Three ways of taking notes

1   **Summarise the key points of a chapter**

2   **Make linear notes**

A list of headings, subdivided with sub-headings listing the key points.

If you use linear notes, you can use different colours to highlight key points and keep topic areas together.

Use plenty of space to make your notes easy to use.

3   **Try a diagrammatic form**

The most common of which is a mind map.

To make a mind map, put the main heading in the centre of the paper and put a circle around it.

Draw lines radiating from this to the main sub-headings which again have circles around them.

Continue the process from the sub-headings to sub-sub-headings.

Highlighting and underlining

You may find it useful to underline or highlight key points in your study text – but do be selective.

You may also wish to make notes in the margins.

Further reading

In addition to this text, you should also read the 'Student section' of the 'Accounting Technician' magazine every month to keep abreast of any guidance from the examiners.

Essential accounting terminology

1

Introduction

The purpose of accounting is to be able to provide financial information about an organisation. For example, managers will want to keep track of the profit made by the organisation in a certain period, and they will also want to see how much the organisation is worth at a specific point in time.

To be able to provide this information it is important that the business transactions of the organisation are recorded and summarised into accounting records.

This chapter will introduce you to the accounting terminology used to record these business transactions.

KNOWLEDGE

Award in Accounting

1.1 Explain the terms assets, liabilities, income and expenditure

1.2 Identify examples of assets, liabilities, income and expenditure

1.3 Explain the terminology associated with the sale and purchase of goods for cash and on credit

1.4 Identify examples of cash and credit transactions

1.5 Explain the terms profit and loss

6.1 Calculate gross profit

6.2 Calculate net profit

Award in Bookkeeping

3 Know the terminology used in bookkeeping (ITB)

3 Understand what is meant by both cash and credit transactions (WWB)

CONTENTS

1 Assets
2 Liabilities
3 Income and expenditure
4 Cash and credit transactions
5 Profit and loss
6 Summary and further questions

1 Assets

1.1 What is an asset?

Assets are items of value which an organisation owns in order to generate profit by selling goods or providing a service.

1.2 Different types of asset

 Examples

Assets include:

Premises – organisations usually need a building from which to carry out their business. These premises could be an office building, a shop, or a factory.

Fixtures and fittings – these are items in the premises which are used to provide goods or services. For example, the computers in an office, the shelving in a shop, or machinery in a factory.

Vehicles – vehicles may be needed to deliver goods or provide a service to customers.

Stock – goods which are ready to sell to customers are kept in stock

Bank – the funds available in the organisation's bank account may be used to purchase more stock to sell.

Cash – some organisations keep money on the premises so that they can buy small items.

Debtors – amounts owed to the organisation by customers as a result of sales made on credit.

1.3 Definition

 Definition

An 'asset' is an item of value owned by an organisation.

2 Liabilities

2.1 What is a liability?

Liabilities are debts owed by the organisation. The money will usually have been used to buy assets for the organisation to use.

Total liabilities are deducted from total assets to calculate an organisation's worth at a specific period in time.

2.2 Different types of liability

 Examples

Liabilities include:

Creditors – amounts owed by the organisation to suppliers of goods and services.

Bank Overdraft – an arrangement that allows an organisation to take more money out of its bank than it has put in. The money is owed to the bank.

Bank Loan – a fixed amount of money an organisation borrows from the bank.

2.3 Definition

 Definition

A 'liability' is a debt owed by an organisation to other organisations, businesses and individuals.

3 Income and expenditure

3.1 Introduction

The purpose of most organisations is to make a profit or to raise funds so that they can continue supplying goods and services to customers. To calculate profit, **expenditure** is deducted from **income**.

3.2 What is income?

Any money received from the supply of goods and services to customers is known as income.

3.3 What is expenditure?

Any money paid for purchasing the goods and services and day to day expenses is known as expenditure.

🔍 Definitions

Income is the money received by an organisation from selling its goods and services.

Expenditure is the money paid by an organisation to purchase goods and services.

Activity 1

Which of the following items are assets, liabilities, income or expenditure? Put a tick in the correct box.

	Asset	Liability	Income	Expenditure
Creditors		✓		
Electricity bill				✓
Money in the bank	✓			
Bank overdraft		✓		
Sales to customers			✓	
Debtors	✓			
Office computers	✓			

KAPLAN PUBLISHING

4 Cash and Credit Transactions

4.1 Recording cash and credit transactions

Income is the amount of money received by an organisation from its sales. Sometimes this money is received immediately and sometimes the money is paid later. It is important that these cash and credit transactions are recorded separately so that the organisation knows how much money it is owed by customers, and how much it owes to suppliers.

4.2 Cash and credit sales

 Definitions

Sales is the exchange of goods or services to an individual or organisation in exchange for money.

A **customer** is an individual or organisation to whom the goods or services have been sold. The organisation supplying the goods or services will then receive money in exchange.

A **debtor** is a customer who has been sold goods on credit.

Cash Sales is the term used to describe a payment at point of sale. The payment itself can be made by cash (currency), cheque, debit or credit card, or bank transfer. An example of a cash sale is when you go into a shop, choose the items you want to buy, and pay for them immediately.

Credit Sales are sales made where the goods or services will be paid later than the point of sale. Many organisations give credit to their regular trade customers so that one payment can be made for all the transactions made in each month.

4.3 Cash and credit customers

With cash sales the organisation gets the money immediately from the customer and the relationship ends there. With credit customers, there is a risk to the organisation that the customer may not pay for the goods. Therefore, before allowing customers to pay on credit the organisation will make certain checks to ensure that the customer can pay.

It is assumed that the money owed by credit customers will be paid and therefore they are classed as debtors (assets) of the organisation.

4.4   Cash and credit purchases

 Definition

Purchases – to buy goods or services from an organisation in exchange for money.

Cash Purchases are when goods or services are paid for at the time of purchase.

A florist may purchase some stock and pay by 'cash'. Although the payment could be by cash (currency), credit card or debit card or bank transfer, if the payment is made immediately it is classed as a cash purchase.

Credit Purchases are when an organisation pays for the goods or services sometime after making the purchase. The money will be sent to the supplier after an agreed amount of time, for example, thirty days.

The supplier is now a creditor (liability) of the organisation.

 Definition

A **supplier** is an individual or organisation providing goods or services to another in exchange for money.

A **creditor** is a supplier who is owed money for goods purchased on credit.

4.5   The Cash Book and Petty Cash Book

The word 'cash' is also used in accounting as a name for recording monetary transactions.

A **Cash Book** is used to keep a record of most of the receipts and payments made by the organisation. The actual monies received and recorded may be by cash (currency), cheque, credit card or debit card, or bank transfer.

A **Petty Cash Book** is used to record the small amount of cash that most businesses hold in order to make small cash payments regularly. Petty cash systems and the management of petty cash are addressed further later in this book.

Activity 2

C Froome's Cycle World

Mr Froome has a small shop selling and repairing bicycles for individual customers.

He buys the spare parts that he needs from a large wholesaler.

Do you think that Mr Froome's income comes from cash sales or credit sales?

Do you think that the expenditure for spare parts is cash purchases or credit purchases?

5 Profit and loss

5.1 Profit and Loss

Organisations need to keep a careful record of their income from sales and their expenditure so that they can calculate if the company has made a profit or a loss.

Profit is the amount of money an organisation earns after expenditure has been deducted from income.

Loss is when an organisation has spent more money than it has earned from income.

5.2 Types of profit

There are two types of profit you will need to know about for this unit.

Gross profit is a very important figure. It can be used as a comparison to see how well the business is doing compared to other businesses, or if it is doing better or worse than in previous years.

To calculate gross profit, the cost of goods sold (purchases) is deducted from income.

Net profit is calculated by deducting all other expenses from gross profit. These other expenses could include wages, rent and rates and other property expenses, and costs for running vehicles. The net profit will show whether a company has covered all its expenses with the income that it has generated.

5.3 Gross profit and net profit calculations

> **INCOME**
>
> From Cash and Credit sales

less

> **COST OF SALES**
>
> The cost of purchasing the goods which have been sold

equals

> **GROSS**
>
> **PROFIT**

less

> **EXPENSES**
>
> Everyday running costs such as wages, lighting, heating, office expenses, etc.

equals

> **NET**
>
> **PROFIT or LOSS**

 Example 1

Your organisation has recorded all sales income and expenditure for the previous month. You have been asked to calculate the gross and net profit for the month.

	£
Sales income from cash and credit sales	125,000
Cost of sales	75,000
Wages	15,000
Premises expenses	3,000
Vehicle expenses	2,500

Solution:

To calculate **gross profit** the cost of sales are deducted from the sales income.

Sales income:	£125,000
– Cost of sales:	-£ 75,000
= Gross profit:	£ 50,000

To calculate **net profit** all other expenses are deducted from the gross profit.

First you will need to add up all the other expenses: wages, premises expenses, vehicle expenses to find total expenditure.

Wages:	£ 15,000
+ Premises expenses:	£ 3,000
+ Vehicle expenses:	£ 2,500
= Total expenditure:	£ 20,500

Then, you need to deduct the total expenditure from gross profit.

Gross Profit:	£ 50,000
-Total expenditure:	-£ 20,500
= Net Profit:	£ 29,500

 Example 2

For the previous month, a business has recorded income of £82,000. The cost of those sales was £66,000 and the other expenses were £25,000. Has the business made a profit or a loss?

Answer: *The business has made a gross profit of £16,000. However, after deducting the remaining expenses of £25,000, the business has made a Net Loss of £9,000.*

 Activity 3

Your organisation has recorded all sales income and expenditure for the previous month. You have been asked to calculate the gross and net profit for the month.

	£
Sales income from cash and credit sales	78,000
Cost of sales	50,700
Wages	7,500
Premises expenses	1,750
Vehicle expenses	2,000

a) Calculate the gross profit for the month

b) Calculate the net profit or loss for the month

Activity 4

An organisation has total income lower than costs of sales plus expenses. Has the organisation made a profit or a loss?

6 Summary and further questions

This chapter has introduced you to some important accounting terminology. You can distinguish between assets, liabilities, income and expenditure. You have also looked at the difference between credit sales and purchases and cash sales and purchases. Finally, the chapter looked at the two different types of profit that an organisation needs to consider.

The further practice questions below test your knowledge of this key terminology.

 Activity 5

Match the definition with the correct term.

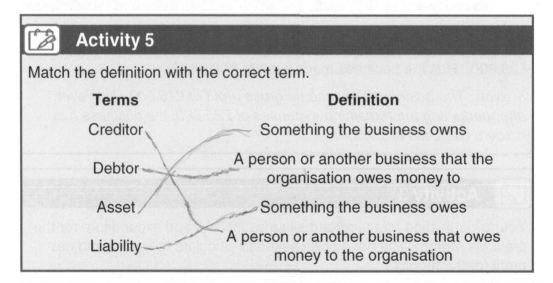

Terms	Definition
Creditor	Something the business owns
Debtor	A person or another business that the organisation owes money to
Asset	Something the business owes
Liability	A person or another business that owes money to the organisation

Activity 6

Fill in the gaps below to complete the sentences. Choose from the Pick list provided.

When an organisation pays for items of expenditure at the time of purchase this is known as a <u>cash purchase</u>

When an organisation allows a customer to pay the amount they owe at a later date this is known as a <u>credit purchase</u>

Pick List

credit sale   cash sale   cash purchase   credit purchase.

Activity 7

Choose the correct option in each of these statements

a. The sum of money spent in making sales is known as [sales/cost of sales]

b. If total income is greater than the cost of sales plus other expenses the organisation has made a [profit/loss]

c. If total income is less than the cost of sales plus other expenses the organisation has made a [profit/loss]

d. Sales income less cost of sales equals [gross profit/net profit]

 Activity 8

Which of the following items are cash or credit sales, or cash or credit purchases? Put a tick in the correct box.

	Cash Sale	Credit Sale	Cash Purchase	Credit Purchase
Goods bought from a supplier and paid for immediately.			✓	
Goods delivered to a customer who will pay at the end of the month.		✓		
Items bought from a supplier on credit.				✓
A payment received from a customer for goods purchased in the shop and paid for at the till.	✓			

Activity 9

Last year your organisation recorded income and expenditure in the table below

Income and Expenditure	£
Sales	156,000
Cost of Sales	93,600
Wages	21,060
Administration Expenses	18,720
Selling Expenses	12,844

Use the income and expenditure figures to complete the following calculations:

Calculate Gross Profit   £ 62,400

Calculate Net Profit   £ 9,776

 Activity 10

Last year your organisation recorded income and expenditure in the table below

Income and Expenditure	£
Sales	152,880
Cost of Sales	91,728
Wages	20,640
Administration Expenses	18,350
Selling Expenses	12,590

Use the income and expenditure figures to complete the following calculations:

Calculate Gross Profit   £ 61,152

Calculate Net Profit   £ 9,572

Answers to chapter activities

 ### Activity 1

	Asset	Liability	Income	Expenditure
Creditors		✓		
Electricity bill				✓
Money in the bank	✓			
Bank overdraft		✓		
Sales to customers			✓	
Debtors	✓			
Office computers	✓			

 ### Activity 2

Mr Froome's income is most likely to be from cash sales. His customers are individuals who will probably pay when they come to pick up their bicycles. They are unlikely to be very regular customers.

His expenditure for the spare parts is likely to be a credit purchase. As Mr Froome will buy regularly from the supplier he may have been given credit so that he can make daily or weekly purchases and then pay for all he owes at a later date.

 ### Activity 3

a) The gross profit for the month is £27,300 (£78,000 - £50,700)

b) The net profit for the month is £16,050 (£27,300 – (£7,500+£1,750+£2,000))

 ### Activity 4

As income is lower than cost of sales plus expenses, the business has made a loss.

Activity 5

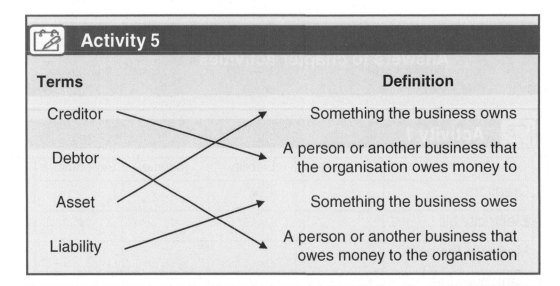

Terms	Definition
Creditor	Something the business owns
Debtor	A person or another business that the organisation owes money to
Asset	Something the business owes
Liability	A person or another business that owes money to the organisation

Activity 6

When an organisation pays for items of expenditure at the time of purchase this is known as a **cash purchase.**

When an organisation allows a customer to pay the amount they owe at a later date this is known as a **credit sale.**

Activity 7

a. The sum of money spent in making sales is known as [**cost of sales**]

b. If total income is greater than the cost of sales plus other expenses the organisation has made a [**profit**]

c. If total income is less than the cost of sales plus other expenses the organisation has made a [**loss**]

d. Sales income less cost of sales equals [**gross profit**]

KAPLAN PUBLISHING

Activity 8

Which of the following items are cash or credit sales, or cash or credit purchases? Put a tick in the correct box.

	Cash Sale	Credit Sale	Cash Purchase	Credit Purchase
Goods bought from a supplier and paid for immediately.			√	
Goods delivered to a customer who will pay at the end of the month.		√		
Items bought from a supplier on credit.				√
A payment received from a customer for goods purchased in the shop and paid for at the till.	√			

 Activity 9

Last year your organisation recorded income and expenditure in the table below

Income and Expenditure	£
Sales	156,000
Cost of Sales	93,600
Wages	21,060
Administration Expenses	18,720
Selling Expenses	12,844

Use the income and expenditure figures to complete the following calculations:

Calculate Gross Profit £ 62,400

Calculate Net Profit £ 9,776

Activity 10

Last year your organisation recorded income and expenditure in the table below

Income and Expenditure	£
Sales	152,880
Cost of Sales	91,728
Wages	20,640
Administration Expenses	18,350
Selling Expenses	12,590

Use the income and expenditure figures to complete the following calculations:

Calculate Gross Profit   £ | 61,152

Calculate Net Profit   £ | 9,572

Business documents for accounting transactions

Introduction

As we have already seen, it is important that customer and supplier transactions are recorded separately so that organisations know how much money they are owed by customers, and how much they owe to suppliers.

Business documents are used to record these transactions and the documents are exchanged between the supplier and the customer so that both parties have a record of each transaction. It is important that both the supplier and the customer keep a copy of each of these documents. Mistakes can happen and each document is proof of each stage of the transaction.

The name of a transaction or document will depend on whether we look at it from the point of view of the seller or the purchaser. Thus an invoice may be called a 'sales invoice' for the seller but a 'purchase invoice' for the purchaser, although it is the same document. Similarly, the same transaction is called a 'sale' by the supplier and a 'purchase' by the customer.

KNOWLEDGE

Award in Accounting

2.1 Identify documents used in the process of buying and selling goods on credit and when they are used

2.2 Identify documents used to process cash sales and cash purchases

4.1 Identify types of codes used when recording financial transactions

Award in Bookkeeping

1 Know how to complete financial documents (BAA)

2 Know the general principles of VAT (WWB)

4 Understand the principles of coding and batch control (WWB)

CONTENTS

1 Documents used to record credit transactions
2 Documents used to record cash transactions
3 Using codes
4 Summary

---

1 Documents used to record credit transactions

1.1 Introduction

This chapter reviews the main documents involved in the flow of business transactions.

1.2 Offering credit and price quotations

Most transactions between business organisations will be on credit terms and this involves an element of risk. The goods are being taken away or delivered to the customer now with the promise of payment in the future. Therefore, suppliers must be confident that payment will be received.

In some organisations it is common practice to quote prices to customers over the telephone particularly if there is a catalogue or price list from which there are no deviations in price. However, some businesses will be prepared to offer certain customers goods at different prices and discounts may be offered and/or given to customers. Therefore, it is often the case that a price quotation is sent to a customer showing the price at which the goods that they want can be bought. The customer can then decide whether or not to buy the goods at that price.

1.3 Purchase Order

If the customer is happy with the price quotation that they have received from the supplier then they will place a purchase order for the goods or services required.

This document will state the details of the goods required, including:

- the quantity and description of the goods
- the price and other terms
- the supplier's code number for the items
- the date the order was placed.

When the supplier receives a purchase order, it is important for them to check all of the details carefully as it forms part of the sales contract.

- Is the price that which was quoted to the customer?
- Are the delivery terms acceptable?
- Are any discounts applicable?

Example

PURCHASE ORDER

Belle's Wedding Planners
11 Mountjoy Street
LONDON W12 6RS
Tel: 0208 741 2962
Fax: 0208 741 2963
Date: 17 March 2012
Purchase order no: P01562

To:
Little Miss Muffin Cake Shop
1 Baker Street
London
WC1 8QT

Delivery address
(if different from above)
Four Hills Hotel
Park Lane
London
W1 1UY

Product	Ref	Quantity	Price per unit (excl. VAT) £	Total (excl. VAT) £
Chocolate Wedding Cake	CWC5	5 Tiers	60.00	300.00

Signed: *J Belle*
           Purchasing Manager

Notes:

a) The customer, Belle's Wedding Supplies has placed an order with the supplier of the cakes, Little Miss Muffin Cake Shop.

b) The purchase order clearly states that the customer wants to purchase 5 tiers of chocolate wedding cake at a price of £60.00 for each tier.

c) The total amount that the customer wants to pay for the cake is £300.00 (5 tiers x £60.00 = £300.00).

d) If Little Miss Muffin Cake Shop does not agree with any of these details they will need to contact Belle's Wedding Supplies immediately. The purchase order has been signed by J Belle, the authorised signatory.

 Definitions

An **authorised signatory** is an individual who has been given permission to sign an official document on behalf of the organisation.

1.4 Delivery note

When the goods or services are supplied, the supplier will prepare a delivery note to give to the customer. This document will show the quantity, description and code number of the goods and services supplied; and the date of the delivery.

The delivery note will be signed by the customer so that the supplier has proof that the customer received the goods or services, in case of any later queries.

1.5 The sales invoice

After the goods have been delivered, the supplier will request payment from the customer by sending an invoice. The invoice will state the code, quantity, description and price of the goods. The invoice will also have a sequential number so that it can be filed in order.

 Example

 Little Miss Muffin Cake Shop

1 Baker Street	Invoice no: 005673
London	Tax point: 25 March 2012
WC1 8QT	VAT reg no: 618 2201 63
Tel: 020 7890 1234 – Fax: 020 7890 1235	Delivery note: DN00673
	Account no: BEL65

INVOICE

To:	**Delivery:**	**Delivery date:**
Belle's Wedding Planners	Four Hills Hotel	25 March 2012
11 Mountjoy St	Park Lane	
London W12 6RS	London W1 1UY	

Date: 25 March 2012   **Sales order number:** 41161

Product	Quantity	Price per unit (£)	Total (£)
Chocolate Wedding Cake	5 tiers	60.00	300.00
		VAT 20%	60.00
		Total	360.00
Payment terms: 14 days net			

Notes

This invoice confirms the price of the goods supplied to the customer

a) 5 Tiers of wedding cake which have been supplied to the Belle's.

b) The price for the goods is £300.

c) Value Added Tax (VAT) of 20%, £60.00 has been added to the cost of the goods.

d) The amount of £360.00 is now due from the customer.

e) The payment is due in 14 days from the date of the invoice.

1.6 Pricing and discounts

Unit prices for goods or services are kept in master files which must be updated regularly. If a price quotation has been sent to a customer then this must be used to determine the price to use on the invoice.

Trade discounts are a definite amount that is deducted from the list price of the goods for the supplies to some customers, with the intention of encouraging and rewarding customer loyalty. As well as checking the actual calculation of the trade discount on the face of the invoice, the supplier's file or the price quotation should be checked to ensure that the correct percentage of trade discount has been deducted.

Even if no trade discount appears on the purchase invoice, the supplier's file or price quotation must still be checked as it may be that a trade discount should have been deducted.

A **bulk discount** is similar to a trade discount in that it is deducted from the list price on the invoice. However, a bulk discount is given by a supplier for orders above a certain size.

A **settlement discount** is offered to customers if they settle the invoice within a certain time period. The discount is expressed as a percentage of the invoice total but is not deducted from the invoice total as it is not certain whether or not it will be accepted. Instead the details of the settlement discount will be noted at the bottom of the invoice.

1.7 The impact of VAT (sales tax)

Sales tax (VAT) is a tax levied on consumer expenditure. The procedure is that it is collected at each stage in the production and distribution chain.

Prices will normally be quoted exclusive of value added tax (VAT), as this is the true selling price to the business. However, if the selling business is registered for VAT, VAT must be charged on taxable supplies.

Most businesses avoid having to treat VAT as an expense as they may deduct the VAT (sales tax) they have paid on their purchases **(input tax)** from the VAT (sales tax) they charge to customers on their sales **(output tax)** and pay only the difference to the tax authorities.

Let us look at a simple illustration. We will assume a standard rate of 20%, and follow one article, a wooden table, through the production and distribution chain.

- A private individual cuts down a tree and sells it to a timber mill for £10. **Tax effect** – none. The individual is not a taxable person in this case.

- The timber mill saws the log and sells the timber to a furniture manufacturer for £100 + VAT.

  Tax effect – Being a taxable person, the mill is obliged to charge its customers VAT at 20% on the selling price (output tax).

  Cash effect – The mill collected £120 from the customer (or has a receivable for this sum). Of this, £20 has to be paid to the tax authorities (HM Revenue and Customs), and therefore only £100 would be recognised as sales.

- The manufacturer makes a table from the wood, and sells this to a retailer for £400 + VAT.

  Tax effect – The manufacturer is obliged to charge VAT at 20% on the selling price (i.e. £80 output tax), but in this instance would be allowed to reduce this amount by setting off the input tax of £20 charged on the purchase of wood from the mill.

  Cash effect – Tax of £60 is paid to the tax authorities (HM Revenue and Customs) (output less input tax = £80 less £20). £400 is recognised as sales and £100 as purchases in the accounts.

- The retailer sells the table to a private customer for £1,000 plus VAT of £200. **Tax effect** – The retailer charges £200 of VAT to the customer but against this output tax may be set off the input tax of £80 charged on the purchase from the manufacturer.

  Cash effect – £120 (£200 – £80) is paid to the tax authorities (HM Revenue and Customs). Purchases would be shown in the books at £400 and sales at £1,000.

- **The private customer** – VAT is a tax levied on consumer expenditure and the chain ends here. The customer is not a taxable person, and cannot recover the tax paid.

KAPLAN PUBLISHING

You will note that everybody else has passed the sales on and, though the customer has paid his £200 to the retailer, the tax authorities (HM Revenue and Customs) has received its tax by contributions from each link in the chain, as shown below:

	£
Timber mill	20.00
Manufacturer	60.00
Retailer	120.00
	200.00

🔍 Definitions

Sales tax (VAT) is charged on the **taxable supply of goods and services** in the United Kingdom by a **taxable person** in the course of a business carried on by him.

Output tax is the tax charged on the sale of goods and services.

Input tax is the tax paid on the purchase of goods and services.

1.8 Rates of VAT (sales tax)

Taxable supply is the supply of all items except those which are **exempt.** Examples of exempt items are as follows:

- certain land and buildings, where sold, leased or hired
- insurance
- postal services

Input tax cannot be reclaimed where the trader's supplies are all exempt.

There are three rates of sales tax (VAT in the UK) on taxable supplies:

1. Some items are 'zero-rated' (similar to exempt except that input tax can be reclaimed), examples of which include:

    - water and most types of food
    - books and newspapers
    - drugs and medicines
    - children's clothing and footwear.

2. There is a special rate of 5% for domestic fuel and power

3. All other items are rated at the standard rate of 20%.

VAT on some items is non-deductible. This means that VAT on any purchases of these items cannot be deducted from the amount of tax payable to the tax authorities (HM Revenue and Customs). The business has to bear the VAT as an expense. Non-deductible items include motor cars and business entertaining.

For our purposes you will normally be dealing with taxable supplies at the standard rate of 20%.

Therefore, if you are given the net price of goods, the price excluding VAT, then the amount of VAT is 20/100 of this price.

Note, VAT is always rounded down to the nearest penny.

 Example

A sale is made for £360.48 plus VAT. What is the amount of VAT to be charged on this sale?

Solution

VAT = £360.48 × 20/100 = £72.09

Remember to round down to the nearest penny.

An alternative way of calculating this would to be to multiply the net amount of £360.48 by 20%.

If a price is given that already includes the VAT then calculating the VAT requires an understanding of the price structure where VAT is concerned.

	%
Selling price incl. VAT (gross)	120
VAT	20
	____
Selling price excl. VAT (net)	100
	____

 Example

Goods have a selling price of £3,000 inclusive of VAT. What is the VAT on the goods and the net price of these goods?

Solution

	£
Net price (£3,000× 100/120)	2,500
VAT (£3,000 × 20/120)	500
	____
Gross price	3,000
	____

1.9   VAT and discounts

When a settlement discount is offered, this makes the VAT calculation slightly more complex.

Invoices should show the VAT payable as 20% (or whichever rate of sales tax is applicable) of the **discounted price**. The amount of VAT paid is always based on the discounted amount even though when the invoice is being prepared it is not known whether the customer will or will not take advantage of the settlement discount.

 Activity 1

What is the amount of VAT on each of the following transactions?

i)   £100 net of VAT

ii)   £250 net of VAT

iii)   £480 including VAT

iv)   £600 including VAT

v)   A sale of £280.00 plus VAT with a settlement discount of 2%

1.10   Preparing a sales invoice

 Example

Thelma Goody is the sales invoicing clerk for a VAT registered clothing wholesaler. Thelma prepares the sales invoices to be sent to the customer from the price list and a copy of the delivery note sent up to her by the sales department. Today she has received the following delivery note from the sales department.

Delivery note: 2685			
To: K Clothes Ltd 9 Port Street MANCHESTER M1 5EX	**A B Fashions Ltd** **3 Park Road** **Parkway** **Bristol** **BR6 6SJ** **Tel: 01272 695221** **Fax: 01272 695222**		
Delivery date: 20 August 20X6			
Quantity	**Code**	**DESCRIPTION**	**Colour**
30	CJA 991	Cashmere jumpers (adult)	Cream
Received by:			
Signature: .... Date:			

Code	Description	Colour	Unit price	VAT rate
CJA 991	Cashmere jumper (adult)	Cream	65.00	Standard
CJA 992	Cashmere jumper (adult)	Pink	65.00	Standard
CJA 993	Cashmere jumper (adult)	Blue	65.00	Standard
CJA 994	Cashmere jumper (adult)	Camel	65.00	Standard

The customer file shows that K Clothes Ltd's account number is KC 0055 and that a trade discount of 10% is offered to this customer.

Thelma must now prepare the sales invoice. Today's date is 22 August 20X6.

Solution

INVOICE

Invoice to:
K Clothes Ltd
9 Port Street
MANCHESTER
M1 5EX

A B Fashions Ltd
3 Park Road
Parkway
Bristol
BR6 6SJ
Tel: 01272 695221
Fax: 01272 695222

Deliver to:

As above

Invoice no:	95124
Tax point:	22 August 20X6
VAT reg no:	488 7922 26
Delivery note no:	2685
Account no:	KC 0055

Code	Description	Quantity	VAT rate %	Unit price £	Amount excl of VAT £
CJA 991	Cashmere jumper (adult) cream	30	20	65.00	1,950.00
					1,950.00
Trade discount 10%					(195.00)
					1,755.00
VAT					351.00
Total amount payable					2,106.00

How did Thelma do it?

Step 1 Enter today's date on the invoice and the invoice number which should be the next number after the last sales invoice number.

Step 2 Enter the customer details – name, address and account number.

Step 3 Refer now to the delivery note copy and enter the delivery note number and the quantities, codes and descriptions of the goods.

Step 4 Refer to the price list and enter the unit prices of the goods and the rate of VAT

Step 5 Now for the calculations – firstly multiply the number of each item by the unit price to find the VAT exclusive price – then total these total prices – finally calculate the trade discount as 10% of this total, £1,950.00 × 10% = £195.00 and deduct it.

Step 6 Calculate the VAT – in this case there is only standard rate VAT on the cashmere jumpers but you must remember to deduct the trade discount (£1,950 – £195) before calculating the VAT amount £1,755 × 20% = £351 – add the VAT to the invoice total after deducting the trade discount.

1.11 Credit Notes

In some cases, the customer may want to return goods to the supplier. For example, if the goods are faulty. When this happens, the supplier will issue a credit note. This credit note will reduce the amount that the customer owes.

Common reasons for credit notes:

- when a customer has returned faulty or damaged goods
- when a customer has returned perfect goods by agreement with the supplier
- to make a refund for short deliveries
- to settle a dispute with a customer.

When a supplier receives returned goods they must be inspected, counted and recorded on receipt. They would normally be recorded on a returns inwards note.

All credit notes must be authorised by a supervisor prior to being issued to the customer.

Some credit notes may be issued without a returns inwards note. For example, an error may have been made in pricing on an invoice but the customer is satisfied with the goods and does not need to return them.

These credit notes must be issued only after written authorisation has been received and must be reviewed and approved before being sent to the customer or recorded.

As credit notes look very similar to invoices, they are often printed in red to make it clear that it is not an invoice.

 Example

 Little Miss Muffin Cake Shop

1 Baker Street

London

WC1 8QT

Tel: 020 7890 1234 – Fax: 020 7890 1235

Credit note no: CN 02542
Tax point: 30 March 2012
VAT reg no: 618 2201 63
Invoice no: 005673
Account no: BEL65

CREDIT NOTE

Credit to:
Belle's Wedding Planners
11 Mountjoy St
London W12 6RS

Date: 30 March 2012

Description	Code	Quantity	Unit price £	Amount exclusive of VAT £
Chocolate Wedding Cake	CWC5	1 tier	60.00	60.00
VAT				12.00
Total amount of credit				72.00
Reason: One tier burnt.				

Notes

In this example, one of the tiers of the cake was burnt, so Belle's Wedding Supplies have requested a credit note.

When the replacement tier has been made and delivered, Little Miss Muffin Cake Shop will raise another invoice for the replacement tier.

1.12 Statement of Account

At the end of each month, the supplier will summarise all the transactions that have taken place with the customer. This could include invoices, credit notes, and any payments received from the customer.

The statement of account will show the outstanding balance owing from the customer at the end of the month.

 Example

 Little Miss Muffin Cake Shop

1 Baker Street
London
WC1 8QT
Tel: 020 7890 1234 – Fax: 020 7890 1235

STATEMENT

To: Belle's Wedding Planners
Date: 31 March 2012

Date	Transaction	Debit £	Credit £	Balance £
1 March	Balance b/d	165.00		165.00
25 March	Invoice 5673	360.00		525.00
30 March	Credit Note 02452		72.00	453.00
31 March	Cash received		165.00	288.00

Notes

a) 1st March — Belle's Wedding Planners owed £165.00 from last month;

b) 25th March — Invoice No 5673 for £360.00 has been added to the £165.00 to show a balance owing of £525.00;

c) 30th March — Credit note No 02452 for £72.00 has been deducted from the £525.00 to show a balance at that date of £453.00;

d)   31st March   Belle's Wedding Planners have paid the amount owing at the beginning of the month, leaving a balance outstanding of £288.00.

1.13   Remittance Advice

The final document in the process is the remittance advice. When the customer pays their outstanding balance they will send a remittance advice to the supplier together with their payment.

The remittance advice will clearly show which invoices are being paid and the date of the payment.

If there are any credit notes, the customer will state which credit notes they are deducting from the payment.

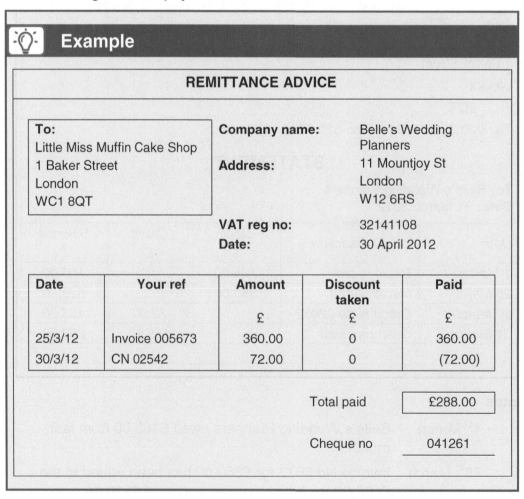

Example

REMITTANCE ADVICE

To:	**Company name:**	Belle's Wedding Planners
Little Miss Muffin Cake Shop		
1 Baker Street	**Address:**	11 Mountjoy St
London		London
WC1 8QT		W12 6RS
	VAT reg no:	32141108
	Date:	30 April 2012

Date	Your ref	Amount	Discount taken	Paid
		£	£	£
25/3/12	Invoice 005673	360.00	0	360.00
30/3/12	CN 02542	72.00	0	(72.00)

Total paid	£288.00
Cheque no	041261

Notes

In this example, on 30th April, 2012, Belle's Wedding Planners paid £288.00 by cheque. This payment is £360.00 for Invoice No 005673 less £72.00 for Credit Note CN02542.

If customers do not send a remittance advice and there are a lot of transactions in the month, it would be difficult for the supplier to know which invoices and credit notes the payment relates to.

1.14 Overview of the flow of transaction

The diagram below shows the typical flow of a transaction including the documents involved.

Dependent on whether it is a credit sale or a credit purchase, we will be looking at it from the perspective of the business or customer.

Customer	Supplier
Purchase order ⟶	
⟵	Sends **delivery note** with goods supplied
Signs delivery note ⟶	
⟵	Sends **invoice**
Returns goods ⟶	
⟵	Sends **credit note**
⟵	Sends **statement of account** (usually on a monthly basis)
Sends **remittance advice** ⟶ with payment	

Activity 2

Which two documents are sent by the customer to the supplier?

Activity 3

Which documents are sent by the supplier to the customer?

2 Documents used to record cash transactions

2.1 Receipt

In a cash sale or purchase, the transaction is much simpler. The customer will probably place an order verbally and payment is always made as soon as the customer receives the goods or services.

The customer will need a copy of the sales receipt in case they need to return them to the supplier.

3 Using codes

3.1 Common systems of codes

To be able to find and process the information quickly and efficiently, abbreviations or codes are often used.

Common systems of codes are:

Alphabetical codes

Codes which are made up of a series of letters only. These are short forms of a full title. For example:

Code Description

AAT   Association of Accounting Technicians

ACS   AAT Access

Numerical codes

Codes which are made up of a series of numbers only. For example, a sequential list of invoice numbers.

4156

4157

4158

Alphanumerical codes

These codes are a mixture of letters and numbers. Alphanumerical codes are often used for customer and supplier codes. For example:

BEL65	Belle's Wedding Planners
FRO02	Froome's Bicycle Repairs
CIR01	Ciro's Light Bites & Nibbles

Activity 4

Draw a line to match the Code provided with the Type of Code which best describes it.

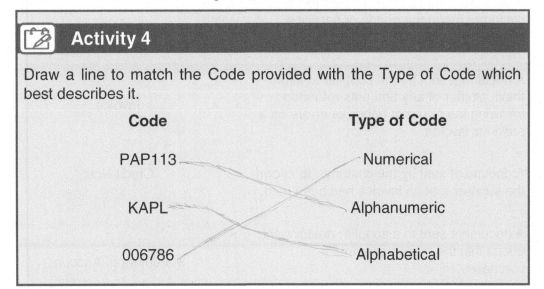

Code	Type of Code
PAP113	Numerical
KAPL	Alphanumeric
006786	Alphabetical

4 Summary and further questions

In this chapter you looked in detail at the documents used to record transactions for credit and cash customers.

You also looked at how codes can be used to process information efficiently and effectively.

Activity 5

Organisations issue and receive different documents when buying and selling goods.

Draw a line to match the document with the transaction

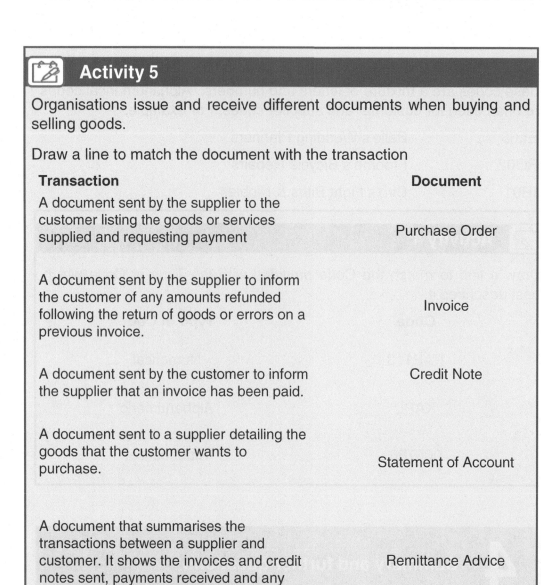

Transaction	Document
A document sent by the supplier to the customer listing the goods or services supplied and requesting payment	Purchase Order
A document sent by the supplier to inform the customer of any amounts refunded following the return of goods or errors on a previous invoice.	Invoice
A document sent by the customer to inform the supplier that an invoice has been paid.	Credit Note
A document sent to a supplier detailing the goods that the customer wants to purchase.	Statement of Account
A document that summarises the transactions between a supplier and customer. It shows the invoices and credit notes sent, payments received and any outstanding balance on the account.	Remittance Advice

Activity 6

Your organisation purchased 24 boxes of paper towels at £12.45 for each box. What is the total of the paper towels?

£

Activity 7

You work for Posies and Roses Florists. A customer purchased 24 red roses at £1.75 each. What is the total cost?

£

Activity 8

The customer who purchased the roses in Activity 7 has complained that 4 of the roses are damaged. Unfortunately, there are no more roses available so the manager has agreed to issue a credit note. How much does the customer owe after the credit note has been issued?

£ _____

Activity 9

You work for Cavalier Beds as a sales invoicing clerk. Your task is to prepare a sales invoice for each customer using the information below.

Today is 28 October, 20X6 and you have received the following delivery note from the sales department.

Use the information from the delivery note, the information from the customer file and the price list below to prepare an invoice for KP Furniture Ltd.

The last invoice issued was Invoice No. 67894.

Delivery Note:

Delivery note: 6785

To: KP Furniture Ltd
9 Paris Street
COLCHESTER
CF25 1XY

Cavalier Beds
3 Brussels Road
County Road
Gloucester
GL6 6TH
Tel: 01456 698271
Fax: 01456 698272

Delivery date: 27 October 20X6

Quantity	Code	DESCRIPTION	Size
5	MAT15K	Deluxe Mattress	King Size

Received by: ....

Signature: .... Date: ....

Customer File:

The customer file shows that KP Furniture Ltd's account number is KP12 and a trade discount of 10% is offered to this customer.

Price List:

Code	Description	Size	Unit price	VAT rate
MAT15S	Deluxe Mattress	Single	58.00	Standard
MAT15D	Deluxe Mattress	Double	74.00	Standard
MAT15K	Deluxe Mattress	King	98.00	Standard

Cavalier Beds
3 Brussels Road
County Road
Gloucester
GL6 6TH
Tel: 01456 698271   Fax: 01456 698272

Invoice to:				
		Invoice no:		
		Date:		
		VAT reg no:	488 7922 26	
		Delivery note no:		
		Account no:		

Code		Quantity	VAT rate	Unit price £	Amount excl of VAT £
			20%	£	
Trade discount 10%					
Subtotal					
VAT					
Total amount payable					

Activity 10

A customer has been sent two invoices totalling £457.98 and £69.65. They have also received a credit note for goods returned to the supplier. This credit note was for a total of £58.60.   During the month, the customer paid £200.00 to the supplier.

a) What is the balance outstanding on this customer's account?

£

b) What is the name of the document which will be sent to the customer to show these transactions and the balance outstanding?

Answers to chapter activities

Activity 1

i)   £100.00 × 20/100   =   £20.00

ii) £250.00 × 20/100   =   £50.00

iii) £480.00 × 20/120   =   £80.00

iv) £600.00 × 20/120   =   £100.00

v)   £(280 – 2% × 280) × 20/100 = £54.88

Activity 2

The customer sends a **purchase order** to state which goods they want to purchase and a **remittance advice** to say which transactions they are paying.

Activity 3

The supplier sends a **delivery note** with the goods when they are supplied; an **invoice** to tell the customer how much the goods cost; and a **statement of account** to summarise all the transactions that have taken place.

Activity 4

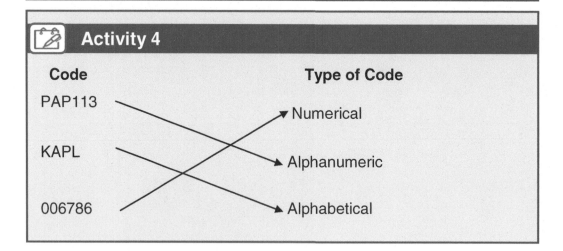

Code	Type of Code
PAP113	Numerical
KAPL	Alphanumeric
006786	Alphabetical

Activity 5

Transaction	Document

A document sent by the supplier to the customer listing the goods or services supplied and requesting payment

Purchase Order

A document sent by the supplier to inform the customer of any amounts refunded following the return of goods or errors on a previous invoice.

Invoice

A document sent by the customer to inform the supplier that an invoice has been paid.

Credit Note

A document sent to a supplier detailing the goods that the customer wants to purchase.

Statement of Account

A document that summarises the transactions between a supplier and customer. It shows the invoices and credit notes sent, payments received and any outstanding balance on the account.

Remittance Advice

Activity 6

Your organisation purchased 24 boxes of paper towels at £12.45 for each box. What is the total of the paper towels?

£ 298.80

Activity 7

You work for Posies and Roses Florists. A customer purchased 24 red roses at £1.75 each. The customer has requested a receipt. What is the total cost?

£ 42.00

Activity 8

The customer who purchased the roses in Activity 7 has complained that 4 of the roses are damaged. Unfortunately, there are no more roses available so the manager has agreed to issue a credit note. How much does the customer owe after the credit note has been issued?

£ | 35.00 |

 Activity 9

Cavalier Beds
3 Brussels Road
County Road
Gloucester
GL6 6TH
Tel: 01456 698271   Fax: 01456 698272

Invoice to:		Invoice no:	67895
		Date:	28/10/X6
KP Furniture Ltd 9 Paris Street COLCHESTER CF25 1XY		VAT reg no:	488 7922 26
		Delivery note no:	6785
		Account no:	KP12

Code		Quantity	VAT rate	Unit price £	Amount excl of VAT £
MAT15K	Deluxe Mattress	5	20%	98.00	490.00
Trade discount 10%					49.00
Subtotal					441.00
VAT					88.20
Total amount payable					529.20

Activity 10

A customer has been sent two invoices totalling £457.98 and £69.65. They have also received a credit note for goods returned to the supplier. This credit note was for a total of £58.60. During the month, the customer paid £200.00 to the supplier.

a) What is the balance outstanding on this customer's account?

£ | 269.03

b) What is the name of the document which will be sent to the customer to show these transactions and the balance outstanding?

Statement of Account

Books of prime entry

Introduction

In the previous chapter you looked at the documents that are used in cash and credit transactions. These documents now need to be summarised in **books of prime entry**.

As the documents are recorded regularly, these books are also known as **day books.**

KNOWLEDGE	CONTENTS
Award in Accounting	1 Documents used to record transactions with customers
3.1 Select appropriate documents to record transactions in the books of prime entry	2 Documents used to record transactions with suppliers
3.2 Select the appropriate book of prime entry to record transactions relating to credit sales and credit purchases	3 Batch control
3.3 Select the appropriate book of prime entry to record payments made and monies received	4 Summary and further questions
3.4 Explain what is meant by a batch control system	
Award in Bookkeeping	
5 Understand how to process information into the books of prime entry (WWB)	

1 Documents used to record transactions with customers

1.1 Overview

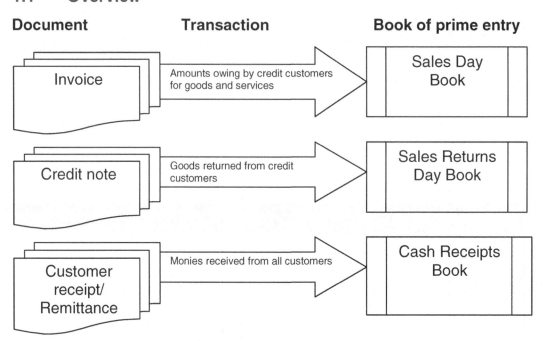

Document	Transaction	Book of prime entry
Invoice	Amounts owing by credit customers for goods and services	Sales Day Book
Credit note	Goods returned from credit customers	Sales Returns Day Book
Customer receipt/ Remittance	Monies received from all customers	Cash Receipts Book

1.2 The sales day book (SDB)

The sales day book records the individual invoices issued to credit customers. It is just a list but it will be used to perform double entry bookkeeping which you will learn about in your Level 2 accounting studies.

Example:

SALES DAY BOOK						
Date	Customer	Reference	Invoice number	Total £	VAT £	Sales £
1 July	Althams Ltd	ALT01	45787	100.00	20.00	120.00
2 July	Broadhurst plc	BRO02	45788	200.00	40.00	240.00
			TOTALS	300.00	60.00	360.00

Notes

- The reference number is the code number of the customer's account in the sales ledger.
- The invoice number is the number of the invoice issued for each sale.
- The Sales column is the total value of the goods sold as shown on the invoice after deducting trade discount including VAT.

- The amount of VAT is recorded in a separate column to show the amount owing to HMRC for these invoices.
- The Total column shows the total amount due from customers.

🔆 Example

An invoice to customer A is made up as follows:

	£
Sale of 50 units at £2 per unit	100.00
Less: 20% trade discount	(20.00)
	80.00
VAT (£80 × 20%)	16.00
Total invoice value	96.00

An invoice to customer B is made up as follows:

	£
Sale of 75 units at £2 per unit	150.00
Less: 10% trade discount	(15.00)
	135.00
VAT (£135.00 × 20%)	27.00
Total invoice value	162.00

The sales day book would therefore look as follows for the example above:

Date	Customer	Reference	Invoice number	Total £	VAT £	Sales £
	A			96.00	16.00	80.00
	B			162.00	27.00	135.00
			TOTALS	**258.00**	**43.00**	**215.00**

1.3 The sales returns day book

Sales returns are usually entered in a 'sales returns day book'. This is similar to the sales day book, and the columns are used in the same way. The only difference is that instead of having a column for the invoice number, there is a column for the 'credit note number'. This is because when the goods are returned by customers a credit note is issued.

SALES RETURNS DAY BOOK						
Date	Customer	Reference	Credit note number	Total £	VAT £	Sales returns £

In some businesses the level of sales returns are fairly low and therefore it is not justified to keep a separate sales returns day book. In these cases any credit notes that are issued for sales returns are recorded as negative amounts in the sales day book.

1.4 The cash book

Definition

The Cash Book records receipts and payment made by cash, cheque, credit or debit card, or bank transfer.

One of the most important books used within a business is the cash book. There are various forms of cash book, a 'two column' and a 'three column' cash book.

A two column cash book records details of cash and bank transactions separately as shown here:

CASH BOOK							
Date	Details	Bank £	Cash £	Date	Details	Bank £	Cash £
		Receipts				Payments	

Notes

- The left hand side of the cash book represents the debit side – money received.
- The right hand side of the cash book represents the credit side – money paid out.
- In practice, there is usually a column on both the debit and the credit side for the date.
- The details column describes the transactions – typically the name of the customer and supplier.

- The bank column on the debit side represents money received (by cheque or other bank payment) whereas the bank column on the credit side represents money paid (by cheque or other bank payment).

Some organisations keep separate cash books to record receipts and payments. These are known as the Cash Receipts Book and Cash Payments Book, respectively.

 Definition

Monies – A term used to describe all types of payments and receipts including cash, cheques and direct bank transfers.

1.5 The petty cash book

 Definition

Petty cash is the small amount of cash that most businesses hold in order to make small cash payments.

The petty cash book is normally set out as a large ledger account with a small receipts side and a larger analysed payments side.

A typical petty cash book is set out below.

Receipts										
Date	Narrative	Total	Date	Narrative	Voucher no	Total	Postage	Cleaning	Tea & Coffee	VAT
						£	£	£	£	£
1 Nov	Bal b/f	35.50								
1 Nov	Cheque 394	114.50	1 Nov	ASDA	58	23.50			23.50	
			2 Nov	Post Office Ltd	59	29.50	29.50			
			2 Nov	Cleaning materials	60	15.07		12.56		2.51
			3 Nov	Postage	61	16.19	16.19			

The receipts side of the petty cash book only requires one column, as the only receipt into the petty cash box is the regular payment into the petty cash box of cash drawn out of the bank account.

From the example of a typical petty cash book (above), we can see that the balance brought forward was £35.50. The petty cash has then been restored up to £150 by paying in an additional £114.50.

Payments out of the petty cash box will be for a variety of different types of expense and an analysis column is required for each type of expense in the same way as the cash payments book is analysed. The example (above) has split the expenses into postage, cleaning, tea & coffee and sundry expenses. Note that a column is also required for VAT, as if a petty cash expense includes VAT this must also be analysed out.

2 Documents used to record transactions with suppliers

2.1 Overview

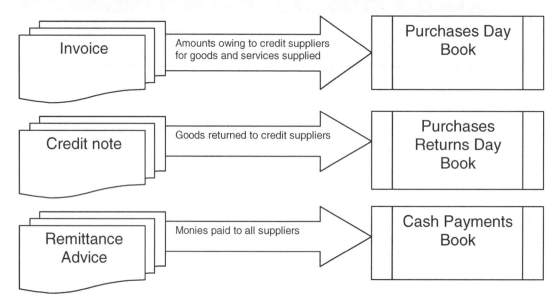

2.2 The purchases day book

As seen earlier in the chapter, credit sales are recorded in the 'sales day book'. In the case of credit purchases, we have the 'purchases day book'.

The purchases day book is simply a list of the purchases invoices that are to be processed for a given period (e.g. a week). In its simplest form, the purchases day book will comprise just the names of the suppliers and the amount of the invoices received in the week.

Purchases returns are entered in a 'purchases returns day book'. This looks similar to the purchases day book, and the columns are used in the same way. The only difference is that instead of having a column for the

KAPLAN PUBLISHING

invoice number, there is a column for the 'credit note number'. This is because when the goods are sent back the business will receive a credit note from the supplier.

In some businesses the level of purchases returns are fairly low and therefore it is not necessary to keep a separate purchases returns day book. In these cases any credit notes that are received for purchases returns are recorded as negative amounts in the purchases day book.

 Example

You work in the accounts department of R Porte Manufacturing Ltd and one of your tasks is to sort the documents before they are entered in to the correct books of prime entry.

From the following documents, identify which book of prime entry it should be recorded in.

Document 1

R Moore Fashions

12 Dutch Corner
High Wycombe
HG4 7NQ

Invoice no: 005673
Tax point:14 July 2016

INVOICE

To: R Porte Manufacturing Ltd
5 Ventoux Crescent, Cardiff, CA2 3HU

Product	Quantity	Price per unit	Total
		£	£
Cargo pants	5	25.00	125.00
T-shirts	10	15.00	150.00
			275.00
		VAT 20%	55.00
		Total	330.00
Payment terms: 30 days net			

Answer: You are dealing with documents for R Porte Manufacturing.

This invoice is sent **to** you at R Porte Manufacturing, so you have received it from R Moore Fashions, who must be the supplier.

Therefore, this is a supplier invoice and should be entered into the **purchases day book.**

Document 2

R Porte Manufacturing Ltd			
5 Ventoux Crescent Cardiff CA2 3HU		Credit Note no: 05876 Tax point: 16 July 2016	
CREDIT NOTE			
To: Birnies Biscuits Elysee Avenue, Mitcham, MA3 6ZT			
Product	Quantity	Price per unit (£)	Total (£)
Packing cases	4	5.00	20.00
		VAT 20%	4.00
		Total	24.00
Payment terms: 30 days net			

Answer: Remember, you are dealing with documents for R Porte Manufacturing.

This credit note is sent **to** Birnies Biscuits, so they must be the customer. Therefore, this is a customer credit note and should be entered into the **sales returns day book.**

Activity 1

Match the following documents to the relevant book of prime entry.

Invoice to customer	Cash Payments Book
Credit note from supplier	Sales Day Book
Cash received from customer	Sales Returns Day Book
Invoice from supplier	Cash Receipts Book
Credit note to customer	Purchases Day Book
Cheque paid to supplier	Purchases Returns Day Book

Activity 2

You work in the accounts department of Armistead & Co and one of your tasks is to sort the documents before they are entered in to the books of prime entry.

Armistead & Co

Ryan's Close	Invoice no: 59870
Lower Meltham	Tax point: 1 July 2016
MT4 3SQ	

INVOICE

To: Pendleton Prisms
Stuart Street, Bristol, BR1 JQ8

Product	Quantity	Price per unit	Total
Anti-rust bike chain	100	£3.99	£399.00
Chainset and cable kit	5	£25.00	£125.00
			£524.00
		VAT 20%	£104.80
		Total	**£628.80**
Payment terms: 15 days net			

The book of prime entry to be used is:

 Activity 3

You work in the accounts department of Birnies Biscuits and your task is to sort the documents before they are entered in to the correct books of prime entry. Which book of prime entry should be used for the following?

R Porte Manufacturing Ltd

5 Ventoux Crescent	Credit Note no: 05876
Cardiff	Tax point: 16 July 2016
CA2 3HU	

CREDIT NOTE

To: Birnies Biscuits
Elysee Avenue, Mitcham, MA3 6ZT

Product	Quantity	Price per unit (£)	Total (£)
Packing cases	4	5.00	20.00
		VAT 20%	4.00
		Total	24.00
Payment terms: 30 days net			

3 Batch control

3.1 Batch processing

A busy accounts office will need to record a lot of transactions and it is important that all the information is entered quickly and accurately into the correct book of prime entry.

Batch processing is a method of entering batches of similar transactions all together rather than individually.   Using this method, all customer invoices, credit notes and receipts and all supplier invoices, credit notes and receipts will be sorted into separate piles before being entered into the relevant book of prime entry.

3.2 Benefits of batch processing

Batch processing will help to save time as it means that accounting staff can concentrate on one task at a time can be rather than swapping between different documents and books of prime entry. By focusing on one task at a time, it also means that fewer mistakes will be made.

Cheques and cash paid listings can be used to quickly record all the money paid out by the organisation each day. The total amount is then entered into the cash payments book.

Cheques and cash received listings can be used to record all the money received out by the organisation each day. The total amount is then entered into the cash receipts book.

4 Summary and further questions

In this chapter you learnt about the different day books used to keep of a record of the documents used in accounting transactions.

You also saw how batch control can help accounting professionals to process information efficiently and effectively.

The following practice questions will test your knowledge of this chapter.

Activity 4

Fill in the gaps below to complete the sentences. Choose from the Pick list provided.

The _____ is used to record invoices from customers.

The _____ is used to record credit notes from customers.

The _____ is used to record invoices to suppliers.

The _____ is used to record credit notes to suppliers.

The _____ is used to record monies received from customers.

The _____ is used to record monies paid to suppliers.

Pick List

Cash receipts book	Sales day book	Cash payments book
Purchases day book	Purchases returns day book	Sales returns day book

Activity 5

You have been asked to enter the invoice below into the sales day book.

P Sagan Cleaning Products

15 Gatehead Road
Maplethorpe
MA1 7GZ

Invoice no: 5698
Tax point: 26 Mar 2016

INVOICE

To: G Thomas (A/C Ref TH02)
5 Holland Crescent, Chesham CA2 3HU

Product	Quantity	Price per unit	Total
Goods (Carpet – Deluxe Cleaner)	5	£50.12	£250.60
		VAT 20%	£50.12
		Total	£300.72
Payment terms: 30 days net			

Complete the Sales Day Book below with the correct information.

_Date	Customer	Reference	Invoice No	Total £	VAT £	Net £

Activity 6

Complete the sentence below with the correct options.

Batch processing is a method of processing financial documents [all together/individually] rather than [all together/individually].

 Activity 7

You work in the accounts department of Foe & Co and one of your tasks is to sort the documents before they are entered in to the books of prime entry.

Foe & Co			
Middlebrow MI4 3SQ		Invoice no: 598 Tax point: 18 July 20X6	
Credit Note			
To: Fi and Fun **Rose Avenue, Cardiff, CT1 JQ8**			
Product	*Quantity*	*Price per unit*	*Total*
KBM15	1	£35.99	£35.99
		VAT 20%	£7.19
		Total	**£43.18**
Payment terms: 15 days net			

Which daybook should this document be entered in?

sale

Activity 8

You work in the accounts department of Diamond Ltd and one of your tasks is to sort the documents before they are entered in to the books of prime entry.

King & Co			
Highbrow HI4 3SQ		Invoice no: 2867 Tax point: 18 June 20X6	
Invoice			
To: Diamond Ltd Platt Avenue, Delph, OL1 JQ8			
Product	*Quantity*	*Price per unit*	*Total*
Item 5	10	£35.50	£355.00
		VAT 20%	£71.00
		Total	£426.00
Payment terms: 15 days net			

Which daybook should this document be entered in? *Purchas*

 Activity 9

You work in the accounts department of Diamond Ltd and you have been asked to send a cheque to a supplier for payment of goods.

Which daybook should the amount be listed in?

 Activity 10

Complete the sentences below by choosing the correct options:

Cheques and cash paid into the organisation can be listed on a **cheques and cash paid/cheques and cash received** listing before entering into the **cash payments book/cash receipts book.**

This is an example of **batch processing/invoice processing** and means that **more/fewer** mistakes will be made.

Answers to chapter activities

 Activity 1

Invoice to customer	=	Sales Day Book
Credit note from supplier	=	Purchase Returns Day Book
Cash received from customer	=	Cash Receipts Book
Invoice from supplier	=	Purchases Day Book
Credit note to customer	=	Sales Returns Day Book
Cheque paid to supplier	=	Cash Payments Book

 Activity 2

You are dealing with documents for Armistead & Co. This invoice is **to** Pendleton Prisms, so they must be the customer.

Therefore, this is a customer invoice and should be entered into the **sales day book.**

 Activity 3

You are dealing with documents for Birnies Biscuits. This credit note is **from** R Porte Manufacturing, so they must be the supplier.

Therefore, this is a supplier credit note and should be entered in the **purchase returns day book.**

KAPLAN PUBLISHING

Activity 4

The **Sales day book** is used to record invoices from customers.

The **Sales returns day book** is used to record credit notes from customers.

The **Purchases day book** is used to record invoices to suppliers.

The **Purchases returns day book** is used to record credit notes to suppliers.

The **Cash receipts book** is used to record monies received from customers.

The **Cash payments book** is used to record monies paid to suppliers.

Activity 5

Date	Customer	Reference	Invoice No	Total £	VAT £	Net £
26 Mar 2016	G Thomas	TH02	5698	300.72	50.12	250.60

Activity 6

Batch processing is a method of processing financial documents [**all together**] rather than [**individually**].

Activity 7

You are dealing with documents for Foe & Co. This credit note is **to** Fi and Fun, so they must be the customer.

Therefore, this is a credit note sent to a customer and should be entered into the **sales returns day book.**

Activity 8

You are dealing with documents for Diamond Ltd. This invoice is sent from King and Co who must be the supplier of the goods.

Therefore, this is an invoice received from a supplier and should be entered into the **purchases day book.**

Activity 9

You work in the accounts department of Diamond Ltd and you have been asked to send a cheque to a supplier for payment of goods. Therefore this is a payment and should be listed in the **cash payments book.**

 Activity 10

Cheques and cash paid into the organisation can be listed on a **cheques and cash received listing** before entering into the **cash receipts book.**

This is an example of **batch processing** and means that **fewer** mistakes will be made.

Cheques and paying-in slips

Introduction

There are many different ways a business can make and receive payments. A lot of businesses make electronic payments, however a lot of customers still pay in cash or by writing a cheque. When physical payments are received by an organisation, the monies will need to be paid into the business's bank account.

This chapter explains how to complete the documents used in banking transactions.

KNOWLEDGE	CONTENTS
Award in Accounting	1 Paying-in slips
5.1 Complete a bank paying-in slip for notes, coins and cheques.	2 Cheques
5.2 Complete a cheque.	3 Summary and further questions

1 Paying-in slips

1.1 Paying-in slips

All business organisations are provided with a paying-in book by the bank. Each paying-in book contains paying-in slips. When money is paid into the bank it is accompanied by one of the completed paying-in slips.

If your job is to pay money into the bank, you will need to complete and sign the bank paying-in slip taken from the paying-in book. The paying-in slip is then given to the bank cashier who will check it against the monies being paid in to the bank.

1.2 Example of a paying-in slip

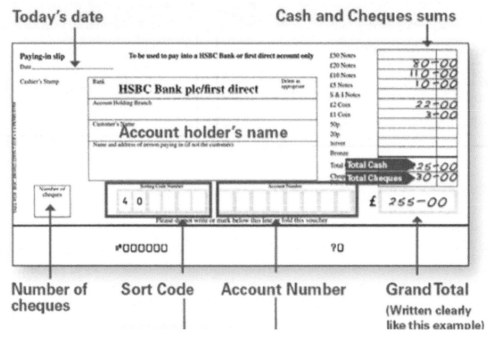

(Source: www.hsbc.co.uk)

1.3 Paying-in requirements and records

You only need to enter the number of cheques being paid in and the total amount on the front of the paying in slip. On the back of the paying in slip you should write a list of the cheques being paid in.

The paying-in stub is the part of the paying-in slip which stays in the paying-in book and is a record for the organisation of the amounts paid into the bank.

Activity 1

Today's date is 19 July 2015.

You have been asked to complete a bank paying-in slip for the money received today, which is as follows:

Notes	Coins	Cheques	
3 x £20 notes	25 x £1 coins	Thomas	£1,500.00
15 x £10 notes	8 x 50p coins	Friebe	£ 750.00
20 x £5 notes	20 x 10p coins		

Complete the paying-in slip below:

Date:	Main Bank plc	£50 notes	
	Cartown	£20 notes	
		£10 notes	
	Account	£5 notes	
	ABC Ltd	£2 coin	
		£1 coin	
No of cheques	Paid in by *AAT Student*	Other coin	
		Total cash	
	Sort Code Account No	Cheques	
	10-11-44 12879065	Total £	

 Activity 2

Why is it important that the paying-in slip is dated and signed?

2 Cheques

2.1 The use of cheques

When a person (or organisation) writes a cheque they are instructing their bank to transfer a specified amount of money from their bank account to the bank account of the recipient of the cheque – the payee.

If the cheque hasn't been completed correctly the bank may return it to the payee. The payee will then have to ask for a replacement cheque from the organisation.

As this causes delays in the payment process, it is important that the cheque is completed correctly in the first place.

2.2 Cheque requirements

For a cheque to be valid it should include:

- **Payee name** The payee is the person or organisation to whom the cheque is written. The payee's name should exactly match the name on their bank account.

- **Date** The date that the cheque is written must include the day, month and the year. A cheque that is more than 6 months old is invalid and the bank will not accept the cheque.

- **Words** The pounds part of the amount being paid must be written in words but the pence part can be written in numbers. If the amount is a whole number of pounds then you should write 'ONLY' after the amount to prevent someone changing the figure.

- **Numbers** The amount being paid should be written in numbers in the box on the right hand side of the cheque. The amount in numbers should exactly match the amount written in words.

- **Signature** The cheque should be signed by an authorised signatory of the organisation.

🔍 Definition

Signatories – a person or persons who are authorised to sign cheques on behalf of an organisation.

💡 Example

ABC Bank PLC	Date: 30th January 20X5

Payee: *Mr John Smith*

	£350.00
Three hundred and fifty pounds only	MISS ANNE JONES

CHEQUE NO	SORT CODE	ACCOUNT NO
04312	25-22-78	30087251

KAPLAN PUBLISHING

Activity 3

Today's date is 29th July 2015 and you have been given the following cheques to complete. Fill in the gaps using the correct numbers, words and/or date.

Cheque A

ABC Bank PLC	Date: 29th July, 2015
Payee: *Mr G Thomas*	
Five hundred pounds ONLY	on behalf of TDF Ltd

CHEQUE NO	SORT CODE	ACCOUNT NO
04312	25-22-78	30087251

Cheque B

ABC Bank PLC	Date: 29th July, 2015
Payee: *Armistead & Co*	
	250.50
	on behalf of TDF Ltd

CHEQUE NO	SORT CODE	ACCOUNT NO
04312	25-22-78	30087251

Cheque C

ABC Bank PLC	Date:
Payee: *Mr P Sagan*	
	25.20
Twenty five pounds and 20p only	on behalf of TDF Ltd

CHEQUE NO	SORT CODE	ACCOUNT NO
04312	25-22-78	30087251

3 Summary and further questions

In this chapter, you were introduced to two documents used in banking procedures.

The paying-in slip should be completed correctly and should match the monies being paid into the bank.

For cheques to be valid they need to be made out to the correct payee, the words and numbers need to match exactly, and the cheques need to be signed by an authorised person.

The following questions will test your knowledge of this chapter:

Activity 4

Write the following words as numbers to two decimal places:

Five hundred and fifty pounds	
Twenty two pounds and thirty four pence	
Five hundred pounds and five pence	
One thousand, two hundred and twenty pounds	

Activity 5

Write the following amounts in words:

£20.50	
£678.90	
£1400.40	
£89.00	

Activity 6

Cheques can be signed by anyone in an organisation. True or False?

Activity 7

Match the definitions with the correct words used in banking

A person who is authorised to sign documents on behalf of an organisation	payee
The person or organisation to whom the cheque is written	stub
A written instruction to transfer a specified sum of money from one bank account to another.	monies
The part of a cheque or paying-in slip kept as a record of the transaction	signatory
The term used to describe different forms of payments and receipts including cash, cheques and direct bank transfers.	cheque

 Activity 8

As long as a cheque has been completed correctly it is valid for ever.

True or False?

Answers to chapter activities

Activity 1

Date:	Main Bank plc		£50 notes	
	Cartown		£20 notes	60.00
			£10 notes	150.00
	Account		£5 notes	100.00
	ABC Ltd		£2 coin	
			£1 coin	25.00
No of cheques	Paid in by *AAT Student*		Other coin	6.00
			Total cash	341.00
	Sort Code	Account No	Cheques	2250.00
	10-11-44	12879065	Total £	2591.00

Activity 2

The paying-in slip must be dated and signed so that the bank cashier can contact the person who paid in the money in to the bank, in case there are any queries.

Activity 3

Cheque A - The amount in numbers should be £500.00

ABC Bank PLC	Date: 29th July, 2015
Payee: *Mr G Thomas*	
	500.00
Five hundred pounds ONLY	on behalf of TDF Ltd

CHEQUE NO	SORT CODE	ACCOUNT NO
04312	25-22-78	30087251

Cheque B - The amount in words should be 'Two hundred and fifty pounds and 50p'

ABC Bank PLC	Date: 29th July, 2015

Payee: *Armistead & Co*	
	250.50
Two hundred and fifty pounds and 50p	on behalf of TDF Ltd

CHEQUE NO	SORT CODE	ACCOUNT NO
04312	25-22-78	30087251

Cheque C - The date should contain the day, the month and the year. For example: 29th July 2015, 29 Jul 15, or 29/07/15 are all correct.

ABC Bank PLC	Date: ***29th July, 2015***

Payee: *Mr P Sagan*	
	25.20
Twenty five pounds and 20p only	on behalf of TDF Ltd

CHEQUE NO	SORT CODE	ACCOUNT NO
04312	25-22-78	30087251

Activity 4

Five hundred and fifty pounds	£550.00
Twenty two pounds and thirty four pence	£22.34
Five hundred pounds and five pence	£500.05
One thousand, two hundred and twenty pounds	£1220.00

Activity 5

£20.50	Twenty pounds and fifty pence
£678.90	Six hundred and seventy eight pounds and ninety pence
£1400.40	One thousand four hundred pounds and forty pence
£89.00	Eighty nine pounds

Activity 6

The statement is false. Cheques can only be signed by authorised signatories.

 Activity 7

Match the definitions with the correct words used in banking

A person who are authorised to sign documents on behalf of an organisation   payee

The person or organisation to whom the cheque is written   stub

A written instruction to transfer a specified sum of money from one bank account to another.   monies

The part of a cheque or paying-in slip kept as a record of the transaction   signatory

The term used to describe different forms of payments and receipts including cash, cheques and direct bank transfers.   cheque

 Activity 8

As long as a cheque has been completed correctly it is valid for ever.

This statement is **false.** Banks will refuse to accept cheques which are banked 6 months after the date written on the cheque.

KAPLAN PUBLISHING

Accounting in a professional environment

Introduction

The accounting department performs a vital role in all organisations, providing financial information to internal and external customers. In this chapter you will learn about the types of organisations in which accounting professionals work and how they provide support to other departments.

As information provided by accounting professionals may be commercially sensitive, it is important to understand how to handle this confidentially.

Finally, you will learn why it is important for accounting professionals and the organisations in which they work to behave in an ethical and socially responsible manner.

KNOWLEDGE

Award in Accounting

1.1 Identify different types of business organisation

1.2 Identify the customers of the accounting function

1.3 Explain how the accounting function can support an organisation

2.1 Explain how to maintain confidentiality of information

2.2 Explain the importance of ethical and professional behaviour to the role of those in the accounting function

3.3 Identify how an employee in the accounting function can ensure that personal information is protected and not disclosed without authority

3.4 Identify the importance of an organisation adopting environmentally and socially responsible policies

Award in Bookkeeping

2 Understand different types of business organisation (ITB)

6.1 Understand the responsibilities relating to security of data when dealing with customers, suppliers and external agencies (WWB)

CONTENTS

1 Business organisations
2 Customers of the accounting function
3 Accounting function support to the organisation
4 Confidentiality
5 Ethical and professional behaviour
6 Environmental and social responsibility
7 Summary and further questions

1 Business organisations

1.1 Business sectors

There are three main sectors in which business organisations operate.
Each of these sectors has a different purpose.

Private sector
The main purpose of business organisations in the private sector is to **make a profit** for their owners. Private sector organisations include sole traders, partnerships and limited companies.

Public sector
The purpose of public sector organisations is to **provide essential services** such as education and health care. They are funded by monies raised through taxation.

Examples include councils, NHS, Police, Fire and Ambulance services.

Charities
Charitable organisations are set up to raise money and awareness **to promote a cause or to provide services** for specific groups.

Examples of these are Save the Children and Guide dogs for the Blind. You can probably name others.

 Activity 1

Write down the names of as many charities you can think of.

Then, write down what you think each charity does for the public or for the 'common good' of society.

Then check their websites to see if what they do is what you think they do.

1.2 Ownership in the private sector

There are three different types of ownership of **private sector** organisations. The main purpose of each of these organisations is to make a profit.

Type of Business	Ownership
Sole Trader	A sole trader business is owned by one person. If the business makes a profit the owner will keep all the profits. However, if the business gets into financial difficulty, the sole trader is responsible for all the debts. A sole trader may work on their own or have several employees. The owner is in direct control of all elements and is legally accountable for the finances of the business. Sole traders may use a trade name or business name other than their own legal name.
Partnership	A partnership is similar to a sole trader business but is owned by between two and twenty people. Each partner will take a share of the profits of the business or be liable for the losses of the business.
Limited companies	When a limited company is set up it is given its own legal identity. The ownership of these companies is divided into shares of the business. Any profit made by the business is allocated to shareholders in the form of dividends, based on how many shares they hold. Shareholders have limited liability which means that they are not liable for the business's debts. If the business gets into financial difficulty, shareholders will only lose the money they originally invested. The shares of private limited companies (Ltd) are usually given to the directors of the organisation or other private individuals. The shares of public limited companies (plc) are sold on the stock exchange which means that anyone from the general public can buy them.

Activity 2

Identify the purpose of each sector by matching the sector in the first column with the purpose in the second column.

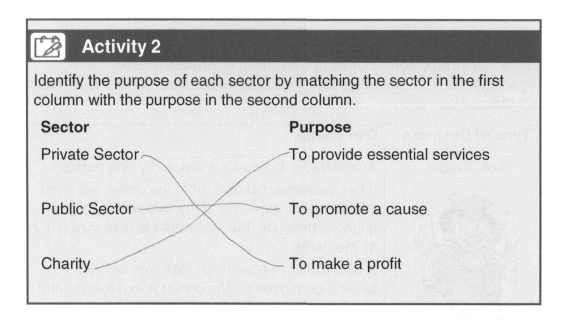

Sector	Purpose
Private Sector	To provide essential services
Public Sector	To promote a cause
Charity	To make a profit

Activity 3

Identify which sector the following organisations belong to:

	Private Sector	Public Sector	Charity
An animal welfare organisation			✓
Local government			
A sole trader	✓		
A limited company			
A primary school		✓	
An environmental conservation organisation			

2 Customers of the accounting function

2.1 The function of the accounts department

The function of the accounts department of an organisation is to provide financial information to its customers. These customers can be from inside the organisation (internal) or outside the organisation (external).

All customers will expect the accounts department to provide information which is accurate and complete, and is delivered on time.

2.2 Information for internal and external customers

Examples of the types of information that internal and external customers need from the accounts department are listed below.

Internal customers:

Sales Department　　　　　may need to know the amount of credit and cash sales for a particular period.

Marketing Department　　　may need to know how much money is available for advertising.

Purchasing Department　　may need to know if and/or when a supplier's invoices have been paid.

External customers:

Suppliers (Creditors)　　　may need to know when an invoice will be paid for goods or services supplied.

Customers (Debtors)　　　may need to know how much they owe the business for goods and services sold.

HMRC
(Her Majesty's Revenue and Customs)　　　may want to check the amount of invoices received and supplied to ensure the correct amount of VAT has been collected.

Definition

Function – an activity carried out in an organisation. For example, the accounting function is carried out by the staff in the accounts department.

 Activity 4

Why is it important for employees in the accounting function to treat internal customers with the same courtesy and respect as external customers?

3 Accounting function support to the organisation

3.1 Support from the accounting function

The accounting function provides help and support to all other functions within the organisation.

The managers of these other functions will rely on the information provided by accounting staff in order to run their departments effectively and contribute to the overall smooth running of the organisation.

It is very important that any information provided by the accounts department to the rest of the organisation is timely (up to date), accurate (free from errors) and complete (nothing is missing).

 Definitions

Working effectively– Completing tasks accurately and on time.

Working efficiently – Completing work as quickly as possible to required standards without making mistakes

3.2   Information from the accounting function

The table below gives examples of the key information provided by the accounts department to other functions in the organisation.

Information	Function
Management will need information about the profit or loss of the organisation. For example, they may want to know whether a particular product is making a profit or a loss, or which department is making the most profit.	Management
The manager of the production department may want to know if the department has spent more or less than budgeted. They may need to know the cost of raw materials, discounts, the cost of any machinery and the budget for any replacements.	Production
The sales function may want to know about the income received from a particular product or the level of sales each sales person has been responsible for.	Sales
Human Resources may want the total salary cost of the staff, if there is a recruitment budget and whether there are any bonuses, overtime or commission due.	Human Resources

Activity 5

The Premises manager has approached you for some help. He has some costs, present and future, that need to be met, and he is unsure of which budgets to use. He has sent you a memo, part of which is below. Fill in the gaps with the correct budget name.

I need to know how much money is left in the _____ budget to plan future repairs to the buildings.

I want to send two members of staff on a course to develop their skills so I need to apply to the _Training_ budget.

A couple of fire extinguishers need servicing by outside contractors. I will put the cost through the _____ budget.

Pick list

Premises	Distribution	Advertising
Training	Production	Health and Safety

4 Confidentiality

4.1 Confidentiality

Most of the information supplied by the accounting function will be financial information that may be both sensitive and/or private. Whether the information is held on paper or held electronically on a computer, accounting staff must make sure that confidential information is kept in a safe and secure way, so that it is only made available to the people authorised to see it.

4.2 Commercial information

Information held by the accounts department may be commercially sensitive. For example, the price paid for a particular product, or discounts given to customers. If a competitor of the business knew this information they might be able to use it as a competitive advantage.

4.3 Personal information

Personal information held about individuals, such as employees and customers, is protected by law. The Data Protection Act sets out rules about how personal data can be used. The Information Commissioner's Office (ICO) is the UK's independent body set up to uphold information rights. You can find out how your personal information is protected by visiting their website: https://www.ico.org.uk

Whether personal and sensitive information is held on computer or in a paper based filing system it must be kept safe and secure. This means it must be kept away from any unauthorised access. It would be wrong to leave personal data open to be viewed by just anyone.

4.4 Security of confidential information

If you have been given sensitive information to work with it is your responsibility to keep it safe and secure. Below are some examples of how you can keep confidential information secure in the situations you will find in an accounting office.

Example

Situation	Paper based filing system	Information held on a computer
Confidential information you are currently working with.	Any confidential information you are responsible for should be kept close by you at all times so that you are aware if anyone tries to read it. To avoid the information being seen by anyone passing by your desk, all confidential paperwork should be kept face down or in a folder until you need to work with it.	You may need to change the position of your computer screen to make sure that unauthorised people cannot see information on your computer screen as you are working. If this is not possible, you may need to move desks or offices to ensure that you can carry out the work. Sensitive information held on computers should be protected by multi-level passwords so that employees only see what is relevant to them. Never share your password with unauthorised people.
If you have to leave your workstation	If you have to leave your desk always put any confidential papers in a locked drawer or filing cabinet.	You should use the screen lock on your computer so that confidential information cannot be read by people passing your desk when you are away.
Storage of confidential information	Sensitive information should be kept in a locked filing cabinet, until it is needed.	Regular back-ups of computer data should be taken and stored in fireproof cabinets.
Out of date information	When confidential information is no longer needed it should be shredded before being recycled.	Data should be removed or deleted from computers by authorised staff from the Information Technology (IT) department.

Definition

Authorised person – Someone who has been given permission to do something on somebody else's behalf. For example, an employee who has been authorised to input confidential information onto a computer.

Activity 6

Commercial information is information that can be sold to anyone, so it does not have to be kept confidential. True or False?

---

5 Ethical and professional behaviour

5.1 Membership of professional bodies

A professional is someone who is qualified to carry out a task with a high level of expertise and skill. Accounting professionals are people who have qualifications in accountancy. They usually belong to a professional body such as the AAT.

All members of professional bodies whether they are students or fully qualified accountants are expected to behave ethically and professionally.

5.2 Ethical behaviour

Behaving ethically means doing the right thing at the right time. Accounting professionals are trusted by their employers to handle confidential and sensitive information in an appropriate manner.

The AAT has published a set of ethical guidelines for accounting professionals to follow, see http://www.aatethics.org.uk/code/. The following fundamental ethical principles form part of these guidelines.

- **Confidentiality** – as described earlier in this chapter, it is important that information is not disclosed to third parties, used for personal gain or shared unless there is a legal or professional duty to do so.

- **Objectivity** – accountants should remain independent and show sound judgement rather than allowing bias, personal interests or pressure from others to influence them.

- **Integrity** - this means being straightforward and honest when you perform your duties.

- **Professional behaviour and competence** – this means that you are able to perform your job to an acceptable level and provide a good service. All accounting professionals should undergo regular training to keep their technical knowledge up-to-date so that they can complete work to agreed standards, without mistakes.

5.3 Continuing Professional Development (CPD)

All accounting professionals perform a continual assessment of their learning needs to keep up to date with professional developments.

The AAT's CPD policy follows a four-stage cycle: Assess, Plan, Action, Evaluate. The AAT recommend that the cycle is followed at least twice each year.

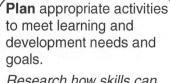

Assess learning and development needs and goals.

What skills do I need to be able to perform my duties effectively?

Plan appropriate activities to meet learning and development needs and goals.

Research how skills can be developed and discuss training opportunities with your manager. It might be by enrolling on a college course, or having informal training from a colleague.

Evaluate whether the activities did meet the developmental goals.

Can I now perform the tasks the organisation needs me to?

Action the plan

Enrol on a college course/ schedule training with a mentor.

Activity 7

In each of the following situations decide whether this is an example of ethical behaviour or not. For each, state which ethical principle is being considered.	Is this ethical behaviour?		Which ethical principle is being considered?
	Yes	No	
Discussing the issues one of your clients is facing when with your friends over dinner.			
Providing advice on an area of tax accounting you are not familiar with to a customer.			
Completing the accounts on time and bearing in mind all recent changes in legislation.			
Changing the contents of a report because your manager offered you a financial bonus to do so.			

Activity 8

Why is it important for accounting professionals to continually develop their skills?

6 Environmental and social responsibility

6.1 Environmental issues in business

Businesses as well as individuals need to think about how they can change the way they work in order to protect the environment for the future. An organisation's customers may consider whether businesses behave in an environmentally, ethically and socially responsible way before they will do business with them.

Many businesses have developed environmental and socially responsible policies and initiatives that benefit the internal and external customers of the business, as well as the wider society.

For example, the Unilever Group, a multinational organisation in the food and beverage industry manufactures some of the world's leading tea brands. One of the sustainability initiatives developed by the company is to work directly with the tea plantation farmers to make sure that they have safe working conditions and learn how to farm in sustainable ways, for example, by reducing the use of chemicals. Unilever also donates trees for planting and helps the local communities by building roads and schools.

http://www.unileverfoodsolutionsarabia.com/sustainability/case-studies/tea

 Definition

Sustainability means meeting the needs of the present generation without compromising the ability of future generations to meet their own needs.

6.2 Environmentally-friendly policies

All companies, large or small, can introduce policies to encourage staff to reduce the negative environmental impact of an organisation.

Examples of these sort of policies are found on the next page.

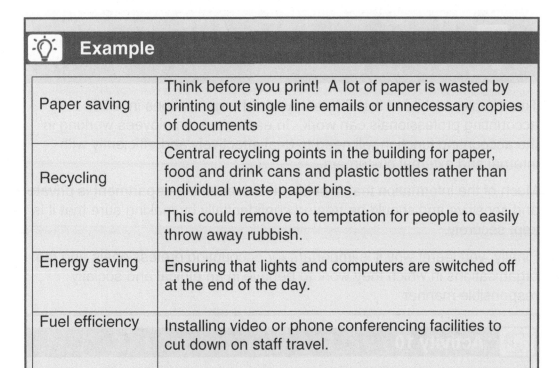

Example

Paper saving	Think before you print! A lot of paper is wasted by printing out single line emails or unnecessary copies of documents
Recycling	Central recycling points in the building for paper, food and drink cans and plastic bottles rather than individual waste paper bins.
	This could remove to temptation for people to easily throw away rubbish.
Energy saving	Ensuring that lights and computers are switched off at the end of the day.
Fuel efficiency	Installing video or phone conferencing facilities to cut down on staff travel.

Definition

Policy – A written document explaining how an organisation does something and the procedures it follows.

Activity 9

Consider your own workplace and suggest ways in which it could become more environmentally and socially responsible.

7 Summary and further questions

This chapter looked at the different types of organisations in which accounting professionals can work. In each case, employees working in the accounting function will need to deal effectively and efficiently with internal and external customers.

Much of the information that is held in the accounting department is private and sensitive and should be treated confidentially by making sure that it is kept securely.

Finally, you learnt why it is important for accounting professionals and the organisations in which they work to behave in an ethical and socially responsible manner.

Activity 10

Complete the sentences below using the pick list provided.

_____ sector organisations are normally concerned with the provision of basic government services.

Sole Traders are private businesses owned by one person.

_____ sector organisations are primarily concerned with making profit from the sale of goods or services. Where these businesses have shareholders they are known as _____.

Pick list

Private	Public	Charity
Sole traders	Partnerships	Limited companies

Activity 11

Match the following definitions with the correct business function.

Business function	Definition
PRODUCTION	This department sells the company's goods and services to customers.
SALES	This department is responsible for typing, collecting and distributing mail, keeping & filing records, organising meetings and maintaining resources
ADMINISTRATION	This department deals with the recruitment of new staff, the training of new and existing staff, pay negotiations and regular staff appraisals
ACCOUNTING	This department is responsible for producing the goods or services that a business provides by making best use of the various inputs.
HUMAN RESOURCES	This department is responsible for keeping records and accounts, for giving advice on budgets to other departments, and for paying wages and salaries

 Activity 12

You have been working on a confidential document on your computer and have to leave the office for ten minutes to deal with a customer. How can you keep the information on your screen confidential?

Tick the most appropriate answer.

Switch the computer off	
Use the screen lock facility to lock the computer screen	
Stay at your desk	
Put some papers over the screen to hide the information from passers by	

Activity 13

Which of the following are principles that a professional accountant should follow in order to demonstrate ethical behaviour?

Tick ALL that apply.

Confidentiality	
Flexibility	
Integrity	
Confidence	
Numeracy	

Activity 14

Which TWO of these options is an example of a socially and environmentally responsible organisation?

Offering free lunches for staff	
Training staff to use the recycling facilities	
Keeping the computers switched on at all times	
Using video conferencing instead of travelling to customers' premises	

Answers to chapter activities

Activity 1

Examples of charities and their goals include:

British Red Cross – to 'mobilise the power of humanity so that individuals and communities have the capacity to prepare for, deal with and recover from crisis'

Make-A-Wish – to 'grant the wishes of children with life-threatening medical conditions to enrich the human experience with hope, strength and joy'.

Oxfam – to 'create lasting solutions to poverty, hunger and social injustice'.

Activity 2

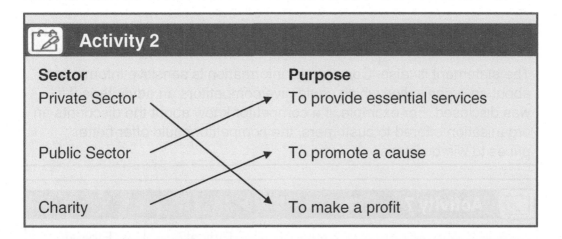

Sector	Purpose
Private Sector	To provide essential services
Public Sector	To promote a cause
Charity	To make a profit

Activity 3

	Private Sector	Public Sector	Charity
An animal welfare organisation			✓
Local government		✓	
A sole trader	✓		
A limited company	✓		
A primary school		✓	
An environmental conservation organisation			✓

Activity 4

The accounting function provides support and an essential service to the rest of the organisation. If they do not provide a good customer service to other departments it can put a strain on internal relationships and result in the organisation not giving a good overall level of service to all its customers.

Activity 5

I need to know how much money is left in the **Premises** budget to plan future repairs to the buildings.

I want to send two members of staff on a course to develop their skills so I need to apply to the **Training** budget.

A couple of fire extinguishers need servicing by outside contractors. I will put the cost through the **Health and Safety** budget.

Activity 6

The statement is false. Commercial information is sensitive information about an organisation which could give competitors an advantage if it was disclosed. For example, if a competitor knew about the discounts an organisation offered to customers, the competitor could offer better prices to win business.

Activity 7

	Ethical?		Ethical principle
	Yes	No	
Discussing the issues one of your clients is facing when with your friends over dinner.		✔	Confidentiality
Providing advice on an area of tax accounting you are not familiar with to a customer.		✔	Integrity
Completing the accounts on time and bearing in mind all recent changes in legislation.	✔		Professional behaviour & competence
Changing the contents of a report because your manager offered you a financial bonus to do so.		✔	Objectivity

Activity 8

Accounting professionals need to ensure that they remain competent for the work they do. They will need to keep up to date with changing regulations that affect their work. They will also need to keep up to date with technologies that help them do their work efficiently and effectively.

 Activity 9

There is no written answer for this activity.

 Activity 10

Public sector organisations are normally concerned with the provision of basic government services.

Sole traders are private business owned by one person.

Private sector organisations are primarily concerned with making profit from the sale of goods or services. Where these businesses have shareholders they are known as **limited companies.**

 Activity 11

Business function	Definition
PRODUCTION	This department is responsible for producing the goods or services that a business provides by making best use of the various inputs.
SALES	This department sells the company's goods and services to customers.
ADMINISTRATION	This department is responsible for typing, collecting and distributing mail, keeping & filing records, organising meetings and maintaining resources.
ACCOUNTING	This department is responsible for keeping records and accounts, for giving advice on budgets to other departments, and for paying wages and salaries.
HUMAN RESOURCES	This department deals with the recruitment of new staff, the training of new and existing staff, pay negotiations and regular staff appraisals.

Activity 12

Switch the computer off	
Use the screen lock facility to lock the computer screen	✔
Stay at your desk	
Put some papers over the screen to hide the information from passers by	

Activity 13

Confidentiality	✔
Flexibility	
Integrity	✔
Confidence	
Numeracy	

Activity 14

Offering free lunches for staff	
Training staff to use the recycling facilities	✔
Keeping the computers switched on at all times	
Using video conferencing instead of travelling to customers' premises	✔

Personal and professional working practices and skills

Introduction

As mentioned earlier in this study text, people working in accounting are trusted employees who are expected to work to high standards.

Accounting professionals have a duty to maintain a safe and effective working environment. In doing so, they will complete their own work efficiently and also contribute to the effectiveness of the team and the organisation.

Anyone working within an accounting environment will need to continually develop their professional and personal skills, attributes and behaviours.

KNOWLEDGE
3.1 Identify the responsibility an organisation has to the health and safety of its employees and of visitors to its premises
3.2 Explain the role of an employee in the accounting function in maintaining safe and effective working practices
4.1 Identify efficient working practices which contribute to the achievement of your own and team goals
4.2 Explain how communication within the team contributes towards its overall efficiency.
4.3 Identify the personal skills required to work in the accounting function
4.4 Identify ways in which new skills and knowledge can be acquired
4.5 Explain how the acquisition of new skills can be agreed and subsequently reviewed with the line manager

CONTENTS

1. Health and safety in the workplace
2. Efficient working practices
3. Team working
4. Professional and personal skills
5. Target setting

Health and Safety in the workplace

1.1   The importance of Health and Safety

Everyone in the workplace has a duty of care to all employees, customers, visitors and anyone on the business premises. If an employer is found to be responsible for an injury, they may be held liable and legal action may be taken against the organisation.

Because health and safety at work is so important all business organisations provide training and written rules that everyone should follow to reduce risks in the workplace. New employees will receive health and safety training as part of their induction to the organisation. If you see something that is unsafe, or could cause an accident it is your responsibility to report it to your manager.

Definition

Induction – a short programme which introduces new employees to the working environment. The process covers key internal and external regulations and policies which all employees must follow.

1.2   Safe and effective working practices

One way that you can help to maintain health and safety in the workplace is to keep your own work area clean and tidy. You should make sure that walkways are not blocked by boxes of papers, or trailing wires that could cause someone to trip.

Many workers find themselves overwhelmed by the amount of clutter on their desks, so by taking a few minutes each day to tidy up your work area you can make your office surroundings more professional, healthier and less stressful.

Keeping your work area tidy will also help you to prevent any confidential information to be left lying around.

Each function within an organisation is subdivided into teams so that all the work can be shared out to ensure it is completed on time. Team working means that the work will be completed more efficiently and effectively rather than each individual working independently.

The team leader will allocate the tasks that the team needs to complete to individual members of the team. Each individual then needs to organise their own workload so that they can make sure that it is completed efficiently within the deadlines set by the team leader.

2 Efficient working practices

2.1 Planning your work

A work plan is simply a list of jobs to complete, organised into the order in which they will be tackled and the time when each will be completed. There are many different methods which can be used to plan your work and the ones you choose may depend on your own personal preference, or be recommended by your team leader.

Some common planning methods which can be used in combination are:

To do Lists

A 'to do' list is a simple check list of all the activities that need to be carried out each day. The first five minutes of each day are set aside to write out the 'to do' list, and as each activity is completed it is crossed off the list. If anything is not completed that day, it can be added to the 'to do' list for the next day. However, if there is a task which cannot be completed within a certain time, then you will need to let your team leader know so that they can reschedule the task if necessary.

Example

THINGS TO DO TODAY

Date.........................

1	....	☐
2	....	☐
3	....	☐
4	....	☐
5	....	☐
6	....	☐
7	....	☐

In Tray

You may have a set of letter trays on your workstation which can be used to organise the different types of documents you are working on.

For example, your job role may involve dealing with purchase orders, purchase delivery notes and purchase invoices. Each tray should be labelled accordingly for each different document so that you, and other members of the team, can find the documents quickly and easily.

A traditional method of using letter trays is to have three trays labelled 'In', 'Out' and 'Pending'. Any new documentation that you receive is put in the 'In' tray, any work that you cannot complete because you need information from someone else is placed in the 'Pending' tray, and any work that has completed and needs filing or passing on to another team member is placed in the 'Out' tray.

Each tray should be clearly labelled so that anyone leaving a document for you can put it into the correct tray without disturbing your work.

Diary

Team members may use individual diaries or a team diary to make a note of tasks that need to be completed on a certain date. For example, you may have a conversation with a customer who has been late in paying an invoice. You can make a note in the diary for a particular time on a day next week to check if the customer's payment has been received.

Weekly Schedule

A schedule is a breakdown of the routine activities you need to complete for the following week as agreed with your team leader. The schedule should include all the planned activities for the week.

Example

	Monday	Tuesday	Wednesday	Thursday	Friday
9am - 10am	Opening and distributing post	Opening and distributing post	Opening and distributing post	Opening and distributing post	Opening and distributing post
10am – 11am	Processing Purchase Orders	Processing Sales Invoices	Processing Purchase Orders	Processing Sales Invoices	Team meeting
11am – 12pm	Processing Purchase Orders	Processing Sales Invoices	Processing Purchase Orders	Processing Sales Invoices	Preparing customers statement of accounts
12pm – 1pm	Preparing Banking	Preparing Banking	Preparing Banking	Preparing Banking	Preparing Banking
1pm – 2pm	Lunch	Lunch	Lunch	Lunch	Lunch
2pm – 3pm	Dealing with email queries	Dealing with email queries	Dealing with email queries	Dealing with email queries	Dealing with email queries
3pm – 4pm	Departmental Reports	Preparing supplier payments	Departmental Reports	Preparing supplier payments	Reconcile Petty Cash
4pm – 5pm	Filing documents	Filing documents	Filing documents	Filing documents	Filing documents

It is important that everyone keeps their colleagues and line managers informed of their progress against deadlines. If a deadline is not met, or is in danger of not being met, this will need to be communicated at the earliest opportunity and in an appropriate manner.

Activity 1

Mary has a series of necessary administrative tasks to complete in the morning before a large departmental meeting in the afternoon. Her manager Betty has informed her that the meeting is extremely important. Tick the ONE most appropriate solution for Mary from the list provided.

Mary should do the straightforward jobs and leave the more difficult ones for her colleagues to complete after she has left for the meeting.	
Mary should make a list of all that she needs to do in the morning and give each a timescale and priority.	
Mary should realise that it will be difficult to perform all of the tasks so she should put them all off until the next day.	
Mary should ignore the regional meeting and devote all her time to the tasks she needs to complete in the shop.	

3 Team working

3.1 Team working skills

To be able to work effectively in a team you will need to develop good team working skills. These skills include mutual support for each other, respect for others opinions, and the sharing of information.

Each member of the team will have certain tasks to do by a specific deadline and in some instances, other members of your team will need information from you before they can complete their work. It is therefore important that you share good communication skills with the team, so that everybody is aware if a task may not be completed on time.

If something happens which means that the team cannot complete a task on time, the team leader will have a **contingency plan.** For example, the team leader may build in some spare time in each team member's weekly schedule to allow them to step in to help other individuals if something has happened which means that they cannot keep to the planned schedule.

Activity 2

Which of the following are characteristics of an effective team?

a)   Mutual respect and support

b)   Lack of communication

c)   Strong pressure for group members to conform

d)   Clear aims and allocated tasks

e)   Dominant individual members

f)   No obvious leader

4 Professional and personal skills

4.1 Professional skills

Professional skills which can be developed over time include:

Professionalism	Accounting professionals should be able to demonstrate a high level of competence in their work and be able to meet the required standards of the profession.
Integrity	Accounting professionals should adopt an approach to work guided by strong moral principles. They are expected to be straightforward, honest and trustworthy.
Numeracy	Accounting professionals are expected to have good numeracy skills. They should be able to process numerical information quickly and accurately and be able to understand and explain calculations.
Literacy	Accounting professionals need to be skilled at dealing with written content.
Communication Skills	Accounting professionals need to be able to speak and deal with a wide range of people using a range of communication skills: e.g. writing, speaking, presenting, and listening.

4.2 Personal skills and attributes

As well as the key skills mentioned above, accounting professionals are expected to display certain personal attributes. These include:

Reliability	Employers and your team workers will need to rely on you to do the work that you promised to do.
Punctuality	Being punctual means being on time, both in terms of arriving at your place of work on time and completing a required task at an agreed time.
Willingness to learn	Showing a willingness to learn demonstrates to others that you are interested in your job role and the organisation. It also means that you are not afraid of learning new skills which will help you and the organisation to develop.
Well – organised	Employers will expect you to be able to complete work within an agreed time frame. If you are well-organised you are more likely to be able to complete your work effectively and efficiently.

4.3 Acquiring new skills

New skills and knowledge can be acquired in a variety of ways.

Accounting professionals will undertake **formal training** to learn technical skills, for example by enrolling on a college course to take AAT qualifications.

Knowledge and experience can also be acquired through **informal training** such as self-study or on the job training.

When setting development goals, it is important to work with your line manager so that they can ensure that your training needs are in line with the goals of the organisation.

The AAT CPD cycle can help you and your line manager to assess, plan, action and evaluate your skills development.

🔆 Example

ASSESS	Your line manager or mentor should discuss your development needs and goals with you to ensure that these are in line with organisational goals.
PLAN	Once the developmental need has been identified both you and your line manager can decide the best method for you to acquire the new skill.
ACTION	Complete the training activity within a scheduled time following SMART targets.
EVALUATE	After the training has been completed, you and your line manager should review the training to check whether it met your developmental needs and those of the organisation, and you can now complete the tasks required.

Job training can either be formal – attending a college course, or informal. Examples of informal training are given below.

🔆 Example

Job Rotation	Job rotation involves switching employees round through a range of jobs. Job rotation can mean that employees are given a wider knowledge of the organisation. It can also help the organisation if cover is needed for absent staff.

KAPLAN PUBLISHING

Job Shadowing	Job shadowing means working with an experienced employee who can pass on the skills and knowledge required to perform the task
Professional Journals	Professional journals are magazines written by professionals in a particular field of interest. For example, the AAT Accounting Technician magazine publishes articles on issues related to accountancy for accounting students.
Internet	The internet is useful for up to date information on financial news.
Newspapers	The business section of daily newspapers contains information relevant to accounting professionals.

5 Target setting

5.1 SMART targets

Any goals that you and your line manager agree should be SMART. SMART is an acronym that relates to the characteristics of sound objectives.

Specific

Measurable

Achievable

Relevant

Timely

For example, you and your line manager have agreed that you need to develop your communication skills when dealing with customer queries. It is decided that the best way to develop this skill will be for you to job shadow an experienced colleague.

The SMART target set is "to handle customer queries effectively by the end of the month".

Specific	To be able to deal with a variety of work related queries from customers.
Measurable	Customers will complete a short questionnaire stating whether they were satisfied with the way you handled their query.
	The experienced colleague will give feedback on your performance to you and your line manager.

Achievable	You have the support of colleagues to help you develop your communication skills.
Relevant	Being able to deal with customer queries effectively is important for the organisation
Timely	By the end of the month, you can deal with customer queries effectively.

If targets are not SMART it will be difficult to achieve them.

 Activity 3

When setting objectives for his staff, these should be SMART. What does SMART stand for?

a) Specific, Manageable, Accountable, Relevant, Timely

b) Specific, Measurable, Achievable, Relevant, Timely

c) Scientific, Measurable, Achievable, Realistic, Timely

d) Scientific, Measurable, Authoritative, Responsible, Timely

 Activity 4

Identify a skill that you would like to improve and complete the table below to help you write a SMART target to achieve the goal.

The skill you want to develop:		
SPECIFIC	What do you want to achieve?	
MEASURABLE	What will you be able to do when you have achieved the goal?	
ACHIEVABLE	Is it a realistic target?	
RELEVANT	Is it relevant to your or your organisation's needs?	
TIMELY	State a date by which time you will have achieved the goal.	

 Activity 5

Write out the SMART target above in a sentence.

(Further activity: Discuss this with your manager/mentor/tutor.)

KAPLAN PUBLISHING

6 Further questions

Activity 6

Health and safety in the workplace is the responsibility of:

The government	
The managers	
The employees	
The managers and the employees	

Activity 7

On your way into work you noticed that there was an electrical cable dangling from the ceiling in reception. What should you do about this?

Nothing – it is not your responsibility	
Report the risk to a manager immediately	
Get a ladder so the receptionist can push the electrical cable back	

Activity 8

What does CPD stand for? Tick the correct box.

Constant Personal Development	
Constant Private Development	
Continuous Private Development	
Continuing Professional Development	

Activity 9

For each of the following examples of ways to develop your knowledge and skills, determine whether it is formal or informal training.

	Formal / informal
Reading professional journals	
Attending a day release course at a local college	
Studying an online course for which you will be awarded a certificate on completion.	
Work shadowing	

Answers to chapter activities

 Activity 1

Mary should make a list of all that she needs to do in the morning and give each a timescale and priority.

 Activity 2

a) Mutual respect and support
d) Clear aims and allocated tasks

 Activity 3

The answer is **B -** Specific, Measurable, Achievable, Relevant, Timely.

 Activity 4 and 5

There is no written answer for these activities as it will depend on the individual's goals and development needs.

 Activity 6

Health and safety in the workplace is the responsibility of the managers and the employees.

 Activity 7

You should report the risk to a manager immediately.

 Activity 8

CPD stands for Continuing Professional Development.

Activity 9

Reading professional journals	**Informal**
Attending a day release course at a local college	**Formal**
Studying an online course	**Formal**
Work shadowing	**Informal**

1 Communication styles

1.1   Formal and informal communication

Formal Language

Business English is the formal language used for business communications, especially when producing documents. Formal language is structured and professional and follows accepted grammatical rules and spelling conventions. You should not use slang or text language and words are written out in full and not abbreviated.

Informal Language

Informal language is less structured than formal language and is most often used in speech. In some cases, it may be acceptable to use informal language in a business setting, for example when you are communicating with your peers. However, even when communicating with people you know well it is still possible for your message to be misunderstood if you use slang or text language. If you are in any doubt you should always use formal language.

Formal language is most commonly used with external customers. Informal language may be used when communicating with internal customers. However, even when using informal language you should make sure that the message is clear and easily understandable by the reader.

Activity 1

Decide when you would use these examples of formal or informal language.

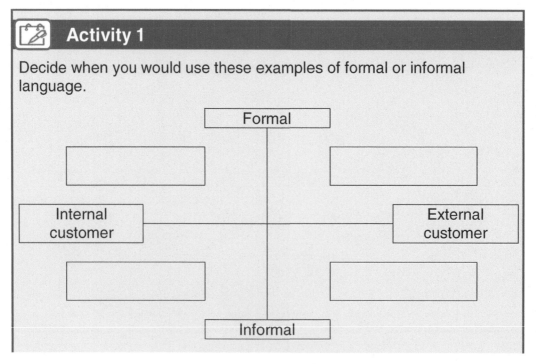

Creating business documents

7

Introduction

Accounting professionals will need to communicate regularly with internal and external customers.

This chapter introduces you to the different types of business documents you will come across in an accounting environment. You will be able to identify the correct communication style to use in each business document.

Finally, you will be able to produce routine business documents accurately and professionally.

KNOWLEDGE

Award in Accounting

1.1 Identify different types of business document and when they might be used

1.2 State why templates are used for some business documents

2.1 State why some businesses adopt a 'house style' for certain documents

2.2 Give examples of when to use a formal or informal communication style

3.1 Produce routine business documents using the appropriate communication style

3.2 Check documents for accuracy

CONTENTS

1 Communication styles
2 Letters
3 E-mails
4 Memos
5 Reports
6 House styles and templates
7 Summary and further questions

A   Thank you for the payment received today.

B   Ok, thanks - that's great.

C   There were some errors in the report you sent over. Can you redo and email it back to me asap?

D   Please let me know if I there is anything else I can help you with.

E   Let's meet up and have a chat about it. About 2 ish?

F   It was great to meet up with you today.

G   Your invoice is now overdue.   Please could you arrange payment by the end of the week.

H   We need to arrange a meeting to discuss staffing over the summer holidays. Please could you let me know when you are free?

1.2   Business writing

Business documents follow a standard structure according to organisational guidelines.

In each case, they should be in the correct format, using clear and concise language, and they should be free from any grammatical or spelling mistakes.

1.3   Paragraphs and structure in business documents

All business documents should be structured by using paragraphs. Paragraphs help the reader to understand your message because:

*   They break text down into manageable proportions

*   Each sentence in a paragraph relates to the same topic

*   Starting a new paragraph makes it clear to the reader that you are moving on to another topic.

In business documents there should be a short introductory paragraph followed by one or two paragraphs with the main content. The final paragraph should be a short conclusion.

When writing business communications the pneumonic STRIPE is a useful structure to follow:

S	Salutation	A greeting, for example 'Dear ....'
T	Topic	The heading or subject
R	Reason	The main purpose of the communication
I	Information	Specific details or a request for information
P	Prompt to action	What you would like the reader to do.
E	End	A complimentary close and signature

2 Letters

2.1 The use of letters in business

Letters are used to communicate with **external** customers and should always be written using **formal** language.

All letters contain similar elements. However, you should also check your organisation's guidelines as it is important that all letters sent out by employees of the organisation are consistent with the organisation's house style.

Definition

House Style - A set of guidelines that explain how all documents produced by an organisation should be set out.

2.2 Letterheads and return addresses

Many organisations have a letterhead which contains the company logo, the postal address, and company website address.

If your organisation does not have a letterhead, the name and address of the organisation should appear on the right side of the document, immediately above the date line in the letter.

2.3   Letter format

Date Line

The date should include the day, the month and the year. The month should always be written in full, e.g. 17 June 2016

Customer Name and Address

The recipient's name and address should be spelt correctly and written on the left hand side of the letter.

Open Salutation

The opening salutation begins with the word 'Dear' and continues with the recipient's title and last name. If you don't know the name of the recipient, you can use 'Dear Sir or Madam'. However, it is better to try to find out the name of the person you are writing to by telephoning the recipient's organisation to ask who you should address the letter to.

Reference

The reference is a short description of the content of the letter.

Body of Letter

The body of the letter should be concise, clear and to the point, and should be divided into paragraphs.

* The first paragraph should state the purpose of the letter.

* The middle paragraph(s) should contain supporting information.

* The final paragraph should state what you would like the recipient to do.

Closing salutation

The choice of closing salutation depends on the opening salutation used.

When you know the name of the person you are addressing, e.g. 'Dear Mr or Mrs …' the closing salutation should be 'Yours sincerely'

If you don't know the addressee's name, and you have used an opening salutation of 'Dear Sir or Madam' the closing salutation should be 'Yours faithfully'

Signature

The letter should be signed above the typed name and job title of the writer.

Activity 2

In a business letter what salutation would you use when writing to somebody whose name is known to you? (His name is James Smith)

a) Sir

b) James

c) Mr Smith

 Activity 3

How would you sign off a business letter to someone whose name is not known to you?

a) Yours faithfully

b) Yours sincerely

c) Yours forever

 Example

Friebe Motors
Top Lane
CHEETHAM
CH5 7TY

17 June 2016

Mr R Moore
Chippendale Lane
CHEETHAM
CH4 8PG

Dear Mr Moore

Re: Cheque Payment of £5,450

Thank you for your cheque payment of £5,450 received today.

Unfortunately, you did not send a remittance advice with the payment so we are not sure which invoices you are paying. Please could you send a remittance advice so that we can make sure that we allocate the payment to the correct invoices?

We look forward to receiving your remittance. In the meantime, if you need any more information please contact me at the above address.

Yours sincerely

D Francis

D Francis
Accounts Administrator

3 E-mails

3.1 The use of e-mails in business

E-mails are an effective way to communicate formal or informal information electronically to internal and external customers. Many business people receive hundreds of e-mails every day and find dealing with emails very time consuming. It is important that any business emails you send are short and to the point so that they can be read and responded to quickly.

3.2 Effective e-mail format

E-mails should have a clear subject line and the message itself should be clear and concise. Some people recommend writing the message in no more than five sentences so that the recipient is more likely to read the e-mail and respond quickly. If an e-mail contains detailed information, it may be more suitable to include the additional information as an attachment.

 Definition

Attachment – An email attachment is a computer file, for example a document or spreadsheet, which is sent with an e-mail message.

3.3 E-mail structure

Although e-mails are less formal that a printed business letter you should always write emails with the same care that you would use to write a formal letter. Remember that people are unlikely to be offended if you are too formal, but some may think you are being rude if you are too informal.

To: droberts@abc.net

Cc: accountsteam@soppo.com

Subject: Returned faulty goods

Hello David

Further to our conversation today, I can confirm that the goods you returned to us have been received in our warehouse.

The warehouse team will check that the goods are faulty and, if so, we will send a credit note to you immediately.

Kind regards

D Marsh

Accounts Administrator

---

4 Memos

4.1 What is a memo?

A memo is a document containing information which is to be communicated to one or more **internal customers**. Memos are generally used to make announcements or notify staff of new policies and procedures. They should be written using **formal** language.

4.2 Structure of a memo

All memos will have the following elements

To: The names of the recipient(s)

From: The name and job title of the sender

Date: The date written in full, e.g. 18 June 2016

Subject: A short description of the content of the memo

The main content of the communication should be broken down into paragraphs.

 Example

> MEMO
>
> To: Accounting Department Staff
>
> From: J Cooke, Health and Safety Manager
>
> Date: 18 May 2015
>
> Subject: Fire Hazard
>
> It has come to my attention that the fire doors at the rear of the Accounts Office are being propped open by boxes of stationery.
>
> This is a serious fire hazard. Please ensure that the fire doors are kept shut and that a safe storage place is found for the stationery boxes.

5   Reports

5.1   The use of reports in business

Business reports are used to communicate information formally to internal and external customers.

Reports are used to present a lot of information all together in one document.

5.2   The structure of reports

The format of the report depends on the information being presented but could include:

Title Page	The report will have a front cover or title page which will include: • The name of the person the report is for • The name of the person the report is from • The date of the report.
Summary	A short overview of what can be found in the full report.
Contents page	An index of page numbers where the information can be found.
Introduction	An outline of the report's structure.
Body	The main content of the report which may be sectioned into sub headings.
Conclusion	The main findings from the report.
Appendix	Graphs and charts which support the information in the main report.

Activity 4

Put the following sections of a report into the order in which you would expect to see them. Complete the boxes below using a), b), c) or d).

a)	Recommendations	First	
b)	Conclusion	Second	
c)	Introduction	Third	
d)	Appendix	Fourth	

6 House styles and templates

6.1 The need for house styles

Most organisations insist that written communication presents a consistent, positive message to customers which also supports the organisation's characteristics. Some organisations may want to project a very formal image whilst others may want to appear more friendly and approachable.

6.2 House style guidelines

House styles are a set of organisational guidelines stating how documents should be formatted. Before producing any business documents you should check whether your organisation has a house style and if it has you should always follow those guidelines.

House style guidelines could include:

Font	The type, size and colour of font to be used for normal text. The house style may also define the size and formatting of any headings and the type of bullet points to use.
Addresses	A house style may state where addresses should appear on a letter and whether they should include punctuation.
Days and dates	The correct order and style for the date may be given. For example, one house style may state that just the number is given for the day: 8 September 2015, whilst another may say that 'th', 'rd' or 'st' should be used. e.g: 8th September 2015
Language	A house style may give guidelines about the type of language that should be used in written communication.
Abbreviations	Some house styles give a list of abbreviations that can be used.

 Activity 5

Think of an organisation that you know and create a set of guidelines for the organisation's house style. What would you include?

6.3 What is a template?

A template is a pre-prepared electronic document set out using an organisation's house style.

6.4 The benefits of using templates

Using templates makes it easier for employees to create business communications that are consistent with the organisation's brand image.

Templates help to save time and reduce errors because common elements are pre-printed and users just have to complete any information that is specific to that particular communication. In this example, only the items in bold need to be completed.

 Example

Dear **[customer name]**

Ref: **[Customer Account Number]**

Please find attached your statement of account for **[month].** The balance outstanding is £ **[balance outstanding].**

We would appreciate payment by the end of this week. If you have any queries regarding any of the amounts on the statement, please contact me as soon as possible.

Yours sincerely

Accounts Assistant

7 Summary and further questions

In this chapter you learnt how to structure some common business documents. You should now understand that it is usually more appropriate to use formal language when communicating with other professionals. The importance of consistency in business communication to present an organisation's brand image effectively was also discussed.

The further questions below are designed to check your knowledge.

Activity 6

Classify the following communication activities as:

- formal or informal
- internal or external

	Formal / Informal	Internal / External
A letter to a member of the public responding to a complaint		
Asking a colleague whether or not an order has been fulfilled		
A report for the directors analysing annual business performance		
A Human Resources policy document for all staff		
An e-mail to all customers regarding a new invoicing system		

 Activity 7

Read through the letter shown below and identify TEN errors.

> Morse Manufacturing
> The Old Mill
> Addison Drive
> Newtown
> NW24 8RP

Christopher Barrie
22 Loring Avenue
Little Hinton
Buckinghamshire
HP99 2AQ

Hello Barrie

Ref: 50% discount on all home furnishings

I am pleased to confirm that we have accepted your credit account application. You're initial credit limit on the account will be £1,500 and you will be required to settle your account within 15 days of purchase.

after a tryal period of three months, if payments have been received in a timely fashion, we will discuss your requirements further!

I hope that the above meets with your approval. If I could of been of any more assistance, please let me know.

Otherwise we look forward 2 hearing from you soon.

Yours faithfully,

Kevin Claydon
kevlovesit@hotmail.com

Activity 8

You have been given the following letter from an unhappy customer.

Required:

i.   Read the contents of the letter and consider how to write an apology with a suggested solution for the customer

ii.   Write a letter to the customer

iii.   Write an e-mail to your colleagues to inform them of your actions.

34 Huckleberry Farm
Parsons Road
Boxted
PR23 6DW

Buttersworth Garden Store
Windmill Lane
Newtown
NW89 6QR   29th December 2014

Dear Sir/Madam

Ref: My recent order for a Turbo 6000 Hedge Trimmer

I write to you regarding my recent online order for a Turbo 6000 Lightweight Hedge Trimmer which I purchased on 1st December 2014.

Firstly, I would like to complain that although the price listed on the website was £75 due to your Christmas Garden Hampers offer, I was still charged the full retail price of £99. The total cost of the order should therefore have been £90 including the £15 home delivery charge, which I was also not aware of until the checkout process began. Naturally, I feel misled by both the offer and the delivery charge and believe I have been overcharged. I therefore would like an immediate refund.

Secondly, having ordered this hedge trimmer as a Christmas gift, I was disappointed that it had not arrived within the three week delivery period. Although I telephoned you to seek advice on the delivery date I was told that you could not promise anything. I was then shocked to find, on return from our Christmas break, three hedge trimmers had been delivered. It is now too late for any more than one of these hedge trimmers to be worthwhile, as Christmas has passed.

Please advise me as to how this error occurred and arrange an immediate refund. I appreciate your assistance with this matter, as due to this incident, I am unlikely to use your website for future purchases.

Yours faithfully,

David D Mooney
07111 423699

Answers to chapter activities

Activity 1

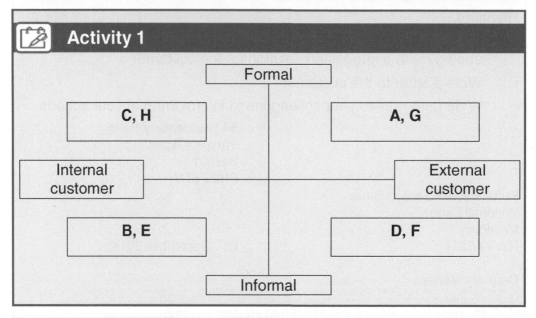

	Formal	
C, H		**A, G**
Internal customer		External customer
B, E		**D, F**
	Informal	

Activity 2

c)   Mr Smith

Activity 3

a)   Yours faithfully

Activity 4

The correct order is:

First	C (Introduction)
Second	A (Recommendations)
Third	B (Conclusion)
Fourth	D (Appendices)

Activity 5

House style guidelines could include any of the following.

- Abbreviations
- Addresses and telephone numbers
- Bullets and lists
- Capital letters
- Charts and tables
- Days and dates
- Font size and type
- Language
- Numbers
- Money
- Punctuation

 Activity 6

	Formal / Informal	Internal / External
A letter to a member of the public responding to a complaint	Formal	External
Asking a colleague whether or not an order has been fulfilled	Informal	Internal
A report analysing annual business performance for the board of directors	Formal	Internal
A Human Resources policy document for all staff	Formal	Internal
An e-mail to all customers informing them of a new invoicing system	Formal	External

Activity 7

The following errors can be identified:

1. There is no date anywhere on the letter

2. The letter should start 'Dear Mr Barrie'. The salutation of Hello is not appropriate in a letter to a customer. 'Barrie' is the customer's surname, so would not be correct even in a less formal form of writing.

3. The subject of the letter has nothing to do with the content (it is about the opening of a trade account, not discounted furnishings).

4. The second paragraph should start with a capital letter ('After' not 'after').

5. The word 'trial' in the first line of the second paragraph is spelt incorrectly.

6. The second paragraph ends with an exclamation mark which is inappropriate in a business context.

7. In the third paragraph, 'could of' should be 'could have'.

8. In the final sentence the number 2 is used instead of the word 'to'. 'Text speak' is not acceptable in any business communications.

9. As the name of the recipient is known, the letter should end with 'Yours sincerely' rather than 'Yours faithfully'.

10. The writer's signature section is not appropriate – it does not include their job title under their name beneath the signature. The e-mail address provided is not a work e-mail address.

 Activity 8

i. In terms of the apology, there are a number of potential means of handling this particular complaint. Assuming that the offer mentioned was valid, it would be appropriate to refund £24 which was overcharged online. As a goodwill gesture, bearing in mind that delivery was not within the time frame given, delivery charges could also be refunded.

There are also customer service problems which require attention – for example, the lack of delivery advice and then error in delivering three trimmers. Although an apology and explanation will go some way to address this, at the very least collecting the extra trimmers would be appropriate.

It may also be advisable to offer a further discount if the customer orders again, or personal service, to try to keep their business given the tone at the end of the letter.

ii.   The exact contents of the letter will depend on the approach taken, but here is an example:

> Buttersworth Garden Store
> Windmill Lane
> Newtown
> NW89 6QR

David D Mooney
34 Huckleberry Farm
Parsons Road
Boxted
PR23 6DW

2nd January 2015

Dear Mr Mooney

Ref: Your recent order for a Turbo 6000 Hedge Trimmer

Thank you for your letter relating to your order for a Turbo 6000 Lightweight Hedge Trimmer. May I take this opportunity to thank you for using our new website and ordering from Buttersworth Garden Stores. I apologise for the problems you have encountered, which hopefully this letter will help to rectify.

In terms of pricing, I am sincerely sorry for the error on the website. As you suggest, the discounted price was £75 and therefore you should not have been charged the full retail price of £99. This error was due to technical difficulties with the new website and I apologise for any inconvenience or confusion caused. I have arranged for an immediate refund of £24 to your credit card.

I also apologise for the customer service issues you describe, especially as we pride ourselves on providing good information to our customers. The customer services team member should have provided you with more information and I have made my manager aware of the inconvenience caused. As a gesture of goodwill we will also refund the £15 delivery charge, as I appreciate that the delivery was not made in time for Christmas. Our standard delivery time in December for specialist items is 3-4 weeks which should have been explained.

I will arrange for the two extra trimmers to be collected immediately. Unless I hear otherwise from you, this will be next Tuesday morning. I am sorry for any storage issues caused by these being delivered and I have escalated the matter to our logistics team.

It is disappointing to hear that you may not consider using our services again and I hope this letter has shown that we value your custom and are looking to improve our service. I am also happy to offer you 10% off your next order, which I will personally process on your behalf.

I hope that this rectifies the situation and look forward to hearing from you soon. Please contact me with any further queries or requests.

Yours sincerely,

Steve Palmer
Customer Services Advisor
Buttersworth Garden Stores
steven.palmer@buttersworth.co.uk
01234 765123

iii.

From: Steve Palmer

To: Mike Andrews (IT Manager); Melanie Parfitt (Customer Services Manager); Simon Elders (Logistics Manager); Sita Mardi (Accounts); Customer Services staff

Hello all

Please find attached a scan letter from one of our customers, David D Mooney. He was incorrectly charged for a 6000 Turbo HT via the web in December, as the Christmas promotion prices were not working correctly. Mike – please could you log the problem; Sita – please could you refund him £39 in total (including a goodwill gesture for shipping).

As you can see, Mr Mooney also did not receive delivery in time and then we sent the order three times. Simon – please could you advise and arrange collection of the two surplus products next Tuesday morning?

When he called the office, it seems he did not receive full information, which has added to the problem. I have asked that for future orders he contacts me and will honour a 10% discount should he allow us an opportunity to make up for this. Please could you forward any calls or communications on to me should he be in touch.

I have obviously passed on apologies to the customer and assured him this will not happen again, but felt you should be aware.

Many thanks,

Steve Palmer

Customer Services

Ext 5123

Mathematics for accounting

Introduction

When you are working in an accounting department you will need to be confident in handling money and working with numbers. You will also be expected to be able to use a calculator effectively

This chapter covers the essential mathematical skills you will need to perform common accounting calculations: addition and subtraction, multiplication and division, percentages, ratios and fractions, and calculating the average of a range of numbers.

KNOWLEDGE
Award in Accounting
1.1 Add and subtract whole numbers and numbers up to two decimal places
1.2 Multiply and divide whole numbers and numbers up to two decimal places
1.3 Calculate the ratio or proportion of two numbers
1.4 Calculate the percentage of one number in relation to another
1.5 Find a percentage of a whole number
1.6 Apply a fraction to whole numbers
1.7 Calculate the average of a range of numbers

CONTENTS

1 Mathematic symbols
2 Decimal places and rounding up and down
3 Addition and subtraction
4 Multiplication and division
5 Fractions and ratios
6 Percentages
7 Summary

1 Mathematic symbols

1.1 Common symbols

The following table shows the most common symbols you will see for the mathematical functions you will be using in this unit.

	Addition	Subtraction	Multiplication	Division
Calculator	+	-	X	÷
Computer keyboard	+	-	*	/
Written	+	- or ( )	X or @	$\frac{2}{3}$

1.2 Currency

For numbers that represent money you should always show the relevant currency symbol. The currency symbol for UK sterling pounds is **£**. Euros are represented by **€**, and for US dollars the symbol is **$**. You can either write the symbol against each amount or the currency symbol can be shown at the top of the list.

1.3 Punctuation

In the UK a full stop [.] is used to separate pounds and pence and a comma [,] is used to separate thousands.   For example, to make it easier to see the difference between £1000000, £100000 and £10000 count 3 zeros back from the right and put a comma, then count another 3 zeros back from the first comma and put another comma, and so on.

£1000000 becomes £1,000,000 or one million pounds

£100000 becomes £100,000 or one hundred thousand pounds

£10000 becomes £10,000 or ten thousand pounds.

When you are dealing with a long list of numbers putting the commas in the right place makes the figures easier to read, and you will be able to perform the calculations more efficiently.

Note:

Some countries use commas for the decimal point and the thousand separator is shown by a full stop. Always follow the convention of the country you are working in.

2 Decimal places and rounding up and down

2.1 Decimal places

For the AAT assessment, the instructions will always tell you whether you should round your answer to the nearest pound (whole number), or to one or two decimal places.

Whole number: £500   Five hundred pounds

Two decimal places: £49.99   Forty nine pounds and ninety nine pence

One decimal place: £2.5 million Two and a half million pounds

Note: If you are using a calculator the display will not show the second decimal point if it is zero. When writing the answer down you should always include the missing zero.

💡 Example

A customer bought 5 items costing £2.50 each. You multiply 5 times £2.50 by keying 5 x 2.50 on the calculator. The display shows 12.5.

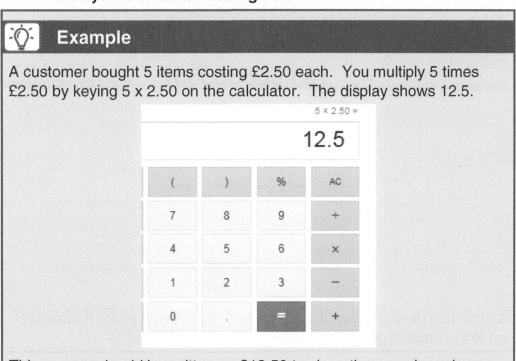

This answer should be written as £12.50 to show the pounds and pence.

In the workplace, always check how many decimal places you should show. If you are not sure, show your answers to two decimal places.

Monetary amounts should always be shown to one or two decimal places, or whole numbers. However, the calculator may show more figures after the decimal place than you need, so you will need to round your answer.

2.2 Showing pounds and pence to two decimal places

Calculations which require the answer to be shown in pounds and pence should always be given to two decimal places. If your calculator shows more than two decimal places, you will need to round the answer.

Look at the number in the third decimal place – if it is 5 or above, round the number in the second decimal place up. If it is below 5, the answer is rounded down – you do not need to change the number in the second decimal place.

2.3 Rounding up

 Example

You have been asked to calculate the cost of one box of a product when 3 boxes cost £500.

You divide £500.00 by 3 by keying 500. ÷ 3 on the calculator. The display shows 166.666666667

As the third decimal place is larger than 5, you should round this answer **up** to the nearest penny - £166.67.

2.4 Rounding down

 Example

A supplier has given you a price of £100.00 for 3 boxes of a product. What is the cost for one box?

You divide £100.00 by 3 by keying 100. ÷ 3 on the calculator. The display shows 33.3333333333

As the third decimal place is below 5, this answer should be rounded **down** to the nearest penny. This means you do not have to change the figure in the second decimal place, so the answer is £33.33.

2.5 Rounding answers to the nearest whole number

To round numbers to the nearest whole number, you need to look at the number in the first decimal place - if the number in the first decimal place is 5 or above, round up the pounds figure. If it is below 5, round down the pounds figure – you do not need to change the pounds figure.

Example

You have been asked to round the following figures to the nearest whole pound.

Original figure	Rounded to the nearest whole pound	Notes
£49.99	£50	The number in the first decimal place is 9 – the pounds figure is rounded up.
£425.20	£425	The number in the first decimal place is 2 – the pounds figure is rounded down. You do not need to change the pounds figure.

3 Addition and subtraction

3.1 Addition and subtraction in accounting

There are many tasks in the accounting function where you will be required to add and subtract lists of numbers. You will need to complete these tasks confidently and efficiently. You should always add up lists of numbers twice to check that you get the same answer both times.

When you are writing down lists of numbers make sure that the decimal points are aligned, so that the figures are easier to read and calculate.

Example - addition

You have been asked to add the weekly credit sales and you have written the following list.

Monday	£15,000.00
Tuesday	£14,500.50
Wednesday	£ 9,250.00
Thursday	£16,700.00
Friday	£18,000.00
Saturday	£25,000.00

Using a calculator effectively

When working with monetary numbers you should always key in the decimal point on the calculator. If you need to add a whole number you do not need to key in the zeros after the decimal place and if the pence are a multiple of 10 you do not need to key in the final zero.

Use this technique to add up the list of weekly credit sales.

The answer on your calculator will be:

15000. + 14500.5 + 9250. + 16700. + 18000. + 25000. =

98450.5

This answer should be written down as **£98,450.50**

KAPLAN PUBLISHING

Activity 1

The Sales department have been given the following information for last week's sales.

Credit Sales	Monday	£ 2,399.00
	Tuesday	£ 3,210.50
	Wednesday	£ 2,225.20
	Thursday	£ 4,375.00
	Friday	£ 6,010.00

Cash Sales	Monday	£ 499.99
	Tuesday	£ 325.50
	Wednesday	£ 769.00
	Thursday	£ 1,005.00
	Friday	£ 247.20

Required:

a) Calculate the weekly credit sales,

b) Calculate the weekly cash sales

c) Calculate the total weekly sales

3.2 Subtraction to calculate profit

 Definition

Cost of Sales – The direct cost of producing the goods and *purchases* services that have been sold.

Gross profit – The profit (or amount of money left) from sales after the cost of sales has been deducted.

Net profit – The amount left from sales income (gross profit) after cost of sales and all other expenses (such as wages, electricity and marketing costs) have been deducted.

To calculate gross profit, cost of sales are subtracted from sales income.

To calculate net profit, all other expenditure is subtracted from gross profit.

Example - subtraction

A business has calculated last month's sales income to be £98,000

The cost of sales came to £58,800, and other expenditure was £25,000

You are to calculate the gross profit and the net profit.

a) Calculate gross profit

Subtract cost of sales, £58,800 from sales income, £98,000

Gross profit is £39,200

b) Calculate net profit

Subtract £25,000 from £39,200

Net profit is £14,200

Example 2 - subtraction

You have been given the following financial information for a business

Sales income	£259,258.75
Cost of sales	£156,540.00
Wages	£85,000.00
Marketing	£5,297.50
Premises costs	£3,200.00
Vehicle costs	£2,785.80

Calculate:

a) Gross profit

b) Net profit

Solution

a) To calculate gross profit, subtract £156,540.00 from £259,258.75

> 259258.75 - 156540. =
>
> ## 102718.75

Gross profit is £102,718.75

b) There are two methods for calculating net profit:

   i. Subtract each expense from the gross profit figure:

   > 102718.75 - 85000. - 5297.5 - 3200. - 2785.80 =
   >
   > ### 6435.45

Net profit is £6,435.45

ii. First add up all the other expenditure, and then subtract that figure from your gross profit figure of £102,748.75

> 85000. + 5297.50 + 3200. + 2785.80 =
>
> ### 96283.3

> 102718.75 - 96283.3 =
>
> ## 6435.45

Net profit is £6,435.45

Activity 2

Tripps Tiles had weekly credit sales of £58,956.50 and weekly cash sales of £25,985.60.

The cost of sales figure was £55,215.35

Other expenses were:

Wages	£ 6,500.00
Advertising	£ 1,576.00
Heat and light	£ 1,040.50
Administration	£ 1,875.70
Vehicle costs	£ 950.75

Calculate:

a) Weekly sales income

b) Gross profit

c) Net profit

4   Multiplication and division

4.1   Multiplying in accounting

Many calculations that you perform in an accounting office will require you to multiply or divide.

 Definition

Multiplying means adding the same amount a number of times. If you need to find the cost of more than one item you multiply the cost of the item by the number of items needed.

Multiplying a number by another will **increase** the original amount.

Example

You are working in the sales department of a computer supplies wholesaler. A customer has bought the following goods and has asked you to calculate the total sales price.

- 5 AG 355 15" laptop computer @ £299.00
- 3 Tamsing 10" Tablet PC @ £199.00
- 8 Shogun USB External Hard Drive @ £50.00
- 1 Tiger Antivirus Pro (10 licenses) @ £29.99

Setting the information out clearly in a table will help you to calculate the prices efficiently and will look more professional.

Item	Quantity	Unit Price (£)	Total Price (£)	Calculation
AG 355 15" laptop computer	5	299.00	1,495.00	5 x 299
Tamsing 10" Tablet PC	3	199.00	597.00	3 x 199
Shogun USB External Hard Drive	8	50.00	400.00	8 x 50
Tiger Antivirus Pro (10 licenses)	1	29.99	29.99	1 x 29.99
Total Sales Price			**2,521.99**	1495.00+ 597.00+ 400.00 +29.99

4.2 Division in accounting

 Definition

Dividing a number means splitting it into parts. If you know the cost of a number of items and want to find the cost of just one of them you will use division.

Dividing a number by another will **decrease** the original amount.

Example

The customer has seen some mouse mats for sale at £12.50 for a pack of 5. The customer would like to know the cost for each mouse mat.

To calculate the cost per unit, divide the total cost by the number of units

Total cost per pack of mouse mats is	£12.50
Divided by the number of units	5

Calculation:

12.5 ÷ 5 =

2.5

Each individual mouse mat costs **£2.50**

 Activity 3

You have been asked to calculate the weekly gross pay for the following employees.

Gross pay is the total amount of money paid to an employee before taxes or other deductions are made.

- Kamal worked for 35 hours and is paid £7.20 per hour.
- Pamela worked for 35 hours and is paid £8.50 per hour.
- Jason worked for 16 hours and is paid £8.50 per hour.
- Sana worked for 8 hours and is paid £7.20 per hour.

Required:

Set the information out in a table and calculate

a)   The gross pay for each employee

b)   The total gross pay for all employees.

 Activity 4

You have been given the following information from the previous payroll.

Kamal is paid £7.20 per hour. Last week Kamal earned £216.00.

Calculate how many hours Kamal worked last week.

5 Fractions and ratios

5.1 Using fractions

 Definition

Fractions are another way of representing parts of whole numbers.

If something is shared out equally between two people, each receives a half of the total, and that is written as $\frac{1}{2}$

The top half of a fraction is the **numerator.** The bottom half of a fraction is the **denominator.**

The numerator is divided by the denominator to show the decimal form of the fraction.

$$\frac{1}{2} = 1 \div 2 = 0.5$$

Fractions are written in the lowest possible terms. The numerator and denominator are reduced as far as possible. For example, four eighths 4/8, or two quarters: 2/4 is shown as one half 1/2

Large fractions can be reduced by dividing both the denominator and the numerator by the largest number that goes into both exactly. Each number in the fraction 18/54 can be divided by 18 so, the fraction is reduced to:

$$\frac{18 \div 18 = 1}{54 \div 18 = 3} \quad \text{or one third}$$

5.2 Calculating a given fraction of a whole number

To calculate the fraction of a whole number:

- divide the whole number by the denominator
- multiply the answer by the numerator.

Example

A business has four branches: South Park, North Park, East Park.

The total sales income for all branches was £2,700,000.

North Park made $\frac{2}{3}$ of the sales.

How much sales income did North Park make?

1. Divide the total by the denominator.

$$\frac{£2,700,000}{3} = £900,000$$

2. Multiply the £900,000 by the numerator.

$$2 \times £900,000 = £1,800,000$$

The calculation can be written as:

$$\frac{£2,700,000}{3} \times 2$$

Tip:

To use your calculator efficiently leave the zeros out of your calculation:

$$\frac{27}{3} \times 2 = 18$$

Just remember to add back the zeros you didn't calculate: 1800000 and to include the currency sign and thousand separators. £1,800,000.

 Activity 5

A business manufactures bath mats in three different colours: Kiwi, Mocha and Rose. The production manager has estimated that 540,000 bath mats will be produced next month and $\frac{3}{5}$ will be Mocha bath mats.

How many Mocha bath mats will be produced?

Activity 6

A business has 45,000 customers. $\frac{2}{3}$ of these customers pay on credit. How many of the business's customers are cash customers?

 Activity 7

Three families have organised a meal in a restaurant. The Morris family consists of two adults and three children. The Kazee family consists of two adults and two children. The Thomas family consist of one adult and one child.

The restaurant bill totals £210.56. How can the bill be split so that each family pays a fair proportion of the £210.56?

5.3 Ratios

Ratios give exactly the same information as fractions but they are written in a different way so that comparisons can be made between two numbers.

The two numbers given in a ratio are the fraction numerators.

The denominator is not shown - it can be calculated by adding together the two numerators

In this ratio, 3 and 1 are the fraction numerators.

The denominator is 4.

This ratio is pronounced 'three to one'.

$$3 : 1$$

A business has two retail outlets with total sales of £56,000. The pattern of sales for Store A and Store B has been given as ratio of 3:1 respectively. This means that Store A has 3 *times* more sales than Store B.

To calculate the ratio the two numerators are added together to find the denominator: 3 + 1 = 4.

We can then apportion the total sales of £56,000 between to the two retail outlets:

Store A $\frac{56}{4}$ x 3 = 42 = £42,000

Store B $\frac{56}{4}$ x 1 = 14 = £14,000

Example

You may be asked to calculate the ratio or proportion of two given numbers. Let's use the numbers from the example above.

You are told that Store A has sales of £42,000 and Store B has sales of £14,000. This time you have been asked to find out the ratio of Store A's sales to Store B's.

First, divide	Store A's sales	$\dfrac{£42,000}{£14,000}$	$= 3$
By	Store B's sales		

We are comparing Store A to Store B, so the ratio is answer is written as 3:1.

Store A has 3 times more sales than Store B.

 Activity 8

A company has two departments who use the canteen. There are 125 employees in the production department and 25 employees in the administration department.

What is the ratio of production department employees to administration staff?

 Activity 9

A company has cost of sales of £75,000 and sales of £250,000.

What is the ratio of cost of sales to sales?

 6 | **Percentages**

6.1 The use of percentages

Percentages are another method used to compare figures. 'Per cent' means 'out of a 100' so the **denominator of the percentage is 100**.

Percentages can be shown as fractions or decimals:

$$25\% = \frac{25}{100} = 0.25$$

$$10\% = \frac{10}{100} = 0.10$$

Tip: It is more efficient to calculate percentages on a calculator by using the decimal equivalent.

 Activity 10

Use your calculator to fill in the missing figures from the table below.

Percentage	Fraction	Decimal
25%	$\frac{25}{100}$	0.25
	$\frac{2}{100}$	0.02
10%	$\frac{10}{100}$	0.10
1%	$\frac{1}{100}$	
50%	$\frac{50}{100}$	0.50
	$\frac{5}{100}$	0.05

6.2 Finding a percentage of a whole number

You will need to be able to find a percentage of a whole number, for example when calculating how much discount to deduct from a sales invoice, or to add VAT to an invoice.

Q Definition

VAT (Value Added Tax) is a government tax on some consumer goods. Organisations that are registered for VAT must collect this tax from customers on behalf of the government. In 2015 the VAT rate was 20%.

To calculate percentages efficiently on a calculator, first convert the percentage to a decimal. You can then use this figure in your calculation.

Example

A customer (Howards Plumbers) has bought goods worth £150.00 and has been offered 10% discount.

VAT of 20% is to be added to the invoice amount.

You are to calculate the total amount the customer owes.

Discount

*   Convert 10% to a decimal: $10\% = \dfrac{10}{100} = 0.10$

*   Multiply £150.00 by 0.10 = £15.00 discount
*   **Subtract** £15.00 from £150.00 to find the net amount = £135.00

VAT

*   Convert 20% to a decimal: $20\% = \dfrac{20}{100} = 0.20$

*   Multiply the net amount of £135.00 by 0.20 = £27.00 VAT
*   **Add** £27.00 to £135.00 to find the total amount = £162.00

These calculations are shown on the following invoice:

Labrey Kitchen Fitters
VAT NO. 456 7656 909

Howards Plumbers	Invoice no: i459009
Bolton Close	Tax point: 24 May 2016
Rochdale	
FG1 3SQ	

Goods for resale	£150.00
Less Discount 10%	£15.00
Total after discount	£135.00
VAT at 20%	£27.00
Total	£162.00

Payment terms: 15 days net

KAPLAN PUBLISHING

Activity 11

Complete the following invoices.

Sunshine Coaches	
VAT NO. 234 5267 456	
Grange Theatre	Invoice no: 5678
Blackburn Avenue	Tax point: 23 September 2016
Diggle	
LF2 689	

Coach hire plus driver	£75.00
Less Discount 5%	£
Total after discount	£
VAT at 20%	£
Total	£
Payment terms: 7 days net	

6.3 Calculating the percentage of one number in relation to another

 Example

A business has sales of £890,000 and gross profit of £267,000. We need to calculate gross profit as a percentage of sales.

Divide gross profit
Into sales
$$\frac{£267,000}{£890,000} = 0.30 \text{ then multiply by } 100 = 30\%$$

Gross profit is 30% of sales.

Check your answer by multiplying sales of £890,000 by 0.30 = £267,000.

Activity 12

The human resources department has analysed the number of employees in a business.

	No of employees	Percentage of the total number of employees
Production department	8	
Marketing department	3	
Accounts department	2	
Sales department	4	
Total number of employees	17	

Calculate the number of employees in each department as a percentage of the total number of employees. Round your answers to one decimal place.

7 Summary

In this chapter you have looked at the common maths functions used in accounting. You will need to practice the techniques learnt in the chapter to make sure you are able to perform the calculations quickly and confidently on a calculator.

Answers to chapter activities

Activity 1

a) Credit sales are £18,219.70

$$2399. + 3210.5 + 2225.2 + 4375. + 6010. =$$

$$18219.7$$

b) Cash sales are £2,846.69

$$499.99 + 325.5 + 769. + 1005. + 247.2 =$$

$$2846.69$$

c) Total weekly sales are £21,066.39

$$18219.7 + 2846.69 =$$

$$21066.39$$

Activity 2

a) Weekly sales income is £84,942.10

$$58956.50 + 25985.60 =$$

$$84942.1$$

b) Gross profit is £29,726.75

$$84942.1 - 55215.35 =$$

$$29726.75$$

c) Net profit is £17,783.80

$$29726.75 - 11942.95 =$$

$$17783.8$$

Activity 3

a)

	Hours worked	Pay per hour	Gross pay	*calculation*
Kamal	35	£7.20	£252.00	*35 x 7.2*
Pamela	35	£8.50	£297.50	*35 x 8.5*
Jason	16	£8.50	£136.00	*16 x 8.5*
Sana	8	£7.20	£57.60	*8 x 7.2*
	Total weekly gross pay		£743.10	*252.+297.5 +136.+57.6*

b) The total weekly gross pay is £743.10.

 Activity 4

The total cost of Kamal's weekly wage was   £216.00

Divided by the cost per hour   £7.20

216. ÷ 7.2 =

30

Last week Kamal worked for **30 hours.**

 Activity 5

$\frac{54}{5}$ x 3 = 32.4 = 324,000 Mocha bath mats

Activity 6

The business has 45,000 customers

$\frac{2}{3}$ of customers pay on credit. $\frac{45}{3}$ x 2 = 30,000 credit customers.

The remainder must be cash customers. 45 – 30 = 15 = **15,000**

You can also work this out by calculating the fraction for cash

customers. If credit customers account for $\frac{2}{3}$, cash customers must

account for $\frac{1}{3}$ so $\frac{45}{3}$ x 1 = 15 = **15,000.**

 Activity 7

Firstly, you need to determine how many people there are in total:

The Morris family has 5 members, the Kazee family has 4 members and the Thomas family has 2 members, so there are 11 people in total. This is the denominator.

The fraction of the total bill that the Morris family should pay is $\frac{5}{11}$, for

the Kazee family it is $\frac{4}{11}$, and for the Thomas's it is $\frac{2}{11}$

The bill should be split as follows:

Morris family $\frac{210.56}{11}$ x 5 = 95.70909, a monetary value of £95.71

Kazee family $\frac{210.56}{11}$ x 4 = 76.56727, a monetary value of £76.57

Thomas family $\frac{210.56}{11}$ x 2 = = 38.28363, a monetary value of £38.28

Check that the total bill will be paid correctly: 95.71 + 76.57 + 38.28 = 210.56

Activity 8

Divide 125 by 25 to give an answer of 5. We are comparing production *to* administration, so the ratio is written as **5:1.** There are 5 times more employees who work in production than in administration.

 Activity 9

Divide 225,000 by 75,000 = 3

We are comparing cost of sales *to* sales, so the ratio is expressed as **1:3.** For every £1 of cost of sales there are £3 of sales.

Activity 10

Percentage	Fraction	Decimal
25%	$\frac{25}{100}$	**0.25**
2%	$\frac{2}{100}$	0.02
10%	$\frac{10}{100}$	0.10
1%	$\frac{1}{100}$	**0.01**
50%	$\frac{50}{100}$	0.50
5%	$\frac{5}{100}$	0.05

KAPLAN PUBLISHING

Activity 11

Sunshine Coaches

VAT NO. 234 5267 456

Grange Theatre
Blackburn Avenue
Diggle
LF2 689

Invoice no: 5678
Tax point: 23 September 2016

Coach hire plus driver	£75.00
Less Discount 5%	£3.75
Total after discount	£71.25
VAT at 20%	£14.25
Total	**£85.50**

Payment terms: 7 days net

Kanga Wholesalers

VAT NO. 456 2121 928

H Kazee
Bristol Street
Gloucester
AL9 867

Invoice no: 35281
Tax point: 26 September 2016

5 HB78 @ £15.00	£75.00
10 AN5787 @ £2.30	£23.00
Sub total	£98.00
Less Discount 15%	£14.70
Total after discount	£83.30
VAT at 20%	£16.66
Total	**£99.96**

Payment terms: 7 days net

Activity 12

	No of employees	Percentage of the total number of employees	Calculation
Production department	8	**47.1%**	$\frac{8}{17}$ x 100 = 47.05 (rounded to 47.1)
Marketing department	3	**17.6%**	$\frac{3}{17}$ x 100 = 17.64 (rounded to 17.6)
Accounts department	2	**11.8%**	$\frac{2}{17}$ x 100 = 11.76 (rounded to 11.8)
Sales department	4	**23.5%**	$\frac{4}{17}$ x 100 = 23.52 (rounded to 23.5)
Total number of employees	17	**100%**	$\frac{17}{17}$ x 100 = 100

The total of all the individual percentages should always equal 100%.

Introduction to bookkeeping

Introduction

This chapter covers the basics of bookkeeping within an organisation, including:

- the role and career progression of a bookkeeper
- the need for keeping information secure within an organisation
- single entry bookkeeping, and when it might be used
- the all-important double entry bookkeeping, and what it represents
- balancing the ledger accounts and compiling the balances to produce
- the Trial Balance

KNOWLEDGE	CONTENTS
Introduction to Bookkeeping	1 The role of the bookkeeper
1 Understand the job role and career path for a bookkeeper	2 Bookkeeping basics
2 Understand different types of business organisation	3 Balancing a ledger account
3.1 Identify the difference between a bookkeeper and an accountant	4 The trial balance
Working within bookkeeping	5 Summary
1 Understand single entry bookkeeping	
3 Understand what is meant by both cash and credit transactions	
6 Understand responsibilities when working in a bookkeeping environment	
Bookkeeping and accounts	
2 Be able to record cash and credit transactions in books of original entry	
5 Be able to extract a trial balance from ledger accounting	

1 The role of the bookkeeper

1.1 Why do we need bookkeepers?

No matter where you live or work in the world, an organisation will always need a bookkeeper.

The main reasons bookkeepers will always be needed are:

- So that the owner/manager knows the income and expenditure of the business (see chapter 2 for definitions).
- So that the owner/manager can make decisions that will improve/expand the business.
- So that the organisation pays the correct amount of taxes due.

All governments need money to finance their activities, and they get that money from businesses and individuals in the form of taxes.

1.2 The role of the bookkeeper

The role of the bookkeeper is to keep an accurate record of all financial transactions carried out by an organisation. In most organisations, each transaction is first recorded in a daybook and then transferred to ledgers using the double entry booking system. Bookkeepers are responsible for keeping these records up to date and accurate.

In larger organisations, the bookkeeping work is often separated into different business activities carried out by clerks. For example, a sales ledger clerk will produce customer invoices and statements and chase up outstanding debts. A purchases ledger clerk will keep a record of all invoices received from suppliers and process payments. Cashiers are responsible for recording all monies received and paid by the business. In smaller organisations, a bookkeeper will perform all of these activities.

Once the data has been entered, the information will be analysed by an accountant who will produce financial reports for the managers of the business. It is essential, therefore, that the information provided by bookkeepers or accounts clerks is accurate and up to date.

Bookkeepers and accounts clerks are entry level job roles, but there are a lot of opportunities for career progression by work experience and gaining bookkeeping and accounting qualifications.

1.3   Career progression - the role of an accountant

An accountant's role is to interpret and analyse the information provided by the bookkeeper or accounts clerk so that the owner/manager can make business decisions. Accountants help this decision-making process by interpreting and offering alternative strategies.

Activity 1

Below is a list of jobs that are typical in an accounts department.

Put them into the correct boxes to show the accounting hierarchy within an organisation.

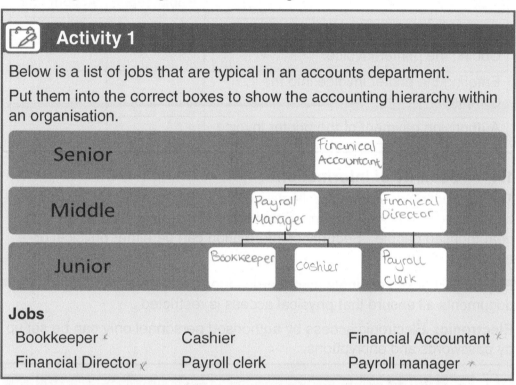

Jobs

Bookkeeper	Cashier	Financial Accountant
Financial Director	Payroll clerk	Payroll manager

Activity 2

Fill in the gaps from the pick list below to complete the paragraph about bookkeepers.

The bookkeeper is responsible for _____ the financial _____ of an organisation. An accountant is responsible for _inputting_ the financial _information_ of an organisation.

The _____ suggests alternative strategies, based on the interpretation of the financial information. The _____ will make the decisions.

A bookkeeper may start as a _bookkeeper_, but, with hard work and study, can progress to _Senior_ accountant

Pick list

Accountant	bookkeeper	information	interpreting
manager	senior	inputting	transactions

Activity 3

Below is a list of duties that are performed in the accounting department. Tick the column to suggest who would typically perform each task.

Role	Bookkeeper	Accountant
Authorising the purchase of a new printer		✓
Coding the printer invoice	✓	
Entering the printer invoice into the computer	✓	
Authorising payment of the printer invoice		✓

1.4 Security of information

The accounting department collects a lot of sensitive financial information which needs to be kept secure so that it cannot be accessed by unauthorised people. Security of information can be either physical or electronic.

Physical: Locked cabinets, cupboards, doors, and the shredding of documents all ensure that physical access is restricted.

Electronic: Electronic access by authorised personnel only can be set up by passwords and encryptions.

 Activity 4

Below is a list of security measures.
Tick the column that you think the security measure belongs in. Some may be both types.

Security measure	Physical	Electronic
Cabinets are locked at all times and the keys held by the office manager		
All employee personal information no longer required is shredded		
Passwords are changed every thirty days		
Access to different areas of the accounting software is restricted according to employee's duties		
Access to the department is restricted by inputting the correct code into a keypad		
ID cards must be worn at all times		

2 Bookkeeping basics

2.1 Single entry bookkeeping

Many small businesses, particularly sole traders, are cash based, or do not have many transactions to record. For this reason the owner will often only use a cash book or spreadsheet to record the income and expenditure of the business.

	A	B
1	Cstd	Sstd
2	0.000	0.00
3	0.100	12.36
4	0.200	24.83
5	0.300	35.91
6	0.400	48.79
7	0.500	60.42

The spreadsheet will often have columns analysed by type. The cash book may not.

It is quicker and easier for the owner to record the transactions this way, but the records are incomplete, and will have to be reconstructed in order to work out the taxable profit.

2.2 Double entry bookkeeping

Most organisations use double entry bookkeeping to record the financial transactions of the business.

Due to the large volume of transactions (and therefore the increased chance of error), the process is divided into three parts.

a)   The transactions are first recorded in a book of prime (first) entry, also referred to as "day books".

b)   The second part is the general ledger itself where the double entry takes place

c)   The third part is, depending on the transaction, the sales ledger or purchase ledger which contains the individual customer and supplier accounts. (These ledgers are also known as the subsidiary (sales/purchase) ledger.

The books of prime entry have already been addressed earlier in this book. Next in the process is the double entry.

Double entry bookkeeping is based upon the principle of the dual effect.

2.3   The dual effect principle

This states that every transaction has two financial effects.

(a)   If, for example, you spend £2,000 on a car and pay for it by a cheque, you will have £2,000 less money in the bank, but you will also have acquired an asset worth £2,000.

This can be viewed as:

Gained: a £2,000 car

Lost: £2,000 in cash.

The accounting terms used for this transaction are: **debit** and **credit**.

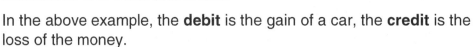

In the above example, the **debit** is the gain of a car, the **credit** is the loss of the money.

Using the accounting terminology, look at the example below:

(b)   If you buy from a supplier £100 of goods and send him a cheque for that amount, you will gain £100 worth of goods, but you will have £100 less money in the bank.

Debit   **£100** of goods

Credit **£100** from the bank account

At first it can seem difficult, but break the transaction into two parts.

Ask:

•   What did I get?

•   What did I lose?

:Ö: **Example 1**

	Debit (gain)	Credit (loss)
a) Purchases goods for resale, paid £800.	Purchases	Bank
b) Pays rent for use of office of £500.	Rent	Bank
c) Buys a van, cost £2,000.	Van	Bank
d) Sells some of the goods for £600.	Bank	Sales
e) Sells some more of the goods for £700.	Bank	Sales
f) Purchases goods for resale for £1,000.	Purchases	Bank
g) Buys stationery for £200.	Stationery	Bank

Explanation for the above example follows:

a)   Gains goods to sell on, loses £800 of money from bank account

b)   Gains office space, but loses £500 of money from bank account

c)   Gains a van, but loses £2,000 of money from bank account

d)   Gains £600, which is paid into bank account, but loses some of the goods previously bought

e)   Gains some money, £700, but more goods go out the door

f)   Gains some more goods to sell on, but spends (loses) £1,000 from bank account

g)   Gains some stationery to write on, but loses £200 from bank account

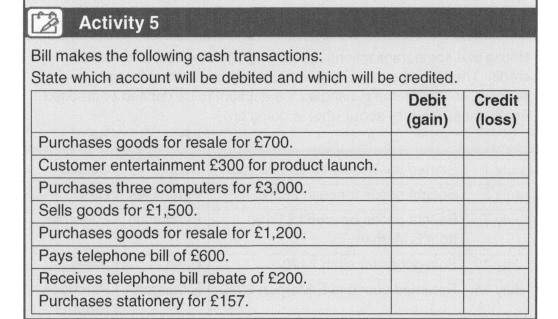

Activity 5

Bill makes the following cash transactions:

State which account will be debited and which will be credited.

	Debit (gain)	Credit (loss)
Purchases goods for resale for £700.		
Customer entertainment £300 for product launch.		
Purchases three computers for £3,000.		
Sells goods for £1,500.		
Purchases goods for resale for £1,200.		
Pays telephone bill of £600.		
Receives telephone bill rebate of £200.		
Purchases stationery for £157.		

2.4   Debit and credit entries

We need to appreciate the effect a debit or a credit entry will have.

Ledger account	
A **debit entry** represents:	A **credit entry** represents:
• An increase in the value of an asset;	• A decrease in the value of an asset;
• A decrease in the value of a liability; or	• An increase in the value of a liability; or
• An increase to an item of expenditure	• An increase to an item of income (revenue)
• A decrease to an item of income	• A decrease to an item of expense.

The mnemonic DEAD CLIC may help to remind you of which side the account balances should be.

Notice that some transactions are for cash (immediate payment) and some are credit transactions (payment will be made at a later date).

DEAD	**CLIC**
Debits:	**Credits:**
Expenses	**L**iabilities
Assets	**I**ncome
Drawings	**C**apital

 Example 2

Notice that some transactions are for cash (immediate) and some for credit. The ones that are credit transactions name the customer or supplier, so their name is used as the account to be debited or credited. Again, think carefully about what is going on.

		DR	CR
July 1	Started business with £3,000 cash	Cash	Capital*
July 3	Bought goods for cash £850	Purchases	Cash
July 7	Bought goods on credit £1,160 from E Morgan	Purchases	E Morgan
July 10	Sold goods for cash £420	Cash	Sales
July 14	Returned goods to E Morgan £280	E Morgan	Purchase Returns
July 18	Bought goods on credit £980 from A Moses	Purchases	A Moses
July 21	Returned goods to A Moses £190	A Moses	Purchase Returns
July 24	Sold goods to A Knight £550 on credit	A Knight	Sales
July 25	Paid E Morgan's account by cash £880	E Morgan	Cash
July 31	A Knight paid us his account in cash £550	Cash	A Knight

*Capital is the name for the money the owner 'lends' to the business, that is why Capital is a credit.

In the example above the individual customer and supplier names are used. All the customers make up the **Sales ledger** or **Debtors** (see chapter 1), and all the suppliers make up the **Purchase ledger** or **Creditors.**

In the above example the Sales ledger and Purchase ledger are made up as follows:

Sales ledger	**Purchase ledger**
A Knight	E Morgan
	A Moses

A business needs to know not only how much an individual customer owes, but also how much is due to the organisation from all the customers added together, so to work out how much in all is owed to the business the customer account balances are added together to get the total amount due.

The total of the customer balances is known as the **Sales ledger control account**, and it is this total figure that goes into the trial balance. The same applies to the purchase ledger. The **Purchase ledger control account** is the total of the money due to all the suppliers.

Let's add some more customers, and some balances (the total amount owed to the organisation by the customers).

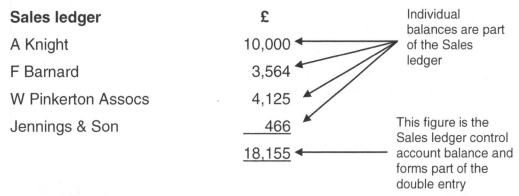

Sales ledger	£	
A Knight	10,000	Individual balances are part of the Sales ledger
F Barnard	3,564	
W Pinkerton Assocs	4,125	
Jennings & Son	466	This figure is the Sales ledger control account balance and forms part of the double entry
	18,155	

The Sales ledger is made up of the individual customer balances, but the **Sales ledger control account** is the grand total, and it's that overall figure that is part of the double entry and forms part of the Trial Balance (see later in the chapter).

The **Purchase ledger** and **Purchase ledger control account** work in the same way.

Activity 6

Now you have a go.

Identify the two accounts needed for each transaction and whether they are a debit or a credit:

		DR	CR
Aug 4	Bought goods on credit £780 from S Holmes		
Aug 5	Bought a motor van by cheque £5,000		
Aug 7	Bought goods for cash £550		
Aug 10	Sold goods on credit £980 to D Moore		
Aug 12	Returned goods to S Holmes £180		
Aug 19	Sold goods for cash £280		
Aug 22	Bought fixtures on credit from Kingston Equipment Co £1,500		
Aug 24	D Watson lent us £1,000 paying us the money by cheque		
Aug 29	We paid S Holmes his account by cheque £600		
Aug 31	We paid Kingston Equipment Co by cheque £1,500		

So far you:

- Understand single entry bookkeeping and why some organisations use it.

- Understand the dual effect of double entry bookkeeping.

- Identified the two 'sides' of a transaction (gain something, lose something).

- Identified the accounts in which to place each side of the transaction.

The next step is to apply this knowledge by placing the entries into the correct accounts.

Example

We will now put debits and credits into the accounts using Example 1:

		Debit	Credit
a)	Purchases goods for resale, paid £800.	Purchases	Bank
b)	Pays rent for use of office of £500.	Rent	Bank
c)	Buys a van, cost £2,000.	Van	Bank
d)	Sells some of the goods for £600.	Bank	Sales
e)	Sells some more of the goods for £700.	Bank	Sales
f)	Purchases goods for resale for £1,000.	Purchases	Bank
g)	Buys stationery for £200.	Stationery	Bank

Debit **Purchases account** **Credit**

Date	Details	£	Date	Details	£
(a)	Bank	800			
(f)	Bank	1,000			

Debit **Bank account** **Credit**

Date	Details	£	Date	Details	£
(d)	Sales	600	(a)	Purchases	800
(e)	Sales	700	(b)	Rent	500
			(c)	Van	2,000
			(f)	Purchases	1,000
			(g)	Stationery	200

Debit **Rent account** **Credit**

Date	Details	£	Date	Details	£
(b)	Bank	500			

Debit **Van account** **Credit**

Date	Details	£	Date	Details	£
(c)	Bank	2,000			

Debit **Sales account** **Credit**

Date	Details	£	Date	Details	£
			(d)	Bank	600
			(e)	Sales	700

Debit **Stationery account** **Credit**

Date	Details	£	Date	Details	£
(g)	Bank	200			

Note:

Notice how when you enter the amount into the account, e.g. Purchases, £800, in the details you have to write where the other half of the transaction is, Bank. Failure to do so will mean that you could get in a muddle and not be able to identify where the other side of the transaction was put, particularly with the longer exercises.

Activity 7

Using the technique from the previous example above, enter the debits and credits into the accounts below.

		DR	CR
July 1	Started business with £3,000 cash	Cash	Capital*
July 3	Bought goods for cash £850	Purchases	Cash
July 7	Bought goods on credit £1,160 from E Morgan	Purchases	E Morgan
July 10	Sold goods for cash £420	Cash	Sales
July 14	Returned goods to E Morgan £280	E Morgan	Purchase Returns
July 18	Bought goods on credit £980 from A Moses	Purchases	A Moses
July 21	Returned goods to A Moses £190	A Moses	Purchase Returns
July 24	Sold goods to A Knight £550 on credit	A Knight	Sales
July 25	Paid E Morgan's account by cash £880	E Morgan	Cash
July 31	A Knight paid us his account in cash £550	Cash	A Knight

Debit   **Capital account**   **Credit**

Date	Details	£	Date	Details	£

Debit   **Purchases account**   **Credit**

Date	Details	£	Date	Details	£

Debit		Cash account				Credit
Date	Details	£	Date	Details	£	

Debit		E Morgan (Supplier) account				Credit
Date	Details	£	Date	Details	£	

Debit		Sales account				Credit
Date	Details	£	Date	Details	£	

Debit		Purchase returns account				Credit
Date	Details	£	Date	Details	£	

Debit		A Moses (supplier) account				Credit
Date	Details	£	Date	Details	£	

Debit		A Knight (customer) account				Credit
Date	Details	£	Date	Details	£	

Please keep your answers for this activity as they will be used later.

3 Balancing a ledger account

3.1 Procedure for balancing a ledger account

An organisation needs to know how much it has spent, and on what. In order to gain that information a balance on each account needs to be calculated:

This is done as follows:

Step 1 Total both the debit and the credit side of the ledger account and make a note of each total.

Step 2 Insert the higher of the two totals as the total on both sides of the ledger account leaving a line beneath the final entry on each side of the account.

Step 3 On the side with the smaller total insert the figure needed to make this column add up to the total. Call this figure the balance carried down (or 'Bal c/d' as an abbreviation).

Step 4 On the opposite side of the ledger account, below the total insert this same figure and call it the balance brought down (or 'Bal b/d' as an abbreviation).

An example of the method is below.

Example

The bank account of a business has the following entries:

Bank

	£		£
Capital	1,000	Purchases	200
Sales	300	Drawings	100
Sales	400	Rent	400
Capital	500	Stationery	300
Sales	800	Purchases	400

Calculate the balance on the account and bring the balance down as a single amount.

Step 1 Total both sides of the account and make a note of the totals. (Note that these totals that are asterisked below would not normally be written into the ledger account itself.)

Bank

	£		£
Capital	1,000	Purchases	200
Sales	300	Drawings	100
Sales	400	Rent	400
Capital	500	Stationery	300
Sales	800	Purchases	400
Sub-total debits*	3,000	Sub-total credits*	1,400

Step 2   Insert the higher total as the total of both sides.

Bank

	£		£
Capital	1,000	Purchases	200
Sales	300	Drawings	100
Sales	400	Rent	400
Capital	500	Stationery	300
Sales	800	Purchases	400
Sub-total debits*	3,000	Sub-total credits*	1,400
Total	3,000	Total	3,000

Step 3   Insert a balancing figure on the side of the account with the lower sub-total. This is referred to as the 'balance carried down' or 'bal c/d' for short.

Bank

	£		£
Capital	1,000	Purchases	200
Sales	300	Drawings	100
Sales	400	Rent	400
Capital	500	Stationery	300
Sales	800	Purchases	400
Sub-total debits*	3,000	Sub-total credits*	1,400
		Bal c/d	1,600
Total	3,000	Total	3,000

Step 4 Insert the balance carried down figure beneath the total on the other side of the account. This is referred to as 'bal b/d' for short.

Bank

	£		£
Capital	1,000	Purchases	200
Sales	300	Drawings	100
Sales	400	Rent	400
Capital	500	Stationery	300
Sales	800	Purchases	400
	_____		_____
*Sub-total debits**	*3,000*	*Sub-total credits**	*1,400*
		Bal c/d	1,600
	_____		_____
Total	3,000	Total	3,000
	_____		_____
Bal b/d	1,600		

The closing balance carried down at the end of the period is also the opening balance brought down at the start of the next period. This opening balance remains in the account as the starting position and any further transactions are then added into the account. In this case the balance brought down is a debit balance as there is money in the bank account making it an asset.

Example

Consider the ledger accounts below and balance them.
The double entry transactions have been numbered to help identify the two sides.

Bank

Date			£	Date			£
1 Jan	Capital	(1)	20,000	1 Jan	Van	(2)	500
5 Jan	Sales	(6)	2,000		Purchases	(3)	1,000
					Drawings	(4)	50
				5 Jan	Purchases	(5)	500
				15 Jan	Rent	(7)	200

Capital

Date			£	Date			£
				1 Jan	Bank	(1)	20,000

Van

Date			£	Date			£
1 Jan	Bank	(2)	500				

Purchases

Date			£	Date		£
1 Jan	Bank	(3)	1,000			
5 Jan	Bank	(5)	500			

Drawings

Date			£	Date		£
1 Jan	Bank	(4)	50			

Sales

Date		£	Date			£
			5 Jan	Bank	(6)	2,000

Rent

Date			£	Date		£
15 Jan	Bank	(7)	200			

Solution

a) **The bank account**

Bank

Date		£	Date		£
1 Jan	Capital	20,000	1 Jan	Van	500
5 Jan	Sales	2,000		Purchases	1,000
				Drawings	50
			5 Jan	Purchases	500
			15 Jan	Rent	200

Step 1 Total both the debit and the credit side of the ledger account and make a note of each total – debit side £22,000, credit side £2,250.

Step 2 Insert the higher of the two totals, £22,000, as the total on both sides of the ledger account leaving a line beneath the final entry on each side of the account.

Bank

Date		£	Date		£
1 Jan	Capital	20,000	1 Jan	Van	500
5 Jan	Sales	2,000		Purchases	1,000
				Drawings	50
			5 Jan	Purchases	500
			15 Jan	Rent	200
		22,000			22,000

Step 3 On the side with the smaller total insert the figure needed to make this column add up to the total. Call this figure the balance carried down (or Bal c/d as an abbreviation).

Step 4 On the opposite side of the ledger account, below the total insert this same figure and call it the balance brought down (or Bal b/d as an abbreviation).

Bank

Date		£	Date		£
1 Jan	Capital	20,000	1 Jan	Van	500
5 Jan	Sales	2,000		Purchases	1,000
				Drawings	50
			5 Jan	Purchases	500
			15 Jan	Rent	200
			31 Jan	Balance c/d	19,750
		_____			_____
		22,000			22,000
		_____			_____
1 Feb	Balance b/d	19,750			

f) **Sales**

Sales

Date		£	Date		£
			5 Jan	Bank	2,000

There is no need to balance the account as there is only one entry – a £2,000 credit balance representing income.

g) **Rent**

Rent

Date		£	Date		£
15 Jan	Bank	200			

As there is only one entry there is no need to balance the account. This is a debit balance indicating that there has been an expense of £200 of rent incurred during the month.

Activity 8

Given below is a bank account ledger account for the month of March. You are required to "balance off" the ledger account.

Bank

Date		£	Date		£
1 Mar	Capital	12,000	3 Mar	Purchases	3,000
7 Mar	Sales	5,000	15 Mar	Non-current asset	2,400
19 Mar	Sales	2,000	20 Mar	Purchases	5,300
22 Mar	Sales	3,000	24 Mar	Rent	1,000
			28 Mar	Drawings	2,000

4 The trial balance

4.1 List of balances

The trial balance is a list showing the balances brought down on each ledger account. An example of a simple trial balance is given below:

	Debit £	Credit £
Sales		5,000
Opening inventory	100	
Purchases	3,000	
Rent	200	
Car	3,000	
SLCAs	100	
PLCA		1,400
	6,400	6,400

The trial balance is produced immediately after the double entry has been completed and the account balances calculated. If the double entry has been done correctly, the total of the debits will equal the total of the credits.

4.2 Reasons for extracting a trial balance

Drafting a trial balance is a way of ensuring that double entries have been correctly completed. It is possible to detect errors with a trial balance, but this is not relevant to the Level 1 Assessment.

Example

The following are the balances on the accounts of Ernest at 31 December 20X8. Prepare Ernest's trial balance as at 31 December 20X8.

	£
Sales	47,140
Purchases	26,500
SLCAs	7,640
PLCA	4,320
General expenses	9,430
Loan	5,000
Plant and machinery at cost	7,300
Motor van at cost	2,650
Drawings	7,500
Rent and rates	6,450
Insurance	1,560
Bank overdraft	2,570
Capital	10,000

Solution

Step 1 Set up a blank trial balance

Step 2 Work down the list of balances one by one using what you have learned so far about debits and credits. Assets and expenses are debit balances and liabilities, income and capital are credit balances.

Trial balance at 31 December 20X8

	Dr £	Cr £
Sales		47,140
Purchases	26,500	
SLCAs	7,640	
PLCA		4,320
General expenses	9,430	
Loan		5,000
Plant and machinery at cost	7,300	
Motor van at cost	2,650	
Drawings	7,500	
Rent and rates	6,450	
Insurance	1,560	
Bank overdraft		2,570
Capital		10,000
	69,030	69,030

Take care with drawings. These are a reduction of the capital owed back to the owner therefore as a reduction of a liability they must be a debit balance.

The bank overdraft is an amount owed to the bank therefore it must be a credit balance.

Activity 9

Refer to your answers in Activity 7. Balance off the accounts, and then draw up a Trial Balance from those balances.

If you have lost your answers, then have another go at Activity 7 and see how much you have improved!

5 Summary

In this chapter we have studied cash and credit transactions. It is important to always start with the bank account and remember that cash received is a debit in the bank account and cash paid out is a credit in the bank account. If you get that right then the rest really does fall into place.

You should also be aware of the definitions of assets, expenses and income and the normal entries you would make in the accounts for these.

Balancing an account is a very important technique which you must be able to master. You must understand how to bring the balance down onto the correct side and what that balance represents.

Answers to chapter activities

Activity 1

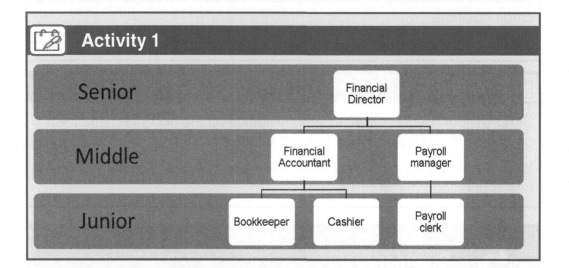

Senior	Financial Director
Middle	Financial Accountant / Payroll manager
Junior	Bookkeeper / Cashier / Payroll clerk

Activity 2

The bookkeeper is responsible for <u>inputting</u> the financial <u>transactions</u> of an organisation. An accountant is responsible for <u>interpreting</u> the financial <u>information</u> of an organisation.

The <u>Accountant</u> suggests alternative strategies, based on the interpretation of the financial information. The <u>manager</u> will make the decisions.

A bookkeeper may start as a <u>bookkeeper</u>, but, with hard work and study, can progress to <u>senior</u> accountant

Activity 3

Role	Bookkeeper	Accountant
Authorising the purchase of a new printer		✓
Coding the printer invoice	✓	
Entering the printer invoice into the computer	✓	
Authorising payment of the printer invoice		✓

Activity 4

Security measure	Physical	Electronic
Cabinets are locked at all times and the keys held by the office manager	✓	
All employee personal information no longer required is shredded	✓	
Passwords are changed every thirty days		✓
Access to different areas of the accounting software is restricted according to employee's duties		✓
Access to the department is restricted by inputting the correct code into a keypad	✓	✓
ID cards must be worn at all times	✓	

Activity 5

	Debit (gain)	Credit (loss)
Purchases goods for resale for £700.	Purchases	Bank
Customer entertainment £300 for product launch.	Entertainment	Bank
Purchases three computers for £3,000.	Computers	Bank
Sells goods for £1,500.	Bank	Sales
Purchases goods for resale for £1,200.	Purchases	Bank
Pays telephone bill of £600.	Telephone	Bank
Receives telephone bill rebate of £200.	Bank	Telephone
Purchases stationery for £157.	Stationery	Bank

Activity 6

		DR	CR
Aug 4	Bought goods on credit £780 from S Holmes	**Purchases**	**S Holmes**
Aug 5	Bought a motor van by cheque £5,000	**Van**	**Bank**
Aug 7	Bought goods for cash £550	**Purchases**	**Cash**
Aug 10	Sold goods on credit £980 to D Moore	**D Moore**	**Sales**
Aug 12	Returned goods to S Holmes £180	**S Holmes**	**Purchase Returns**
Aug 19	Sold goods for cash £280	**Cash**	**Sales**
Aug 22	Bought fixtures on credit from Kingston Equipment Co £1,500	**Fixtures**	**Kingston Equipment**
Aug 24	D Watson lent us £1,000 paying us the money by cheque	**Bank**	**D Watson - Loan**
Aug 29	We paid S Holmes his account by cheque £600	**S Holmes**	**Bank**
Aug 31	We paid Kingston Equipment Co by cheque £1,500	**Kingston Equipment**	**Bank**

Activity 7

Debit			**Capital account**		**Credit**
Date	Details	£	Date	Details	£
			July 1	Cash	3,000

Debit			**Purchases account**		**Credit**
Date	Details	£	Date	Details	£
July 3	Cash	850			
July 7	E Morgan	1,160			
July 18	A Moses	980			

Debit   **Cash account**   **Credit**

Date	Details	£	Date	Details	£
July 1	Capital	3,000	July 3	Purchases	850
July 10	Sales	420	July 25	E Morgan	880
July 31	A Knight	550			

Debit   **E Morgan (Supplier) account**   **Credit**

Date	Details	£	Date	Details	£
July 14	Purchases returns	280	July 7	Cash	1,160
July 25	Cash	880			

Debit   **Sales account**   **Credit**

Date	Details	£	Date	Details	£
			July 10	Cash	420
			July 24	A Knight	550

Debit   **Purchase returns account**   **Credit**

Date	Details	£	Date	Details	£
			July 14	E Morgan	280
			July 21	A Moses	190

Debit   **A Moses (supplier) account**   **Credit**

Date	Details	£	Date	Details	£
July 21	Purchase returns	190	July 18	Purchases	980

Debit   **A Knight (customer) account**   **Credit**

Date	Details	£	Date	Details	£
July 24	Sales	550	July 31	Cash	550

Activity 8

Bank

Date		£	Date		£
1 Mar	Capital	12,000	3 Mar	Purchases	3,000
7 Mar	Sales	5,000	15 Mar	Non-current asset	2,400
19 Mar	Sales	2,000	20 Mar	Purchases	5,300
22 Mar	Sales	3,000	24 Mar	Rent	1,000
			28 Mar	Drawings	2,000
			31 Mar	Balance c/d	8,300
		22,000			22,000
1 Apr	Balance b/d	8,300			

Activity 9

Trial balance at 31 August 20X9

	Dr £	Cr £
Capital		3,000
Purchases	2,990	
Cash	2,240	
Purchase ledger control account		790
Sales		970
Purchase returns		470
	5,230	5,230

From the day books to the general ledger

Introduction

The general ledger is the place where the double entry takes place in the appropriate ledger accounts.

KNOWLEDGE	CONTENTS
Bookkeeping and accounts 2 Be able to record cash and credit transactions in books of original entry	1 The general ledger 2 Credit sales 3 Sales returns 4 Credit purchases 5 Purchases returns 6 Summary and further questions

1 The general ledger

1.1 The general ledger

The general ledger contains all the accounts you have become familiar with so far, for example:

- Capital
- Drawings
- Van
- Rent
- Electricity
- Purchases
- Bank

Each account contains a record of transactions over a given period. At the end of each period, usually each month, the accounts are balanced off to give a total of the transactions in each account. The account balances are then transferred to a trial balance.

Two of these typical accounts are the Customer and Supplier accounts but now we will call these the **sales ledger control account** and the **purchases ledger control account**.

The sales ledger control account shows the total amount outstanding from customers and the purchases ledger control account shows the total amount owing to suppliers.

Note: the AAT refers to this ledger as the general ledger. In some businesses it is referred to as the 'main ledger' or the 'nominal ledger'. Be prepared to use any one of these terms when you are at work.

1.2 The sales ledger

Not only is it important to track how much money the customers in total owe the business, we also have to keep track of how much each individual customer owes the organisation. How much was the customer invoiced? How much has the customer paid? How much does the customer owe?

A separate account for each customer is held in a separate subsidiary sales ledger. This ledger is not part of the general ledger and is not part of the double entry system. Transactions with credit customers are recorded in both the sales ledger control account in the general ledger and the customers' individual account in the subsidiary sales ledger.

The sales ledger contains a separate ledger account for each individual customer. Every individual invoice and cash receipt is posted to an individual's account in the sales ledger.

1.3 The purchases ledger

As we require information about individual customers, the same applies to individual suppliers. How much have we been invoiced? What have we paid? How much do we owe?

A separate account for each supplier is held in a separate subsidiary purchases ledger. Transactions with credit suppliers are recorded in both the purchases ledger control account in the general ledger and the suppliers' individual account in the subsidiary purchases ledger.

The purchases ledger contains a separate ledger account for each individual supplier. Every individual purchase invoice and cash payment is posted to an individual's account in the purchases ledger.

At the end of each period, the subsidiary ledgers are reconciled to check that the totals of the individual accounts are the same amounts showing in the sales ledger and purchases ledger control accounts.

2 Credit sales

2.1 Credit sales and the sales ledger

We have now looked at the three elements of a typical accounting system. We must now see how it all fits together.

We will first consider three credit sales invoices

Customer	Amount
A	£1,500
B	£2,000
C	£2,500

Step 1

Each invoice is recorded in the sales day book (SDB) and in the personal account of each customer in the sales ledger. The entry required for each invoice is a debit in each customer account to indicate that this is the amount that each one owes us.

Step 2

At the end of the period the sales day book is totalled and the total is entered into the sales ledger control account (SLCA) (total customers account) in the general ledger.

The full double entry is as we saw in the previous chapter (ignoring VAT):

Debit   Sales ledger control account

Credit   Sales

Step 3

Now consider the following cheques being received against these debts.

Customer	Amount
A	£1,000
B	£2,000

Each receipt is recorded in the cash book (see later chapter) and in the personal account of each customer in the sales ledger. The entry for cash received in the individual accounts is a credit entry to indicate that they no longer owe us these amounts.

Step 4

At the end of the period the cash book is totalled and the total is entered into the sales ledger control account (total customers account) in the general ledger.

The full double entry is:

Debit   Cash account (money in)

Credit   Sales ledger control account

This is illustrated on the next page.

Summary

1   The invoices are entered into the SDB and the cheques are entered into the cash book.

2   The totals from the cash book and SDB are posted to the SLCA.

3   The individual invoices and cash received are posted to the sales ledger.

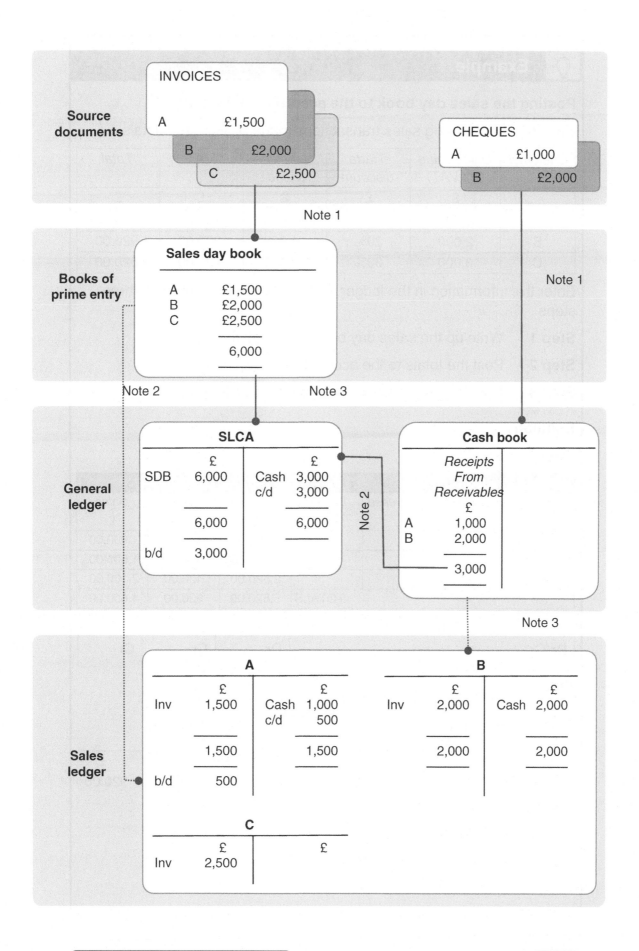

Example

Posting the sales day book to the accounts in the ledgers

Consider the following sales transactions made by Roberts Metals.

Customer	Sales value (ex VAT)	Trade discount	Net sales value	VAT	Total
	£	£	£	£	£
A	1,000	10%	900	180.00	1,080.00
B	2,000	20%	1,600	320.00	1,920.00
C	3,000	30%	2,100	420.00	2,520.00

Enter this information in the ledger accounts using the following three steps.

Step 1   Write up the sales day book, and total the columns.

Step 2   Post the totals to the accounts in the general ledger.

Step 3   Post the individual invoices to the sales ledger.

Solution

Step 1

SALES DAY BOOK						
Date	Customer	Reference	Invoice number	Total £	VAT £	Sales £
	A			1,080.00	180.00	900.00
	B			1,920.00	320.00	1,600.00
	C			2,520.00	420.00	2,100.00
			TOTALS	5,520.00	920.00	4,600.00

Dr/Cr				Dr	Cr	Cr

Step 2

General ledger

Sales

	£			£
		SDB	4,600.00	

VAT

	£			£
		SDB	920.00	

SLCA

	£		£
SDB	5,520.00		

Step 3

Sales ledger

A			B	
	£	£	£	£
SDB	1,080.00		SDB 1,920.00	

C	
	£	£
SDB	2,520.00	

Note to solution

(a) The totals of the SDB are entered in the general ledger.

(b) The individual invoices (total value including VAT) are entered in the individual customers accounts in the sales ledger. This is the amount that the customer will pay.

(c) Note that there are no entries for trade discounts either in the SDB or in the ledger accounts.

Activity 1

A sales day book has the following totals for a week.

Date	Invoice no	Customer name	Code	Total	VAT	Sales
				£	£	£
23/04/X0		Total		65,340	10,890	54,450
Dr/Cr						

Write the double entry for each column in the boxes above.

3 Sales returns

3.1 Recording transactions for returned goods

When customers return goods, the accounting system has to record the fact that goods have been returned. If the goods were returned following a cash sale then cash would be repaid to the customer.

If goods were returned following a credit sale then the SLCA in the general ledger and the customer's individual account in the sales ledger will need to be credited with the value of the goods returned.

 Example

Returns following a cash sale

X sells £500 of goods to A for cash plus £100 VAT

X subsequently agrees that A can return £200 worth of goods (excluding the VAT)

Record these transactions in the ledger accounts.

Solution

Step 1

First of all we need to set up a new account called the 'sales returns account' in the general ledger. This will be used in addition to the sales account and cash book with which you are familiar.

Step 2

Enter the cash sale in the accounts.

Debit bank account for cash received	£600.00
Credit sales with net amount	£500.00
Credit VAT account with VAT	£100.00

Bank account

	£		£
Sales	600.00		

Sales

	£		£
		Cash book	500.00

Sales returns

	£		£

VAT

	£		£
		Cash book	100.00

Step 3

X will repay A £200 plus VAT of (£200 × 20%) = £40. We therefore need to enter the sales return, the cash and the VAT in the accounts.

Debit sales returns account	£200.00
Debit VAT account £200 × 20%	£40.00
Credit bank account with cash paid out	£240.00

Bank account

	£		£
Sales	600.00	Sales returns	240.00

Sales

	£		£
		Cash book	500.00

Sales returns

	£		£
Cash book	200.00		

VAT

	£		£
Cash book	40.00	Cash book	100.00

3.2 Sales returns for credit sales – no VAT

When a credit customer returns goods, he does not receive cash for the return. Instead the seller will issue a credit note to record the fact that goods have been returned. The amount of the credit note will reduce the amount owed by the customer. This credit note is sent to the customer and is entered in the seller's books.

Example

X sells goods on credit to A for £500. A returns goods worth £200. X sends a credit note for £200 to A. Enter these transactions in the general ledger of X's books. There is no VAT.

Solution

Step 1

Record the invoice issued for the credit sale for £500:

Debit the SLCA in the general ledger with £500.

Credit the sales account in the general ledger with £500.

SLCA

	£		£
Sales	500.00		

Sales

	£		£
		SLCA	500.00

Step 2

Record the credit note for £200. The return is debited to a 'sales returns account' to reflect the reduction in sales. The SLCA is credited to show that the amount owed by the customer has been reduced.

SLCA

	£		£
Sales	500.00	Sales returns	200.00

Sales

	£		£
		SLCA	500.00

Sales returns

	£		£
SLCA	200.00		

3.3 Sales returns with VAT

When a return is made and we include VAT, the VAT has to be accounted for both on the invoice when the sale is made, and on the credit note when the goods are returned. This VAT has to be entered in the books.

Example

X sells goods on credit to B for £1,000 + VAT at 20%.

B returns goods worth £400 + VAT at 20%.

Enter these transactions in the general ledger of X's books.

Solution

Step 1

Enter the invoice in the usual way, including the VAT.

SLCA

	£		£
Sales	1,200.00		

Sales

	£		£
		SLCA	1,000.00

VAT

	£		£
		SLCA	200.00

Step 2

Enter the credit note. The VAT on the return will be £400 × 20% = £80.

SLCA

	£		£
Sales	1,200.00	Sales returns	480.00

Sales

	£		£
		SLCA	1,000.00

VAT

	£		£
SLCA	80.00	SLCA	200.00

Sales returns

	£		£
SLCA	400.00		

The books will reflect the position after the return. The balance on the SLCA is £720. This is made up as:

	£
Sales	1,000
Sales return	400
	600
VAT 600 × 20%	120
	720

 Example

A and B are credit customers of Ellis Electricals. The balances on their accounts in the sales ledger are £1,200 and £2,400 (VAT inclusive amounts) because both A and B have made earlier purchases which have not yet been paid.

A returns goods which cost £600 excluding VAT. B returns goods which cost £400 excluding VAT.

Enter the above transactions in the sales returns day book and in the general and sales ledgers of Ellis Electricals.

Solution

Step 1

Enter the original sales invoices in the general ledger.

SLCA

	£		£
SDB	3,600.00		

Sales

	£		£
		SDB	3,000.00

VAT

	£		£
		SDB	600.00

A

	£		£
SDB	1,200.00		

B

	£		£
SDB	2,400.00		

Step 2

Write up the sales returns day book.

SALES RETURNS DAY BOOK						
Date	Customer	Reference	Credit note number	Total £	VAT £	Sales returns £
	A			720.00	120.00	600.00
	B			480.00	80.00	400.00
				1,200.00	200.00	1,000.00

Dr/Cr		Cr	Dr	Dr

Step 3

Enter the SRDB totals in the general ledger accounts.

SLCA

	£		£
SDB	3,600.00	SRDB	1,200.00

Sales

	£		£
		SDB	3,000.00

VAT

	£		£
SRDB	200.00	SDB	600.00

Sales returns

	£		£
SRDB	1,000.00		

Step 4

Enter the individual amounts in the sales ledger.

A

	£		£
SDB	1,200.00	SRDB	720.00

B

	£		£
SDB	2,400.00	SRDB	480.00

Activity 2

Given below are the totals of a sales returns day book for a week.

Date	Customer name	Credit note no	Code	Total	VAT	Sales returns
				£	£	£
23/04/X0				3,360	560	2,800

Dr/Cr			

Post these totals to the general ledger accounts.

4 Credit purchases

4.1 Introduction

When we studied accounting for sales earlier, we dealt with the three parts of the accounting records as they affected sales.

In the case of purchases, the parts are exactly the same except that instead of a 'sales day book' we have the 'purchases day book', and instead of the sales ledger we have the purchases ledger. The third part, namely the general ledger, is exactly the same and contains all the general ledger accounts with which you are familiar.

Remember that, as for sales, the double entry goes through the general ledger, and the purchases ledger is just a memorandum ledger that holds the details of the individual supplier's accounts (it is sometimes called the subsidiary (purchases) ledger).

On the next page we will illustrate how these parts fit together with a diagram.

4.2 Fitting it all together

Consider these three credit purchases invoices

Supplier	Amount
X	£4,000
Y	£5,000
Z	£6,000

Step 1

Each invoice is recorded in the purchases day book.

Step 2

At the end of the period the purchases day book is totalled and the total is entered into the purchases ledger control account in the general ledger. The individual entries are recorded in the individual supplier accounts in the purchases ledger.

Now consider these cheques being paid to the suppliers.

Customer	Amount
X	£2,000
Y	£3,000

Step 1

Each payment is recorded in the cash book.

Step 2

At the end of the period the cash book is totalled and the total is entered into the purchases ledger control account in the general ledger. The individual entries are recorded in the individual supplier accounts in the purchases ledger.

This is illustrated on the next page.

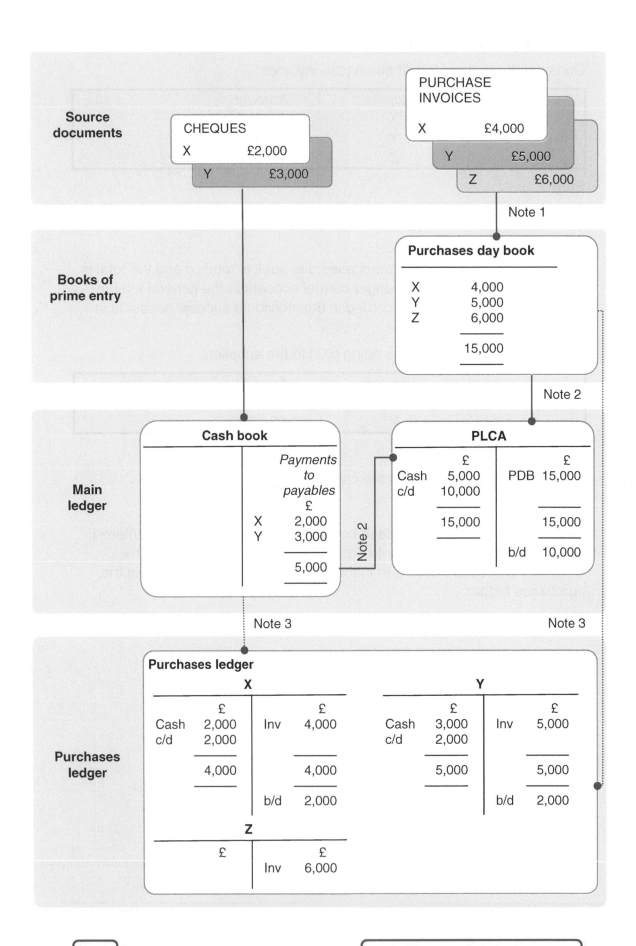

Summary

1 The invoices are entered into the PDB and the cheques are entered into the cash book.

2 The totals from the cash book and PDB are posted to the PLCA.

3 The individual invoices and cash received are posted to the purchases ledger.

 Example

Posting the purchases day book to the accounts in the ledgers

Consider the following purchase invoices received from suppliers by Roberts Metals.

Customer	Purchases value (ex VAT)	Trade discount	Net purchases value	VAT	Total
	£	£	£	£	£
X	500	10%	450.00	90.00	540.00
Y	1,750	20%	1,400.00	280.00	1,680.00
Z	5,000	30%	3,500.00	700.00	4,200.00

The following three steps are needed to enter this information in the ledger accounts.

Step 1 Write up the purchases day book, and total the columns.

Step 2 Post the totals to the accounts in the general ledger.

Step 3 Post the individual invoices to the purchases ledger.

Solution

Step 1

PURCHASES DAY BOOK						
Date	Supplier	Reference	Invoice number	Total £	VAT £	Purchases £
	X			540.00	90.00	450.00
	Y			1,680.00	280.00	1,400.00
	Z			4,200.00	700.00	3,500.00
			TOTALS	6,420.00	1,070.00	5,350.00

Dr/Cr				Cr	Dr	Dr

Step 2

General ledger

Purchases				VAT			
	£		£		£		£
PDB	5,350.00			PDB	1,070.00		

PLCA			
	£		£
		PDB	6,420.00

Step 3

Purchases ledger

X				Y			
	£		£		£		£
		PDB	540.00			PDB	1,680.00

Z			
	£		£
		PDB	4,200.00

Note to solution

(a)   The totals of the PDB are entered in the general ledger.

(b)   The individual invoices (total value including VAT) are entered in the individual supplier accounts in the purchases ledger. This is the amount that will be paid to the supplier.

(c)   Note that there are no entries for trade discounts either in the PDB or in the ledger accounts.

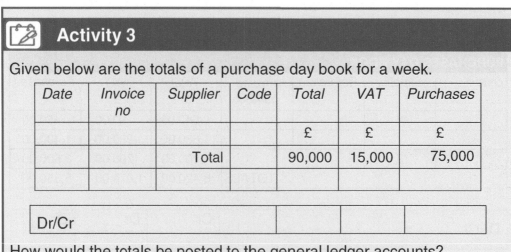

Activity 3

Given below are the totals of a purchase day book for a week.

Date	Invoice no	Supplier	Code	Total	VAT	Purchases
				£	£	£
		Total		90,000	15,000	75,000

Dr/Cr			

How would the totals be posted to the general ledger accounts?

5 Purchases returns

5.1 Introduction

When a business buys and then returns goods to a supplier, the accounting system has to record the fact that goods have been returned. If the goods were returned following a cash purchase then cash would be repaid by the supplier to the customer who had bought the goods.

If goods were returned following a credit purchase then the PLCA in the general ledger will need to be debited and the individual supplier's account in the purchases ledger will need to be debited with the value of the goods returned to reduce the amount owed to the supplier. (We shall see the other entries required below).

 Example

Returns following a cash purchase

Y buys £1,000 of goods from B for cash plus £200 VAT (at 20% standard rated)

B subsequently agrees that Y can return £500 worth of goods (excluding VAT).

Record these transactions in the ledger accounts of Y.

Solution

Step 1

First of all we need to set up a new account called the 'purchases returns account' in the general ledger.

Step 2

Enter the cash purchases in the accounts of Y.

Credit cash book for cash paid	£1,200.00
Debit purchases with expense	£1,000.00
Debit VAT account with VAT	£200.00

Purchases			
	£		£
Cash book	1,000.00		

Purchases returns

	£		£

VAT

	£		£
Cash book	200		

Cash book

	£		£
		Purchases and VAT	1,200.00

Step 3

B will repay Y £500 plus VAT of £100. We therefore need to enter the purchases returns, the cash and the VAT in the accounts.

Cash book

	£		£
Purchases return + VAT	600.00	Purchases and VAT	1,200.00

Purchases

	£		£
Cash book	1,000.00		

Purchases returns

	£		£
		Cash book	500.00

VAT

	£		£
Cash book	200.00	Cash book	100.00

5.2 Purchases returns for credit purchases with VAT

When a credit customer returns goods, he does not receive cash for the return; the seller will issue a credit note to record the fact that goods have been returned. This credit note is sent to the customer and is entered in the customer's books.

When a return is made for goods that incur VAT, we include VAT; the VAT was accounted for on the invoice when the purchase was made, and now has to be accounted for on the credit note when the goods are returned. This VAT has to be entered in the books.

Example

D buys goods from Z for £800 + VAT at 20% (= £960).

D returns goods worth £200 + VAT at 20%.

Enter these transactions in the general ledger of D's books.

Solution

Step 1

Enter the invoice in the usual way, including the VAT.

PLCA

	£		£
		Purchases	960.00

Purchases

	£		£
PLCA	800.00		

VAT

	£		£
PLCA	160.00		

Step 2

Enter the credit note. The VAT on the return will be £200 × 20% = £40. This gives a total credit note of £240.

PLCA

	£		£
Purchases returns + VAT	240.00	Purchases	960.00

Purchases

	£		£
PLCA	800.00		

VAT

	£		£
PLCA	160.00	PLCA	40.00

Purchases returns

	£		£
		PLCA	200.00

The books will reflect the position after the return. The balance on the PLCA is £720. This is made up as:

	£
Purchase	800
Purchase return	(200)
	600
VAT 600 × 20%	120
	720

Example

John bought goods for £750 + VAT from X and £1,000 + VAT from Y.

John returns goods which cost £200 excluding VAT to X, and goods which cost £400 excluding VAT to Y.

Enter the above purchases and returns in the general and purchases ledger of John, using a purchases returns day book.

Solution

Step 1

Enter the original purchases invoices in the general ledger.

PLCA

	£		£
		PDB	2,100.00

Purchases

	£		£
PDB	1,750.00		

VAT

	£		£
PDB	350.00		

X

	£			£
		PDB (£750 + VAT)		900.00

Y

	£			£
		PDB (£1,000 + VAT)		1,200.00

Step 2

Write up the purchases returns day book.

PURCHASES RETURNS DAY BOOK						
Date	Supplier	Reference	Credit note number	Total £	VAT £	Purchases returns £
	X			240.00	40.00	200.00
	Y			480.00	80.00	400.00
				720.00	120.00	600.00

Dr/Cr				Dr	Cr	Cr

Step 3

Enter the PRDB totals in the general ledger accounts.

PLCA

	£		£
PRDB	720.00	PDB	2,100.00

Purchases

	£		£
PDB	1,750.00		

VAT

	£		£
PDB	350.00	PRDB	120.00

Purchases returns

	£		£
		PRDB	600.00

Step 4

Enter the individual amounts in the purchases ledger. The amounts will be debited to the individual supplier accounts as the return is reducing the amount that is owed to the supplier.

X	£		£
PRDB	240.00	PDB (£750 + VAT)	900.00

Y	£		£
PRDB	480.00	PDB (£1,000 + VAT)	1,200.00

✎ Activity 4

Given below are the totals of a purchases returns day book for a week.

Date	Supplier	Credit note no	Code	Total	VAT	Purchase returns
				£	£	£
23/04/X0				9,600	1,600	8,000

Dr/Cr				

Post these totals to the general ledger accounts.

6 Summary and further questions

In this chapter we have reviewed how transactions are recorded.

Initially a transaction is recorded in the relevant book of prime entry (day book).

The double entry takes place in the general ledger, with the total of the gross sales being recorded in a sales ledger control account (SLCA) which we have previously called customers. The total of the gross purchases is recorded in a purchases ledger control account (PLCA) which we have previously called suppliers.

Subsidiary sales ledgers contain individual entries for individual customers whereas the subsidiary purchases ledgers contain individual entries for individual suppliers.

Below are further practice questions to test your knowledge of the above.

Activity 5

Below is a list of documents. Tick the box to which you think each belongs.

	Sales day book	Sales return day book	Purchase day book	Purchase returns day book	None of them
Sales invoice					
Purchase invoice					
Purchase credit note					
Remittance advice					
Sales credit note					

Activity 6

Your supervisor has gone on holiday and left you to transfer the purchase daybooks to the general ledger. You have been provided with the following information:

Date 20X5	Details	Invoice	Total	VAT	Net
	Total		910.44	151.74	758.70

a) Complete the appropriate boxes provided to ensure the correct double entry using the correct wording from the Pick list provided and debit and credit values

Statement	Debit	Credit

Pick list

Purchases	Sales return	Purchases return
VAT	Sales ledger control account	Purchase ledger control account

b) Is the following statement true or false?

Statement	True	False
The total will be a **credit** in the Purchase ledger		

Answers to chapter activities

Activity 1

The required double entry is as follows:

Debit	Sales ledger control account	£65,340
Credit	VAT	£10,890
	Sales	£54,450

Note that it is the net amount that is credited to each sales account and the gross amount (including VAT) that is debited to the sales ledger control account. The VAT total is credited to the VAT account.

The ledger entries would appear as follows:

Sales ledger control account

	£		£
SDB	65,340		

VAT

	£		£
		SDB	10,890

Sales

	£		£
		SDB	54,450

Activity 2

Sales returns

	£		£
SRDB	2,800		

VAT account

	£		£
SRDB	560		

Sales ledger control account

	£		£
		SRDB	3,360

Note that it is the net amount that is debited to each returns account and the gross amount to the sales ledger control account. The difference, the VAT, is debited to the VAT account.

Activity 3

The required double entry is as follows:

Debit	VAT	£15,000
	Purchases	£75,000
Credit	Purchases ledger control account	£90,000

Note carefully that it is the net amount that is debited to each purchases account and the gross amount (including VAT) that is credited to the purchases ledger control account. The VAT total is debited to the VAT account.

The ledger entries would appear as follows:

Purchases ledger control account

	£			£
		PDB		90,000

VAT

	£		£
PDB	15,000		

Purchases

	£		£
PDB	75,000		

 Activity 4

Purchases returns – Department 1 account

	£			£
		PRDB		8,000

VAT account

	£			£
		PRDB		1,600

Purchases ledger control account

	£		£
PRDB	9,600		

Note that it is the net amount that is credited to each returns account and the gross amount to the purchases ledger control account. The difference, the VAT, is credited to the VAT account.

Activity 5

	Sales day book	Sales return day book	Purchase day book	Purchase returns day book	None of them
Sales invoice	✔				
Purchase invoice			✔		
Purchase credit note				✔	
Remittance advice					✔
Sales credit note		✔			

Activity 6

a)

Statement	Debit	Credit
Purchases	758.70	
VAT	151.74	
Purchase ledger control account		910.44

b)

Statement	True	False
The total will be a **credit** in the Purchase ledger	✔	

The cash book

Introduction

The Cash book is the organisation's record of all the money flowing into, and leaving the business. This chapter covers the transactions within the cash book.

KNOWLEDGE	CONTENTS
Bookkeeping and accounts 2 Be able to record cash and credit transactions in books of original entry	1 Recording cash receipts and cash payments 2 The cash book as part of the general ledger

1 Recording cash receipts and cash payments

1.1 Recording cash receipts

 Definition

A cash book is a record of all monies received and paid by the business. The cash book can be used as a book of prime entry and also part of the double entry system acting as a ledger with monies received recorded on the debit side of the book and monies paid out recorded on the credit side of the book. If the cash book is used as a book of prime entry only, the transactions are transferred to a separate Cash Book or Bank account in the general ledger.

Example

The following is an example of the general and sales ledgers, including entries from the sales and sales returns day books.

General ledger

Sales				VAT			
	£		£		£		£
		SDB	4,600.00	SRDB	140.00	SDB	805.00

SLCA				Sales returns			
	£		£		£		£
SDB	5,405.00	SRDB	940.00	SRDB	800.00		

Sales ledger

A				B			
	£		£		£		£
SDB	1,057.50			SDB	1,880.00		

C			
	£		£
SDB	2,467.50	SRDB	940.00

The following transactions took place:

Customers A pays **£1,057.50**

Customers B pays **£1,000.00**

Enter this information in the cash receipts book and in the ledger accounts given above.

Solution

The following steps are needed.

Step 1 Enter these transactions in the cash book.

Step 2 Total the cash book and post the totals to the general ledger.

Step 3 Post the individual amounts of cash paid by customers to the individual accounts in the sales ledger.

Step 1

Date	Narrative	Reference	Total	VAT	SLCA	Cash sales
			£	£	£	£
	A		1,057.50	See Note 2	**1,057.50**	
	B		1,000.00	of Step 2	**1,000.00**	
		TOTALS	2,057.50		**2,057.50**	

Step 2

We have brought forward the balances from the general ledger in the earlier example and now post the cash received book (CRB) totals to the general ledger.

General ledger

Sales			VAT			
£		£		£		£
	SDB	4,600.00	SRDB	140.00	SDB	805.00

SLCA			Sales returns		
£		£		£	£
SDB 5,405.00	SRDB	940.00	SRDB	800.00	
	CRB	**2,057.50**			

Note 1: We have posted the total of the SLCA column of the CRB to the sales ledger control account. The entry to the sales ledger control account is a credit entry as this is reducing the amount owed by our customers.

Note 2: A common confusion is for people to wonder about the VAT – surely some of the money paid by A and B is actually paying the VAT part of the invoice. Yes it is, but we have already accounted for this VAT element when we entered the invoices themselves into the ledger accounts via the sales day book.

The total of the invoices in the SDB were debited to the SLCA and the VAT and sales were the corresponding credits. We therefore now post the total cash including VAT to the sales ledger control account but nothing is posted to the VAT account as this has already been done when dealing with the invoices.

Note 3: This is now the full double entry for the cash received completed.

Debit   Bank account (cash receipts book)

Credit   Sales ledger control account

We have credited the sales ledger control account and the entry in the cash receipts book itself is the related debit entry. So there is no need for any further debit entry.

Step 3

We have brought forward the balance from the sales ledger in the earlier example and now post the cash received to the individual sales ledger accounts. Again, as with the sales ledger control account, the amounts paid are credited to each customer as they reduce the amount owed by each customer.

A				B			
	£		£		£		£
b/f	1,057.50	CRB	**1,057.50**	b/f	1,880.00	CRB	**1,000.00**

C			
	£		£
b/f	2,467.50	SRDB	940.00

Activity 1

Below is the debit side of the cash book. The cash book is a book of prime entry **only**. There was no opening bank balance at the start of the month.

Cash book debit side

Details	Total	VAT	Sales ledger	Cash Sales
Totals	17,856	430	15,276	2,150

What would be the FOUR entries in the general ledger? Choose the account names from the Pick list provided.

Account name	Amount	Debit	Credit

Pick list

Bank

Purchase ledger

Purchase ledger control

Cash purchases

VAT

Cash book

Sales ledger

Sales ledger control

Cash sales

 Activity 2

Your organisation receives a number of cheques from customers through the post each day and these are listed on the cheque listing. It also makes some sales to non-credit customers each day which include VAT at the standard rate of 20% and are paid for by cheque.

Today's date is 28 April 20X1 and the cash receipts book is given below:

Date	Narrative	SL Code	Bank	SLCA	Sales	VAT 20%
20X1			£	£	£	£
28/4	G Heilbron	SL04	108.45	108.45		
	L Tessa	SL15	110.57	110.57		
	J Dent	SL17	210.98	210.98		
	F Trainer	SL21	97.60	97.60		
	A Winter	SL09	105.60	105.60		
	Cash Sales		270.72		225.60	45.12
	Total		**903.92**	**633.20**	**225.60**	**45.12**

Required:

Show what the entries in the sales ledger will be:

Account name	Amount £	Dr ✓	Cr ✓

Show what the entries in the general ledger will be:

Account name	Amount £	Dr ✓	Cr ✓

1.2 Recording cash payments

The Purchases Day Book (PDB) is often used only for invoices from suppliers of purchases, i.e. goods for resale. Invoices for rent, electricity, telephone and similar items will typically not be entered in the PDB. They will be paid by cheque, and the double entry will be made directly between the cash payments book and the relevant expense account in the general ledger.

The reason for this is that the purchases day book (like the sales day book) is used to record purchases made on credit. Purchases of goods made on cash terms will be recorded in the cash book. Payment of expenses also tend to be on a cash basis and therefore will be recorded in the cash book.

☀ Example

Parma Products buys goods for resale from two suppliers on credit. The business buys £1,000 + VAT at 20% of goods from X and £3,000 + VAT at 20% of goods from Y.

Parma also buys goods for resale from a retail supplier with whom he does not have credit terms, and pays for the goods, £500 + VAT at 20%, at the till. Parma also pays X's invoice in full.

KAPLAN PUBLISHING

Enter these transactions in the accounts of Parma Products. The cash purchase is not entered in the PDB.

Solution

Step 1   Enter the invoices for goods in the PDB.

PURCHASES DAY BOOK						
Date	Supplier	Reference	Invoice number	Total £	VAT £	Purchases £
	X			1,200	200	1,000
	Y			3,600	600	3,000
			TOTALS	4,800	800	4,000

Step 2 Enter the totals of the PDB in the general ledger.

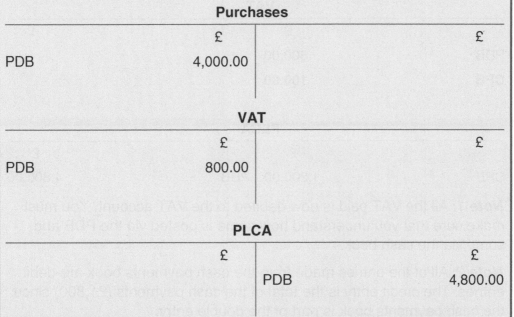

Purchases

	£		£
PDB	4,000.00		

VAT

	£		£
PDB	800.00		

PLCA

	£		£
		PDB	4,800.00

Step 3 Enter the cash paid in the analysed cash payments book.

Date	Narrative	Reference	Total	VAT	PLCA	Cash purchase
			£	£	£	£
	X		1,200.00		1,200.00	
	Cash purchase		600.00	100.00		500.00
		TOTALS	1,800.00	**100.00**	1,200.00	**500.00**

Note that the VAT on the payment to the supplier has already been accounted for in the general ledger via the entries in the PDB. However, the cash purchase was not entered in the PDB and so the VAT has to be entered in the VAT column of the cash book from where it will be posted to the VAT account (see Step 4).

Step 4 Post the cash paid totals from the cash book to the general ledger.

Purchases

	£		£
PDB	4,000.00		
CPB	**500.00**		

VAT

	£		£
PDB	800.00		
CPB	**100.00**		

PLCA

	£		£
CPB	1,200.00	PDB	4,800.00

Note 1: All the VAT paid is now debited to the VAT account. You must make sure that you understand how some is posted via the PDB and some via the cash book.

Note 2: All of the entries made from the cash payments book are debit entries. The credit entry is the total of the cash payments (£1,800) since the cash payments book is part of the double entry.

Step 5: Enter the amounts in the purchases ledger.

X

	£		£
CPB	1,200.00	PDB	1,200.00

Y

	£		£
		PDB	3,600.00

The entries to the purchases ledger from the cash payments book are debit entries in the individual Supplier accounts as the payment means that less is owed to the Supplier.

2 The cash book as part of the general ledger

2.1 The cash book in the assessment

The assessment may show the cashbook as a ledger account format. This means that the cashbook actually forms a part of the general ledger, with the entries being one side of the double entry required within the general ledger.

Therefore a typical assessment requirement will be to complete the other side of the entry within the general ledger, and to update the individual accounts in the subsidiary ledger.

Example

Date	Detail	Bank £	Date	Detail	Bank £
30/6/X9	Bal b/d	16,173	30/6/X9	Supplier P	5,500
30/6/X9	Customer A	13,200	30/6/X9	Cash purchase	1,500
			30/6/X9	Bal c/d	22,373
		29,373			**29,373**

We need to appreciate that the bank account has already been completed with one side of the entries, and the other side of the entry is all that is required to complete the double entry postings.

It is also important to note that the discount column is still to be treated as a memorandum column, requiring both the debit and the credit entries.

Postings to general ledger (ignoring VAT)

Account	Amount	Dr or Cr
SLCA	13,200	Cr
PLCA	5,500	Dr
Purchases	1,500	Dr

Postings to the sales ledger

Account	Amount	Dr or Cr
Customer A account	13,200	Cr

Postings to the purchase ledger

Account	Amount	Dr or Cr
Supplier P	5,500	Dr

 Activity 3

Below is the debit side of the cash book. The cash book is a book of prime entry **and** part of the double entry bookkeeping system. There was no opening bank balance at the start of the month

Cash book debit side

Details	Total	VAT	Sales ledger	Cash Sales
Totals	17,856	430	15,276	2,150

What would be the THREE entries in the general ledger? Choose the account names from the Pick list provided.

Account name	Amount	Debit	Credit

Pick list

Bank	Cash book	Cash purchases
Purchase ledger	Purchase ledger control	Cash sales
Sales ledger	Sales ledger control	VAT

Activity 4

Date	Detail	Bank £	Date	Detail	Bank £
30/6/X9	Bal b/d	24,067	30/6/X9	Cash purchase	20,000
			30/6/X9	Supplier B	2,500
			30/6/X9	Bal c/d	1,567
		24,067			**24,067**
1/7/X9	Bal b/d	1,567			

What are the postings to the general and purchases ledgers based on the accounts above?

Postings to general ledger (ignoring VAT)

Account	Amount	Dr or Cr

Postings to the purchase ledger

Account	Amount	Dr or Cr

Activity 5

You may be asked to only record transactions for one side of the cash book.

Cashbook – debit side

Details	Bank £
Balance b/f	2,568
Edwards Ltd	3,864
Andrews Associates	4,223

(a) Record the TWO transactions within the sales ledger.

(b) Record the ONE transaction within the general ledger.

It is important to appreciate that the above is still the cashbook as a ledger account, but only one half is required. Therefore, the entries will be the same as previously shown.

a) **Sales ledger**

Details	Amount £	Debit/Credit

b) **General ledger**

Details	Amount £	Debit/Credit

Activity 6

Cashbook – credit side

Details	VAT £	Bank £
Cash purchases	60	360
PLCA		4,785

Record the THREE transactions provided within the general ledger.

Details	Amount £	Debit/Credit

 Activity 7

Tick the statements below which you think are correct.

Statement	True	False
The cash book is a book of prime entry ONLY		
The credit side of the cash book is for money paid INTO the business		
A customer receipt of £250.00 is credited to the Sales ledger control account and debited to the Purchase ledger		
A customer receipt is debited to the cash book and credited to the Sales ledger control account		
The VAT showing on the credit side of the cash book is the VAT calculated on cash purchases ONLY		
A supplier payment is debited to the Purchase ledger control account and also to the purchase ledger		

Answers to chapter activities

Activity 1

Account name	Amount	Debit	Credit
Cash book	17,856	✓	
VAT	430		✓
Sales ledger control	15,276		✓
Cash sales	2,150		✓

Activity 2

Account name	Amount £	Dr ✓	Cr ✓
G Heilbron	108.45		✓
L Tessa	110.57		✓
J Dent	210.98		✓
F Trainer	97.60		✓
A Winter	105.60		✓

Account name	Amount £	Dr ✓	Cr ✓
SLCA	633.20		✓
Sales	225.60		✓
VAT	45.12		✓

Activity 3

Account name	Amount	Debit	Credit
VAT	430		✓
Sales ledger control	15,276		✓
Cash sales	2,150		✓

 Activity 4

Postings to general ledger (ignoring VAT)

Account	Amount	Dr or Cr
Purchases	20,000	Dr
PLCA	2,500	Dr

Postings to the purchase ledger

Account	Amount	Dr or Cr
Supplier B account	2,500	Dr

 Activity 5

a) **Sales ledger**

Details	Amount £	Debit/Credit
Edwards Ltd	3,864	Cr
Andrews Associates	4,223	Cr

b) **General ledger**

Details	Amount £	Debit/Credit
SLCA	8,087	Cr

Activity 6

Details	Amount (£)	Debit/Credit
Cash purchases	300	DR
VAT	60	DR
PLCA	4,785	DR

Activity 7

Statement	True	False
The cash book is a book of prime entry ONLY		✓
The credit side of the cash book is for money paid INTO the business		✓
A customer receipt of £250.00 is credited to the Sales ledger control account and debited to the Purchase ledger		✓
A customer receipt is debited to the cash book and credited to the Sales ledger control account	✓	
The VAT showing on the credit side of the cash book is the VAT calculated on cash purchases ONLY	✓	
A supplier payment is debited to the Purchase ledger control account and also to the purchase ledger	✓	

Petty cash

12

Introduction

This chapter considers petty cash and explains why a business may need it and how to account for it.

KNOWLEDGE
Bookkeeping and accounts
4 Be able to understand the petty cash imprest system

CONTENTS

1 Petty cash payments and vouchers

1.1 What is petty cash?

Definition

Petty cash is the small amount of cash that most businesses hold in order to make small cash payments, such as payment for coffee and milk for the staff kitchen.

1.2 Petty cash box

Holding cash on business premises is a security risk and therefore it is important that the petty cash is secure. It should be kept in a locked petty cash box and usually this itself will be held in the safe.

Only the person responsible for the petty cash should have access to the petty cash box.

1.3 Payment of petty cash

Petty cash is usually reimbursed to employees who have already incurred a small cash expense on behalf of the business. These payments should be made for valid business expenses only.

For this reason, the petty cashier should pay out to the employee on receipt of an authorised petty cash voucher and, where appropriate, VAT receipt.

Definition

A petty cash voucher is an internal document that details the business expenditure that an employee has incurred out of his own money.

This voucher must be authorised by an appropriate person before any amounts can be paid to that employee out of the petty cash box.

A typical petty cash voucher is shown below.

Signature of person authorising voucher

PETTY CASH VOUCHER

Authorised by F R Clarke	Received by L Kent	No 4173	
Date	Description	Amount	
4 April 20X1	Train Fare	12	50
Total		12	50

Signature of claimant

Sequential voucher number

Details of expenditure including the date and the nature of the expense

Total paid to employee

1.4 Maintaining petty cash records

The cashier, on receipt of the petty cash voucher should check that the receipt is genuine and that the voucher amounts add up to the total. Once the petty cash vouchers have been received, checked, authorised and the employee reimbursed, the details are recorded in the petty cash book. Earlier in this book we were briefly introduced to the petty cash book as a book of prime entry. In this chapter we will look how petty cash transactions are recorded in the petty cash book.

1.5 Writing up the petty cash book

When cash is paid into the petty cash book it will be recorded on the receipts side (debit side) of the petty cash book.

Each petty cash voucher will then in turn be written up in the petty cash book on the payments (credit) side.

To ensure that no vouchers have been mislaid, petty cash vouchers are pre-numbered sequentially.

Each voucher is then entered into the petty cash book in the correct order, with each item of expenditure being recorded in the correct expense analysis column.

> ### 💡 Example
>
> A business has just started to run a petty cash system with an amount of £100. £100 is withdrawn from the bank account and paid into the petty cash box on *3* April 20X1.
>
> During the first week the following authorised petty cash vouchers were paid. These transactions will now be recorded in the petty cash book.

PETTY CASH VOUCHER

Authorised by T Smedley	Received by P Lannall	No	0001
Date	Description	Amount	
3 April 20X1	Tea/coffee/milk	4	73
	Total	4	73

PETTY CASH VOUCHER

Authorised by T Smedley	Received by R Sellers	No	0002
Date	Description	Amount	
3 April 20X1	Train fare	14	90
	Total	14	90

PETTY CASH VOUCHER

Authorised by T Smedley	Received by F Dorne	No	0003
Date	Description	Amount	
4 April 20X1	Stationery	4	00
	VAT	0	80
	Total	4	80

PETTY CASH VOUCHER

Authorised by T Smedley	Received by P Dent	No	0004
Date	Description	Amount	
5 April 20X1	Postage costs	16	35
	Total	16	35

PETTY CASH VOUCHER			
Authorised by T Smedley	Received by H Polly	No	0005
Date	Description	Amount	
7 April 20X1	Train fare	15	30
	Total	15	30

PETTY CASH VOUCHER			
Authorised by T Smedley	Received by P Lannall	No	0006
Date	Description	Amount	
8 April 20X1	Milk/biscuits	3	85
	Total	3	85

Solution

Petty cash book										
Receipts			**Payments**							
Date	Narrative	Total	Date	Narrative	Voucher no	Total	Postage	Travel	Tea & coffee	Sundry	VAT
20X1		£	20X1			£	£	£	£	£	£
03/04	Cash	100.00	03/04	Tea/coffee	0001	4.73			4.73		
			03/04	Train fare	0002	14.90		14.90			
			04/04	Stationery	0003	4.80				4.00	0.80
			05/04	Postage	0004	16.35	16.35				
			07/04	Train fare	0005	15.30		15.30			
			08/04	Milk/biscuits	0006	3.85			3.85		

2 The imprest system

2.1 The use of an imprest system

Many businesses use the imprest system for petty cash. Using an imprest system makes petty cash easier to control and therefore reduces the possibility of error and fraud.

An imprest system is where a business decides on a fixed amount of petty cash (the imprest) which is just large enough to cover normal petty cash expenditure for a period of time decided by the management of the business (usually a week or a month). This amount of petty cash is withdrawn from the bank.

Claims are paid out of petty cash by a voucher being completed for each amount of petty cash paid out. The vouchers are kept in the petty cash box so that the amount of cash held decreases and is replaced by vouchers.

At any given time, the total contents of the box (i.e. petty cash plus amounts withdrawn represented by vouchers) should equal the amount of the imprest.

At the end of the period, a cheque is drawn for the total of the vouchers which restores the petty cash float to the amount of the imprest. The vouchers are removed from the petty cash box and filed.

 Example

The imprest amount for a petty cash system is £150, which is the amount paid into the petty cash box on 1 March. At the end of the week the total of the vouchers in the petty cash box is £125.05. How much cash is required to replenish the petty cash box to the imprest amount?

Solution

£125.05, the amount paid out on the basis of the petty cash vouchers.

2.2 Non-imprest petty cash system

An imprest petty cash system as in the previous example is the most common method of dealing with and controlling petty cash. However, some businesses may use a non-imprest system. This is where a set amount of cash is withdrawn every so often and paid into the petty cash box no matter what the level of expenditure in that week.

For example it may be an organisation's policy to cash a cheque for £50 each Monday morning for use as petty cash for the week. The danger here is either that petty cash requirements are more than £50 in the week in which case the petty cash box will run out of money. It could also be that week after week expenditure is a lot less than £50 each week, leading to a large amount of cash building up in the petty cash box.

3 Posting petty cash

3.1 Posting the petty cash book

Now that the petty cash book has been written up, we must now post the totals of the petty cash book to the general ledger accounts.

The petty cash book, like the cash book, can either be used either just as a prime entry with postings made to a petty cash account in the general ledger, or a book of prime entry and as a ledger account forming part of the double entry bookkeeping system.

3.2 Posting the petty cash receipt

The receipt into the petty cash box has come from cash being withdrawn from the bank account. This will have been done by writing out a cheque for cash and it from the bank. Therefore, the cheque should be recorded in the cash payments book as a payment (credit) when the cash payments book is written up and as a receipt (debit) when the petty cash book is written up.

3.3 Posting the petty cash payments

We will consider an example where the petty cash book is part of the double entry bookkeeping system as well as being a book of prime entry.

Example

A petty cash book to be posted to the general ledger accounts:

Petty cash book											
Receipts			Payments								
Date	Narrative	Total	Date	Narrative	Voucher no	Total	Postage	Travel	Tea & coffee	Sundry	VAT
20X1		£	20X1			£	£	£	£	£	£
20/08	Bal b/d	100.00	20/08	Tea/coffee	0001	13.68			13.68		
20/08	Bank	50.00	21/08	Train fare	0002	6.80		6.80			
			21/08	Stationery	0003	19.20				16.00	3.20
			22/08	Postage	0004	16.35	16.35				
			23/08	Train fare	0005	15.30		15.30			
			24/08	Milk/biscuits	0006	3.85			3.85		

Solution

Step 1   Each of the columns in the petty cash payments side must be totalled.

Petty cash book											
Receipts			Payments								
Date	Narrative	Total	Date	Narrative	Voucher no	Total	Postage	Travel	Tea & coffee	Sundry	VAT
20X1		£	20X1			£	£	£	£	£	£
20/08	Bal b/d	100.00	20/08	Tea/coffee	0001	13.68			13.68		
20/08	Bank	50.00	21/08	Train fare	0002	6.80		6.80			
			21/08	Stationery	0003	19.20				16.00	3.20
			22/08	Postage	0004	16.35	16.35				
			23/08	Train fare	0005	15.30		15.30			
			24/08	Milk/biscuits	0006	3.85			3.85		
25/08	Bal b/d	150.00		Totals		75.18	16.35	22.10	17.53	16.00	3.20

Check the totals:

	£
Postage	16.35
Travel	22.10
Tea and coffee	17.53
Sundry	16.00
VAT	3.20
Total	75.18

Step 2 Each of the analysis column totals must now be entered into the general ledger accounts as debit entries.

VAT account

	£		£
Petty cash book (PCB)	3.20		

The entry has come from the petty cash book and this is the reference – this is now shortened to PCB.

Postage account

	£		£
PCB	16.35		

Travel account

	£		£
PCB	22.10		

Tea and coffee account

	£		£
PCB	17.53		

Sundry expenses account

	£		£
PCB	16.00		

Bank account

	£		£
		PCB	50.00

The balancing amount of £74.82 should represent the cash that is now in the petty cash tin (£150-75.18).

There is no need for an entry to the petty cash control account as the petty cash book acts as the general ledger account and the closing balance on the account is taken from it when the trial balance is prepared (£74.82 closing Petty cash balance).

3.4 Where the petty cash book is not part of the double entry bookkeeping system

When the petty cash book is not part of the double entry system, the accounting entries must show the impact on the expense accounts, the VAT account and the petty cash control account.

In the event of there being a top up to the petty cash, a separate entry will be required. We would need to show the money being withdrawn from the bank and deposited into petty cash.

We will now consider the earlier illustration to review the general ledger postings required when the petty cash book is not part of the double entry accounting system.

 Example

A petty cash book is give below. This is to be posted to the general ledger accounts.

Petty cash book											
Receipts			Payments								
Date	Narrative	Total	Date	Narrative	Voucher no	Total	Postage	Travel	Tea & coffee	Sundry	VAT
20X1		£	20X1			£	£	£	£	£	£
20/08	Bal b/d	100.00	20/08	Tea/coffee	0001	13.68			13.68		
20/08	Bank	50.00	21/08	Train fare	0002	6.80		6.80			
			21/08	Stationery	0003	19.20				16.00	3.20
			22/08	Postage	0004	16.35	16.35				
			23/08	Train fare	0005	15.30		15.30			
			24/08	Milk/biscuits	0006	3.85			3.85		

Solution

Step 1 Each of the columns in the petty cash payments side must be totalled.

Petty cash book										
Receipts			**Payments**							
Date	Narrative	Total	Date	Narrative	Voucher no	Total	Postage	Travel	Tea & coffee	Sundry	VAT
20X1		£	20X1			£	£	£	£	£	£
20/08	Bal b/d	100.00	20/08	Tea/coffee	0001	13.68			13.68		
20/08	Bank	50.00	21/08	Train fare	0002	6.80		6.80			
			21/08	Stationery	0003	19.20				16.00	3.20
			22/08	Postage	0004	16.35	16.35				
			23/08	Train fare	0005	15.30		15.30			
			24/08	Milk/biscuits	0006	3.85			3.85		
				Bal c/d		74.82					
		150.00				150.00					
25/08	Bal b/d	74.82					16.35	22.10	17.53	16.00	3.20

Check the totals:

	Dr/Cr	Cr	Dr	Dr	Dr	Dr	Dr

	£
Postage	16.35
Travel	22.10
Tea and coffee	17.53
Sundry	16.00
VAT	3.20
	————
Total	75.18
	————

We have been told that the petty cash book is not part of the double entry accounting system. The expense accounts of postage, travel, tea and coffee, sundry and the VAT account will be debited; the impact on the petty cash control account will be to credit it (to reduce the balance) by £75.18 in total that has been paid out.

Remember that the account name in the general ledger should always match the analysis column headings in the petty cash-book and not the description of the expense given in the 'Details' column.

We must also record the impact of the top-up to the petty cash from the bank account. This will be shown as a credit from the bank ledger account and a debit to the petty cash control account.

Step 2 We will now make the entries required into the general ledger accounts

VAT account

	£		£
Petty cash book (PCB)	3.20		

The entry has come from the petty cash book and this is the reference – this is now shortened to PCB.

Postage account

	£		£
PCB	16.35		

Travel account

	£		£
PCB	22.10		

Tea and coffee account

	£		£
PCB	17.53		

Sundry expenses account

	£		£
PCB	16.00		

Bank account

	£		£
		PCB	50.00

Petty cash control

	£		£
Balance b/d	100.00	PCB	75.18
Bank	50.00		

Activity 1

Summary of petty cash vouchers in hand at 31 October 20X7

Date	Description	Total £	VAT incl £
1/10	Envelopes (Administration)	19.72	3.28
4/10	Cleaner (Administration)	8.75	
6/10	Food for staff lunch (Marketing)	17.13	
6/10	Taxi fares (Marketing)	16.23	
6/10	Rail fares (Marketing)	43.75	
10/10	Postage (Administration)	4.60	
15/10	Tea and coffee (Production)	4.39	
17/10	Light bulbs and refuse sacks (Distribution)	8.47	1.41
20/10	Flowers for reception (Administration)	21.23	
26/10	Cleaner (Administration)	8.75	

(a) Write up the payments side of the petty cash book for October 20X7 from this information using the blank petty cash book below.

You should allocate a sequential voucher number to each entry in the petty cash book. The last voucher number to be allocated in September was 6578.

(b) Total each column in the petty cash book and cross-cast them.

PETTY CASH BOOK – PAYMENTS							
Date	Voucher no	Total £	Production £	Distribu-tion £	Marketing £	Administ-ration £	VAT £

(c)   Post the totals to the general ledger accounts given.

Production expenses account

	£		£

Distribution expenses account

	£		£

Marketing expenses account

	£		£

Administration expenses account

	£		£

VAT account

	£		£

4   Reconciling the petty cash

4.1   Reconciling the petty cash

We saw earlier in the chapter that when an imprest system is being used for petty cash then at any point in time the amount of cash in the petty cash box plus the total of the vouchers in the petty cash box should equal the imprest amount.

At regular intervals, usually at the end of each week, this check will be carried out.

4.2   Procedure for reconciling the petty cash box

The total amount of cash in the petty cash box will be counted. The vouchers that have been paid during the week are also in the petty cash box and they must also be totalled.

When the amount of cash is added to the total of the vouchers in the box they should equal the imprest amount.

The petty cash vouchers for the week will then be removed from the box and filed.

 Example

The amount of cash remaining in a petty cash box at the end of a week is as follows:

Notes/coins	Quantity
£10	1
£5	2
£2	3
£1	7
50p	9
20p	11
10p	15
5p	7
2p	16
1p	23

The imprest amount is £100 and the vouchers in the petty cash box at the end of the week are as follows:

PETTY CASH VOUCHER				
Authorised by	Received by		No	0467
C Alexi	P Trant			
Date	Description		Amount	
4 May 20X3	Window cleaner		15	00
		Total	15	00

PETTY CASH VOUCHER				
Authorised by	Received by		No	0468
C Alexi	F Saint			
Date	Description		Amount	
5 May 20X3	Train fare		9	80
		Total	9	80

PETTY CASH VOUCHER				
Authorised by C Alexi	*Received by* A Paul		*No*	0469
Date	*Description*		*Amount*	
5 May 20X3	Stationery		8	00
	VAT		1	40
		Total	9	40

PETTY CASH VOUCHER				
Authorised by C Alexi	*Received by* P Peters		*No*	0470
Date	*Description*		*Amount*	
7 May 20X3	Postage		6	80
		Total	6	80

PETTY CASH VOUCHER				
Authorised by C Alexi	*Received by* C Ralph		*No*	0471
Date	*Description*		*Amount*	
5 May 20X3	Train fare		16	90
		Total	16	90

The cash and vouchers in the petty cash box at the end of the week are to be reconciled.

Solution

The petty cash must be totalled:

Notes/coins	Quantity	Amount (£)
£10	1	10.00
£5	2	10.00
£2	3	6.00
£1	7	7.00
50p	9	4.50
20p	11	2.20
10p	15	1.50
5p	7	0.35
2p	16	0.32
1p	23	0.23
		—————
		42.10
		—————

Now the vouchers must be totalled.

	£
0467	15.00
0468	9.80
0469	9.40
0470	6.80
0471	16.90
	57.90

Finally, total the cash and the vouchers to ensure that they add back to the imprest amount.

	£
Cash	42.10
Vouchers	57.90
	100.00

 Activity 2

Your business runs a petty cash box based upon an imprest amount of £60. This morning you have emptied the petty cash box and found the following notes, coins and vouchers.

Notes		Coins		Vouchers	
Value	Quantity	Value	Quantity	No	£
£5	2	£1	3	2143	10.56
		50p	5	2144	3.30
		20p	4	2145	9.80
		10p	6	2146	8.44
		5p	7	2147	2.62
		2p	10	2148	6.31
		1p	8	2149	1.44

Required:

Reconcile the cash and the vouchers in the petty cash box.

Activity 3

Given below is a business' petty cash book for the week.

Petty cash book											
Receipts			Payments								
Date	Narrative	Total	Date	Details	Voucher no	Amount	Postage	Staff welfare	Station-ery	Travel expenses	VAT
						£	£	£	£	£	£
5/1/X1	Bal b/d	150.00	12/1/X1	Postage	03526	13.68	13.68				
				Staff welfare	03527	25.00		25.00			
				Stationery	03528	15.12			12.60		2.52
				Taxi fare	03529	12.25				10.21	2.04
				Staff welfare	03530	6.40		6.40			
				Postage	03531	12.57	12.57				
				Rail fare	03532	6.80				6.80	
				Stationery	03533	8.16			6.80		1.36
				Taxi fare	03534	19.20				16.00	3.20
				Bal c/d		30.82					
		150.00				150.00					
25/08	Bal b/d	30.82					26.25	31.40	19.40	33.01	9.12

Required:

The Petty Cash Book is part of the double entry bookkeeping system.

Show what the entries in the general ledger will be:

Account name	Amount £	Dr ✓	Cr ✓

5 End of chapter questions

Activity 4

a) Below is a statement about petty cash. Carefully read the statement and tick the box that you think is most appropriate.

Statement	Correct	Incorrect
Petty cash is used for buying very expensive purchases		

b) Below is a list of different types of organisations. Which of the organisations do you think would deal mainly with cash? Tick the box you think is correct.

Organisation	Yes	No
A newsagent		
A business trading with many different countries and currencies		
A market stall		
A business that buys and sells on credit terms		

c) Below are some statements. Carefully read the statements and tick the box that you think is correct.

Statement	Correct	Incorrect
An imprest system is one where the petty cash is topped up to a set amount at regular intervals		
The petty cash box can be left out in the office, as everyone is very honest and trustworthy		
If the balance on the petty cash imprest system should be £100.00, and there are vouchers totalling £53.60, then the amount needed to top up the petty cash is £46.40		
VAT cannot be claimed on purchases made via petty cash		
The petty cash book can be a book of prime entry AND part of the double entry bookkeeping system		
You are reconciling the petty cash. You find that though there should be £46.40 in cash in the box, there is only £45.20. Your supervisor says it doesn't matter		

 KAPLAN PUBLISHING

Answers to chapter activities

Activity 1

(a), (b)

PETTY CASH BOOK – PAYMENTS														
Date	*Voucher no*	*Total*		*Production*		*Distribution*		*Marketing*		*Administration*		*VAT*		
		£		£		£		£		£		£		
01/10/X7	6579	19	72							16	44	3	28	
04/10/X7	6580	8	75							8	75			
06/10/X7	6581	17	13					17	13					
06/10/X7	6582	16	23					16	23					
06/10/X7	6583	43	75					43	75					
10/10/X7	6584	4	60							4	60			
15/10/X7	6585	4	39	4	39									
17/10/X7	6586	8	47			7	06					1	41	
20/10/X7	6587	21	23							21	23			
26/10/X7	6588	8	75							8	75			
		153	02	4	39	7	06	77	11	59	77	4	69	

(c)

Production expenses account

	£		£
PCB	4.39		

Distribution expenses account

	£		£
PCB	7.06		

Marketing expenses account

	£		£
PCB	77.11		

Administration expenses account

	£		£
PCB	59.77		

VAT account

	£		£
PCB	4.69		

Activity 2

Notes and coins

	£	£
£5 × 2	10.00	
£1 × 3	3.00	
50p × 5	2.50	
20p × 4	0.80	
10p × 6	0.60	
5p × 7	0.35	
2p × 10	0.20	
1p × 8	0.08	
		17.53

Vouchers

2143	10.56	
2144	3.30	
2145	9.80	
2146	8.44	
2147	2.62	
2148	6.31	
2149	1.44	
		42.47
Imprest amount		60.00

Activity 3

The entries in the general ledger will be:

Account name	Amount £	Dr ✔	Cr ✔
Postage	26.25	✔	
Staff Welfare	31.40	✔	
Stationery	19.40	✔	
Travel Expenses	33.01	✔	
VAT	9.12	✔	

Activity 4

a)

Statement	Correct	Incorrect
Petty cash is used for buying very expensive purchases		✔

b)

Organisation	Yes	No
A newsagent	✔	
A business trading with many different countries and currencies		✔
A market stall	✔	
A business that buys and sells on credit terms		✔

c)

Statement	Correct	Incorrect
An imprest system is one where the petty cash is topped up to a set amount at regular intervals	✔	
The petty cash box can be left out in the office, as everyone is very honest and trustworthy		✔
If the balance on the petty cash imprest system should be £100.00, and there are vouchers totalling £53.60, then the amount needed to top up the petty cash is £46.40	✔	
VAT cannot be claimed on purchases made via petty cash		✔
The petty cash book can be a book of prime entry AND part of the double entry bookkeeping system	✔	
You are reconciling the petty cash. You find that though there should be £46.40 in cash in the box, there is only £45.20. Your supervisor says it doesn't matter		✔

Bank reconciliations

Introduction

Completion of this chapter will ensure we are able to correctly prepare the cash book, compare the entries in the cash book to details on the bank statement and then finally to prepare a bank reconciliation statement. We will explore the concept of the bank reconciliation, producing an updated cash book using this knowledge.

KNOWLEDGE
Bookkeeping and accounts
3.1 Update a cash book (bank balance) using details from a bank statement.
3.2 Recalculate the closing bank balance.
3.3 Be able to prepare bank reconciliations.

CONTENTS
1   Writing up the cash book
2   Preparing the bank reconciliation statement

1 Writing up the cash book

1.1 Introduction

Most businesses will have a separate cash receipts book and a cash payments book which form part of the double entry system. If this form of record is used, the cash balance must be calculated from the opening balance at the beginning of the period, plus the receipts shown in the cash receipts book for the period and minus the payments shown in the cash payments book for the period.

1.2 Balancing the cash book

The following brief calculation will enable us to find the balance on the cash book when separate receipts and payments book are maintained.

	£
Opening balance per the cash book	X
Add: Receipts in the period	X
Less: Payments in the period	(X)
	——
Closing balance per the cash book	X
	——

 Example

Suppose that the opening balance on the cash book is £358.72 on 1 June. During June the cash payments book shows that there were total payments made of £7,326.04 during the month of June and the cash receipts book shows receipts for the month of £8,132.76.

What is the closing balance on the cash book at the end of June?

Solution

		£
Opening balance at 1 June		358.72
Add:	Receipts for June	8,132.76
Less:	Payments for June	(7,326.04)
		————
Balance at 30 June		1,165.44
		————

Activity 1

The opening balance at 1 January in a business cash book was £673.42. During January payments totalled £6,419.37 and receipts totalled £6,488.20.

What is the closing balance on the cash book?

Activity 2

Below is a cash book that needs updating with the following receipts:

	£
10 May BACS	6,200
25 May Bank interest	40
31 May BACS	460

Enter the amounts into the cash book

Date	Details	£	Date	Chq	Details	£
1 May	Balance b/d	526	1 May			
6 May	Shaws	630	3 May	0041	Bills Farm	2,000
6 May	Andrew Ltd	880	3 May	0042	Cows Head	3,240
			5 May	0043	Adam Ant	840
			30 May	0044	Miles to Go	700

2 Preparing the bank reconciliation statement

2.1 Introduction

At regular intervals (normally at least once a month) the cashier must check that the cash book is correct by comparing the cash book with the bank statement.

2.2 Differences between the cash book and bank statement

At any date the balance shown on the bank statement is unlikely to agree with the balance in the cash book for two main reasons.

(a) **Items in the cash book not on the bank statement**

Certain items will have been entered in the cash book but will not appear on the bank statement at the time of the reconciliation. Examples are:

- Cheques received by the business and paid into the bank which have not yet appeared on the bank statement, due to the time lag of the clearing system. These are known as **outstanding lodgements** (can also be referred to as "uncleared lodgements").

- Cheques written by the business but which have not yet appeared on the bank statement, because the recipients have not yet paid them in, or the cheques are in the clearing system. These are known as **unpresented cheques**.

- Errors in the cash book (e.g. transposition of numbers, addition errors).

(b) **Items on the bank statement not in the cash book**

At the time of the bank reconciliation certain items will appear on the bank statement that have not yet been entered into the cash book. These can occur due to the cashier not being aware of the existence of these items until receiving the bank statements. Examples are:

- Direct debit or standing order payments that are in the bank statement but have not yet been entered in the cash payments book.

- BACS or other receipts paid directly into the bank account by a customer that have not yet been entered in the cash received book.

- Bank charges or bank interest that are unknown until the bank statement has been received and therefore will not be in the cash book.

- Errors in the cash book that may only come to light when the cash book entries are compared to the bank statement.

- Returned cheques i.e. cheques paid in from a customer who does not have sufficient funds in his bank to 'honour' the cheque (see later in this chapter).

2.3 The bank reconciliation

 Definition

A bank reconciliation is simply a statement that explains the differences between the balance in the cash book and the balance on the bank statement at a particular date.

A bank reconciliation is produced by following a standard set of steps.

Step 1: Compare the cash book and the bank statement for the relevant period and identify any differences between them.

You should begin with agreeing the opening balances on the bank statement and cash book so that you are aware of any prior period reconciling items that exist.

This is usually done by ticking in the cash book and bank statement items that appear in both the cash book and the bank statement. Any items left unticked therefore only appear in one place, either the cash book or the bank statement. We saw in 2.2 above the reasons why this might occur.

Step 2: Update the cash book for any items that appear on the bank statement that have not yet been entered into the cash book.

Tick these items in both the cash book and the bank statement once they are entered in the cash book.

At this stage there will be no unticked items on the bank statement.

(You clearly cannot enter on the bank statement items in the cash book that do not appear on the bank statement – the bank prepares the bank statement, not you. These items will either be unpresented cheques or outstanding lodgements – see 2.2 above.)

Step 3: Bring down the new cash book balance following the adjustments in step 2 above.

Step 4: Prepare the bank reconciliation statement.

This will typically have the following layout:

Bank reconciliation as at 31.0X.200X

	£
Balance as per bank statement	X
Less unpresented cheques	(X)
Add outstanding lodgements	X
Balance as per cash book	X

Think for a moment to ensure you understand this layout.

We deduct the unpresented cheques (cheques already entered in the cash book but not yet on the bank statement) from the bank balance, because when they are paid into the bank the bank balance will be reduced.

We add outstanding lodgements (cash received and already entered in the cash book) because when they are paid into the bank they will increase the bank balance.

It is also useful to remember that the bank reconciliation can be performed by starting with the cash book balance and reconciling to the bank statement:

Bank reconciliation as at 31.0X.200X

	£
Balance as per cash book	X
Add unpresented cheques	(X)
Less outstanding lodgements	X
Balance as per bank statement	X

If we start with the cash book balance, to reconcile this to the bank statement balance we add back the unpresented cheques as though they haven't been paid out of the cash book (as the bank statement has not recognised these being paid out).

We deduct outstanding lodgements as though we haven't recognised these in the cash book (as the bank statement has not recognised these receipts). The cash book balance should then agree to the bank statement balance that is, we have reconciled these balances.

KAPLAN PUBLISHING

2.4   Debits and credits in bank statements

When comparing the cash book to the bank statement it is easy to get confused with debits and credits.

- When we pay money into the bank, we debit our cash book but the bank credits our account.

- This is because a debit in our cash book represents the increase in our asset 'cash'. For the bank, the situation is different: they will credit our account because they now owe us more money; in the bank's eyes we are a payable.

- When our account is overdrawn, we owe the bank money and consequently our cash book will show a credit balance. For the bank an overdraft is a debit balance.

On the bank statement a credit is an amount of money paid into the account and a debit represents a payment. A bank statement shows the transactions from the bank's point of view rather than the business' point of view.

 Example

On 30 April Tomasso's received the following bank statement as at 28 April.

Today's date is 30 April.

QC Bank				
QC Street, London				
To: Tomasso's Account No 92836152			30 April 20x2	
Date	**Details**	**Payments**	**Receipts**	**Balance**
20x2		£	£	£
2 April	Bal b/f			100
3 April	Cheque 101	55		45
4 April	Cheque 103	76		(31)
6 April	Bank Giro Credit		1,000	969
9 April	Cheque 105	43		926
10 April	Cheque 106	12		914
11 April	Cheque 107	98		816
21 April	Direct Debit RBC	100		716
22 April	Direct Debit OPO	150		566
23 April	Interest received		30	596
24 April	Bank charges	10		586
28 April	Bank Giro Credit DJA		250	836

The cash book at 28 April is shown below.

Date 20x2	Details	Bank £	Date 2012	Cheque number	Details	Bank £
	Balance b/f	100	01 April	101	Alan & Co	55
06 April	Prance Dance Co.	1,000	02 April	102	Amber's	99
23 April	Interest received	30	02 April	103	Kiki & Company	76
23 April	Graham Interiors	2,000	05 April	104	Marta	140
25 April	Italia Design	900	06 April	105	Nina Ltd	43
			07 April	106	Willy Wink	12
			08 April	107	Xylophones	98

Firstly, we see that the opening balance is £100 per both the bank statement and the cash book. Secondly, we must tick off the items in the bank statement to the cash book.

The effect of this on the bank statement can be seen below.

Date	Details	Payments £	Receipts £	Balance £
2 April	Bal b/f			100
3 April	Cheque 101	✓55		45
4 April	Cheque 103	✓76		(31)
6 April	Bank Giro Credit		✓1,000	969
9 April	Cheque 105	✓43		926
10 April	Cheque 106	✓12		914
11 April	Cheque 107	✓98		816
21 April	Direct Debit RBC	100		716
22 April	Direct Debit OPO	150		566
23 April	Interest received		✓30	596
24 April	Bank charges	10		586
28 April	Bank Giro Credit DJA		250	836

This leaves 4 items unticked on the bank statement. These transactions need to be added to the cash book and the cash book can then be balanced off.

The cash book is updated for these below:

Date 2012	Details	Bank £	Date 2012	Cheque number	Details	Bank £
	Balance b/d	100	01 April	101	Alan & Co	✓55
06 April	Prance Dance Co.	✓1,000	02 April	102	Amber's	99
23 April	Interest received	✓30	02 April	103	Kiki & Company	✓76
23 April	Graham Interiors	2,000	05 April	104	Marta	140
25 April	Italia Design	900	06 April	105	Nina Ltd	✓43
28 April	**DJA**	**250**	07 April	106	Willy Wink	✓12
			08 April	107	Xylophones	✓98
			21 April	–	**DD – RBC**	**100**
			22 April	–	**DD – OPO**	**150**
			24 April	–	**Bank charges**	**10**
			28 April	–	**Balance c/d**	**3,497**
		4,280				4,280
29 April	Balance b/d	3,497				

Once the cash book has been updated, there are 4 items unticked on the cash book.

These are the items that will go onto the bank reconciliation, as shown below.

Bank reconciliation statement as at 28 April	£
Balance per bank statement	836
Add:	
Name: Graham's Interior	2,000
Name: Italia Design	900
Total to add	2,900
Less:	
Name: Amber's	99
Name: Marta	140
Total to subtract	239
Balance as per cash book	3,497

The bank reconciliation statement proves that the difference between the balance on the bank statement and the balance on the cash book is due to outstanding lodgements and unpresented cheques.

Activity 3

FELICITY HOWE BOUTIQUE

Below is the cash book (bank columns only) of Felicity Howe Boutique for the month of April 20x4 together with her bank statement for the same period.

CASH BOOK

20x4		£	20X4		£
1 Apr	Balance b/d	1,470	2 Apr	Cheque 101129	930
9 Apr	Sales	606	4 Apr	Cheque 101130	506
12 Apr	Sales	1,048	9 Apr	Cheque 101131	834
30 Apr	Sales	550	29 Apr	Cheque 101132	410
			30 Apr	Balance c/d	994
		3,674			3,674
1 May	Balance b/d	994			

BANK STATEMENT

NORBURY BANK PLC
Southborough Branch
In account with: Felicity Howe   Account no 34578900

20X4		Payments	Receipts	Balance
01-Apr	balance b/f.			1,470
02-Apr	Cheque No. 129	930		540
05-Apr	Cheque No. 130	506		34
09-Apr	Counter Credit		606	640
12-Apr	Cheque No. 131	834		-194
12-Apr	Counter Credit		1,048	854
16-Apr	STO Hamble Comms.	75		779
17-Apr	BACS - Honey Bee		948	1,727
18-Apr	BACS - Goldfish CC	534		1,193
25-Apr	Overdraft fee		125	1,068
29-Apr	BGC S. May		610	1,678

Required:

a. Bring up to date the Cash Book making any adjustments necessary

b. Update the Cash Book and bring the balance down

c. Prepare a bank reconciliation statement as at 30 April 20x4

Activity 4

Graham

The cash book of Graham showed a debit balance of £204 on 31 March 20X3. A comparison with the bank statements revealed the following:

		£
1	Cheques drawn but not presented	3,168
2	Amounts paid into the bank but not credited	723
3	Entries in the bank statements not recorded in the cash account	
	(i) Standing orders	35
	(ii) Interest on bank deposit account	18
	(iii) Bank charges	14
4	Balance on the bank statement at 31 March	2,618

Tasks

a) Show the appropriate adjustments required in the cash book of Graham bringing down the correct balance at 31 March 20X3.

b) Prepare a bank reconciliation statement at that date.

Activity 5

Below is a list of statements about bank reconciliations. Tick whether the statement is True or False.

Statement	True	False
Cheques take three (or more) days to clear		
An outstanding lodgement is a cheque that has been received by the business, paid into the bank, and has appeared on the bank statement		
An outstanding lodgement is a cheque that has been received by the business, paid into the bank, but has not yet appeared on the bank statement		
An unpresented cheque is one that has been written by the business but which has not yet appeared on the bank statement		
Direct debits that only show on the bank statement should be ignored		
Direct debits and standing orders that only show on the bank statement should be written into the cash book		
Bank charges are receipts to be entered into the cash book on the debit side		
Errors in the cash book may only come to light when the cash book entries are compared to the bank statement		

Answers to chapter activities

 Activity 1

	£
Opening balance	673.42
Payments	(6,419.37)
Receipts	6,488.20
Closing balance	742.25

The closing balance is £742.25 cash surplus.

 Activity 2

Updated cash book:

Date	Details	£	Date	Chq	Details	£
1 May	Balance b/d	526				
6 May	Shaws	630	3 May	0041	Bills Farm	2,000
6 May	Andrew Ltd	880	3 May	0042	Cows Head	3,240
10 May	BACS	6,200	5 May	0043	Adam Ant	840
25 May	Bank Interest	40	30 May	0044	Miles to Go	700
31 May	BACS	460				
			31 May		Balance c/d	1,956
		8,736				8,736
1 June	Balance b/d	1,956				

Activity 3

a. Bring up to date the Cash Book making any adjustments necessary

CASH BOOK

20x4		£	20x4		£
1 Apr	Balance b/d	1,470✓	2 Apr	Cheque 101129	930✓
9 Apr	Sales	606✓	4 Apr	Cheque 101130	506✓
12 Apr	Sales	1,048✓	9 Apr	Cheque 101131	834✓
30 Apr	Sales	550	29 Apr	Cheque 101132	410
			30 Apr	Balance c/d	994
		3,674			3,674
1 May	Balance b/d	994✓			

BANK STATEMENT

20x4		Payments	Receipts	Balance
01 Apr	Balance b/f			1,470✓
02 Apr	Cheque 101129	930✓		540
05 Apr	Cheque 101130	506✓		34
09 Apr	Counter credit		606✓	640
12 Apr	Cheque 101131	834✓		(194)
12 Apr	Counter credit		1,048✓	854
16 Apr	STO Hamble Comms	75✓		779
17 Apr	BACS – Honey Bee		948✓	1,727
18 Apr	BACS – Goldfish CC	534✓		1,193
25 Apr	Overdraft fee	125✓		1,068
29 Apr	BGC S May		610✓	1,678

b. Update the Cash Book and bring the balance down

FELICITY HOWE BOUTIQUE

CASH BOOK

20x4			20x4		
30 April	Balance b/d.	994.00✓			
				Hamble	
	Honey Bee	948.00✓	16 April	Comms.	75.00✓
	S. May	610.00✓	18 April	Goldfish CC	534.00✓
				Bank	
			25 April	charges	125.00✓
				Balance c/d.	1,818.00
		£ 2,552.00			£ 2,552.00

| 1 May | Balance b/d. | 1,818.00 | | | |

c. Prepare a bank reconciliation statement as at 30 April 20x4

Felicity Howe Boutique Bank reconciliation statement as at 30 April	£
Balance per bank statement	1,678
Add:	
Name: Sales	550
Total to add	550
Less:	
Name: 101132	410
Total to subtract	410
Balance as per cash book	1,818

Activity 4

a)

Cash account

	£		£
Balance b/d	204	Sundry accounts	
Interest on deposit account	18	Standing orders	35
		Bank charges	14
		Balance c/d	173
	222		222
Balance b/d	173		

b)

BANK RECONCILIATION STATEMENT AT 31 MARCH 20X3

	£
Balance per bank statement	2,618
Add Outstanding lodgements	723
	3,341
Less Unpresented cheques	(3,168)
Balance per cash account	173

Activity 5

Statement	True	False
Cheques take three (or more) days to clear	✓	
An outstanding lodgement is a cheque that has been received by the business, paid into the bank, and has appeared on the bank statement		✓
An outstanding lodgement is a cheque that has been received by the business, paid into the bank, but has not yet appeared on the bank statement	✓	
An unpresented cheque is one that has been written by the business but which has not yet appeared on the bank statement	✓	
Direct debits that only show on the bank statement should be ignored		✓
Direct debits and standing orders that only show on the bank statement should be written into the cash book	✓	
Bank charges are receipts to be entered into the cash book on the debit side		✓
Errors in the cash book may only come to light when the cash book entries are compared to the bank statement	✓	

An introduction to computerised accounting

Introduction

The aim of this text book is to guide you through the computerised accounting aspects of your studies.

To complete this unit you will need copy of Sage which is an integrated computerised software package for accounts. There are a number of versions of Sage - here we use **Sage 50 Accounts Professional 2012 version 18**.

If you have another version of Sage, or even another accounting package, you should still be able to proceed without too much difficulty, although you may find that some of the screen-shots used differ.

The book uses a **case study approach** to guide you step-by-step. It assumes that you have never used a computerised accounting package before. Even if you have, it is worth starting at the beginning to ensure that you don't 'jump ahead' too quickly.

You will find learning objectives detailed at the start of every chapter under the knowledge heading, which are extracted from the AAT's published 'study and assessment guide' for this particular unit.

KNOWLEDGE	CONTENTS
3.1 Calculate batch controls as required 3.2 Reconcile batch controls as required	1 Computerised accounting systems 2 Accounting documents 3 Batch control and coding 4 Risks of a computerised system 5 Sage software

1 Computerised accounting systems

1.1 The use of computerised accounting systems

For very small organisations, a simple spreadsheet to record monies in and out of the business may be sufficient. However, once a business becomes larger or more complex, it can be more effective to use a computerised bookkeeping system.

There are many proprietary versions on the market, each of which works in a similar way. However, they will each offer different approaches to data entry, presentation of reports and so on, as well as different 'extras' such as stock management modules, budgeting and tax planning.

Some systems also allow a company to integrate a computerised payroll function.

1.2 The benefits of computerised accounting systems

The main benefits of using a computerised bookkeeping system are:

- It enables quicker, more efficient processing of data.

- Fewer mathematical errors – because the system completes all the double entry and other mathematical functions (e.g. calculation of percentages) there is reduced opportunity for human error.

- Accounting documents (e.g. invoices, statements etc) can be generated automatically, using tailored documents designed to incorporate company details, logos etc.

- The range of information that can be easily produced in reports is wide and varied, meaning businesses can report to various internal and external groups (e.g. management, directors, shareholders, banks etc) in an appropriate format.

- There is no need for manual processing of data – computerised bookkeeping systems complete all the double entry automatically.

- Hardware and software prices have fallen dramatically over the last thirty years, making a computerised system affordable to all organisations.

- Allow data to be easily transferred into other programs – e.g. a spreadsheet or word processing package.

2 Accounting documents

2.1 Types of accounting documentation

Business organisations rely on relevant documentation to record the transactions that it undertakes. Without an appropriate piece of supporting documentation, there is no way of knowing what has been bought, from whom and for how much, nor indeed what has been sold.

With a high proportion of modern transactions being on credit, an accurate and comprehensive system of recording transactions is essential.

Accounting documents are referred to as '**Source documents'**. They include:

- purchase orders
- delivery notes
- purchase invoices
- credit notes
- sales invoices
- remittance advices

For example, if an organisation wishes to purchase a new computer printer, it may first raise a purchase order which is sent to the supplier. The supplier would issue or deliver the printer along with a delivery note, to record the safe receipt of the goods. A supplier invoice requiring payment would follow. If the printer was faulty, it could be returned and a credit note issued. When the payment is sent it is accompanied by a remittance advice which itemises each transaction which is being paid.

This process and the nature of these documents are covered in more depth in Chapter 2.

3 Batch control and coding

3.1 Batch control systems

In order for a transaction to be correctly recorded in a computerised accounting system, the appropriate documentation must first be raised and then the details entered into 'the system'. Rather than enter each document on to the computer as it is received, many organisations use a batch control system.

In a batch control system all similar documents are collected and processed together in one batch. For example, purchase invoices and sales invoices will be sorted into separate batches and each batch will be processed separately.

A batch control system will save time as the data processer is just focusing one task at a time.

3.2 Batch control sheets

Batch control can also help to make sure that computer entries are accurate.

First, a manual calculation is made to total each batch of documents. These totals are then checked against the computer system.

 Example

Akddus works in the accounting department of Armistead & Co. One of Akddus' daily tasks is to make sure that all sales invoices notes are entered on to the computer.

Each day Akddus works through the previous day's sales invoices. He calculates the total net amounts, the total VAT amounts, and the total gross amounts. He then enters these totals on to a batch control sheet.

Today, Akddus has three invoices to process:

Armistead & Co

Ryan's Close
Lower Meltham
MT4 3SQ

Invoice no: 59870
Tax point: 16th June 2016

To: Pendleton Prisms
    Stuart Street, Bristol, BR1 JQ8

	£
Goods	399.00
VAT 20%	79.80
Gross amount for payment	478.80

Payment terms: 15 days net

Armistead & Co

Ryan's Close

Invoice no: 59871

Lower Meltham

Tax point: 16th June 2016

MT4 3SQ

To: Wiggins Plc
    Prism Lane, Huddersfield, HT1 JQ3

	£
Goods	3,500.00
VAT 20%	700.00
Gross amount for payment	4,200.00

Payment terms: 15 days net

Armistead & Co

Ryan's Close

Invoice no: 59872

Lower Meltham

Tax point: 16th June 2016

MT4 3SQ

To: Dribbles Ltd
    Dowsett Street, Farnborough, FG6 5AD

	£
Goods	85.60
VAT 20%	17.12
Gross amount for payment	102.72

Payment terms: 30 days net

Akddus calculates the total net amounts, total VAT amounts, and total gross amounts and enters the figures on to a batch control sheet.

Sales invoice batch totals	Total net amounts £	Total VAT amounts £	Total gross amounts £
Tuesday 16th June 2016	3,984.60	796.92	4781.52

Akddus checks that the net amount and VAT amounts equal the total on the batch control sheet: 3984.60 + 796.92 = 4782.52

Akddus then enters the batch of invoices on to the computer and checks that the totals are the same as the figures on his batch control sheet.

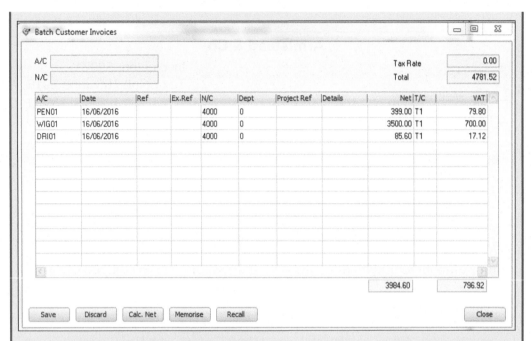

After Akddus has entered the sales invoices onto the computer he will check that the computer-generated batch totals match the total on the batch control sheet. If the totals are not the same, Akddus should check both the batch control totals and the computer entries.

Definitions

Net amount - the total value of goods and services supplied, after discount and before VAT.

VAT (Value Added Tax) - A consumer tax collected by businesses on behalf of the government.

Gross amount – the total cost due from the customer including VAT.

3.3 Coding

All computerised bookkeeping systems work by the use of codes. Each supplier and each customer must be given a unique code by which the computer software can recognise them. It is vital that there can be no confusion between two suppliers with similar names. For example, you may be fully aware that John Green and John Greenwood are entirely different people, but it could be easy for a computer to mix them up. Each must therefore be given a unique code by which they can be identified.

Similarly, each product manufactured or sold by an organisation may be given a unique code. Also, employees are usually 'coded' – you could check your pay slip to find your own Employee Reference Number.

Finally, every type of income or expense, asset or liability, is given a unique code to identify it. This makes entering transactions quite straightforward, since you need only refer to the relevant four digit code rather than a long narrative description.

Codes must be unique. However, they should also be recognisable by the person dealing with the system. For example, if a supplier was coded "SMITH006", this would be far more recognisable than a purely numeric code such as "0827329".

Care must be taken to issue codes that are not ambiguous. The use of a combination of letters and numbers (an alphanumeric code) often achieves this.

In Sage, when you create a new customer or supplier record, the program will automatically suggest a code for that supplier. It does this by taking the first eight characters of the name. The suggested code for a customer called Greenwood would therefore be "GREENWOO". You may decide this is not the most appropriate code (think what the problem might be if you had two different suppliers called Greenwood), in which case you can easily change it. Many organisations have a set structure for coding, and if this is the case in your organisation you should follow it.

4 Risks of using a computerised system

4.1 Potential risks

Computerised accounting systems may offer a lot of advantages to businesses, but organisations must also be aware of the potential risks posed by such systems. These risks can be categorised as:

- **Physical risks** – caused by system failure, theft, damage or loss or corruption of data, and access to systems or data by unauthorised users.

- **Virus threats** – the risk of a computer virus (or similar) being introduced to a network, with the resultant loss of or damage to data.

- **Legal threats** – from contravention of legislation such as the Data Protection Act (1998) by an organisation in the way that it stores or uses personal data.

Accounting data is particularly at risk, because it is highly confidential and potentially highly valuable to other people. Hence you must remain especially vigilant to risks to data security.

4.2 Backups

Occasionally data is lost, whether through an unforeseen circumstance such as a fire or through computer failure. It is therefore essential that organisation's take appropriate steps to minimise the risk of data loss, and to minimise the impact of data loss if it does happen.

Backups should be taken on a regular basis, and at least once a day in most businesses. In addition, individual files should regularly be backed up whilst working on them. There is little more frustrating than spending an hour producing a document or a spreadsheet only to lose it and not to have a backup.

Copies of backups should be kept securely to prevent unauthorised access or accidental damage. It is good practice to keep a backup at a secondary location (i.e. off-site). This way, if there is a fire or a burglary the backup data will not be destroyed or stolen. Some businesses may still take physical backups off site (such as a CD), but this increases the risk of that back up being lost or stolen while away from the office. It is becoming increasingly common for organisations to pay an IT company to keep remote backups electronically.

5 Sage Software

5.1 Installing Sage

Although you will not be required to install Sage as part of the AAT assessment, it is important to understand the initial installation process that will enable you to start using 'Sage 50 Accounts Professional 2012' for the first time as part of your Computerised Accounting studies.

When you load Sage v18 for the first time you should see the following screen:

Assuming you are entering a new company (as you will be doing here, make sure that the "Open Your Company's Data" is marked. Don't worry at this stage about the other options – just press the [OK] button.

You should now see this screen:

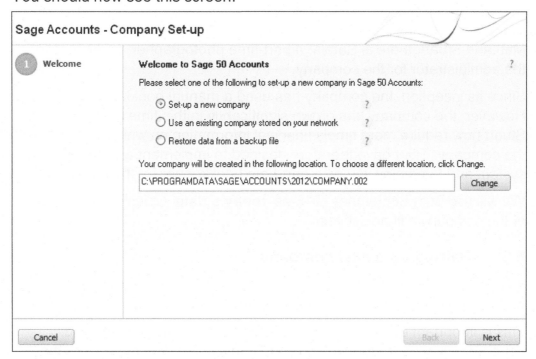

Your choice here depends on whether you are setting up a new company, or uploading existing data.

For now, you will be starting with a completely new company, so click on the "**SET UP A NEW COMPANY**" button as shown.

Once you have company details set up and saved in Sage, it will default to that company each time you start up. However, it is easy to return to this point if you wish to enter a new company.

5.2 Company case study

You will be given a case study throughout this book which will form the basis for activities for you to practice on Sage. It relates to a fictitious company called **TotalPhoto Ltd**.

By completing the activities and entering the relevant transactions, you will learn how to do lots of tasks that are available on Sage. This will help prepare you for the AAT Level 1 computer based assessment as part of your AAT studies.

Background to TotalPhoto Ltd

TotalPhoto Ltd is a small company based in the market town of Miltonby, in Lancashire. It is owned by two directors, Matt Evans and Stuart Lincoln. It was established in 2004 when both Matt and Stuart left Art College.

They specialise in contemporary family photography, most of which takes place in their rented studio on a small industrial estate on the outskirts of town. In addition, they also undertake a varied and increasing range of contracted photography, including weddings, dance shows, football competitions etc.

TotalPhoto Ltd has four members of staff, excluding yourself. In addition to Matt and Stuart, there is Sarala, a part-time photographer, and Michelle, the administrator for the company.

Since its inception, the company has used a manual bookkeeping system. However, the company has grown significantly in this time and Matt and Stuart now require more timely financial information on which to manage the company. They have therefore decided to implement a computerised system and to employ you as a part-time bookkeeper for the business.

We will use 30th September 2016 as '**today's date**' which is the last day of the company's financial year.

5.3   Setting up a new company

When you start using Sage for your case study company, you must firstly enter some information about the company itself.

This is important because it will identify this particular company and appear on various reports. In addition, at this stage, you must enter the dates of the company's financial year. This is vitally important, as Sage will use this information in producing your annual accounts.

You will need the following information for this session:

Company Name:	TotalPhoto Ltd
Company Address:	Unit 63
	Bailey Industrial Estate
	Fornby Road
	Miltonby
	Lancashire
	LD37 7QZ
Telephone:	01949 969 378
Fax:	01949 969 379
E-mail:	info@totalphotoltd.webnet.uk
Website:	www.totalphotoltd.co.uk
Company Reg. Number:	376 096 823
VAT Number:	734928107
Accounting Period:	1st October – 30th September

Now we can begin entering the data for our company, TotalPhoto Ltd.

Activity

Enter the information onto the computerised system using the information provided in the previous box. Guidance follows.

Step One – Initial set up

You will be requested to complete the company details using the information given above.

As you enter the details, be sure to check for accuracy – but don't worry if you make a mistake because you can always amend it later (we will look at how you can amend errors in a later chapter).

Once you are happy with your entries click on the [Next] button.

Step Two – Selecting the business type

On this screen you can choose a business type for your business, this amends the nominal codes so they are specific for your business. For this exercise we are going to choose the Limited Company type.

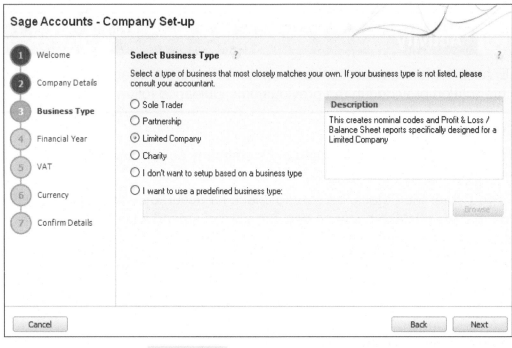

Click the next button [Next]

Step Three – Entering the details of the Financial Year

This is a really important stage. You need to enter the dates of your company's Financial Year. Remember, for TotalPhoto Ltd the company's Financial Year is 1st October to 30th September.

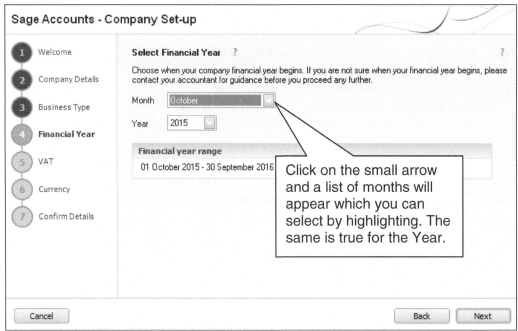

The data in this manual all refers to the year 2015-16, and so our Financial Year will start in **October 2015**. Enter this, using the drop down boxes. In the real computer based test you will be asked to decide on a suitable year to use based on the dates given. You will need to be consistent throughout the test to ensure your dates are correct.

Again, when you have done this press the [Next] button.

Step Four – Entering the VAT Details

Enter the VAT Registration Number as provided in the data (the number is *376096823*). The standard VAT rate is 20%.

Step Five – Entering the currency details

At this stage you can enter the currency details. All of TotalPhoto Ltd's transactions take place in the UK, so their base currency is "Pound Sterling".

You should check that this option is correctly checked.

Again, click the [Next] button to proceed.

Note: During your studies for computerised accounting as part of the AAT qualification, you will not be required to deal with any currency other than £ Sterling.

Step Six – Confirming the information

At this stage is very important that you check the details you have entered so far. If you are happy with the details on this screen, click

[Next] to confirm the information.

Step Seven – Active Setup

You have now set up Sage with the basic information needed for the company TotalPhoto Ltd.

The name of the company should appear at the top of the screen, with the dates at the bottom, as shown below.

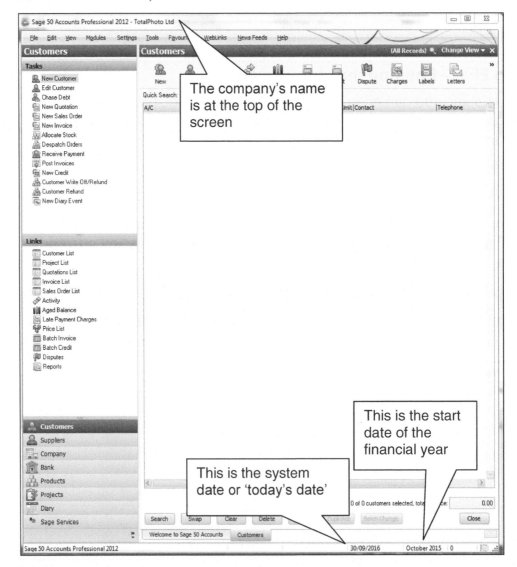

5.4 Navigating Sage

When you open Sage you will see this screen.

This 'window' (or screen) is the one that will now appear every time you open SAGE. You will explore it in more detail as you progress through the manual. For now, just take the time to familiarise yourself with this screen. You can also change the view of the screen to different options by clicking on 'change view' which will be at the top right hand side of your screen.

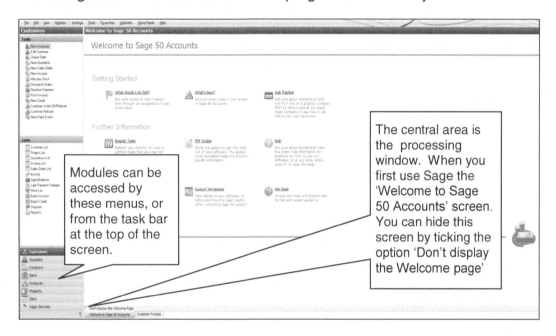

Modules can be accessed by these menus, or from the task bar at the top of the screen.

The central area is the processing window. When you first use Sage the 'Welcome to Sage 50 Accounts' screen. You can hide this screen by ticking the option 'Don't display the Welcome page'

5.5 Modules

Sage uses modules to differentiate different transactions. As you move through the different modules the processing area, tasks, and links will change depending on which module you are working on.

The modules that you will be using for the assessment are: Customers, Suppliers, Company and Bank.   The table below identifies the modules you will be using in the AAT assessment, the accounting term typically used for the module, and the main tasks which are carried out in each module.

Module	Ledger term	Main tasks
Customers	Sales Ledger	• Enter and amend customer details • Enter sales invoices • Enter sales credit notes • Produce invoices and statements • Produce customer reports

Suppliers	Purchase Ledger	• Enter and amend supplier details • Enter purchase invoices • Enter purchase credit notes • Produce supplier reports
Company	Nominal or General ledger	• Enter and amend nominal account records • Produce nominal ledger account reports *In the AAT assessment you not be required to enter any nominal ledger transactions.*
Bank	Cash book	• Enter receipts from cash and credit customers • Enter payments to cash and credit suppliers. • Produce reports

You will be exploring these modules in more detail as you work through the case study.

5.6 Checking your data

If you work steadily and carefully, you should not encounter many problems with your data entry. However, no matter how carefully you work, you will undoubtedly have to make corrections at some time – either because of human error in inputting data, or simply because new information comes to light.

One important feature of Sage is the ability to check your data. This will help to identify any issues with data corruption (which can occur after a power cut, for example), missing data and date errors.

You can access the DataCheck facility by clicking on **FILE** in the main menu bar, then **MAINTENANCE**, and then **CHECK DATA.**

Sage will check the validity of your data and advise you of any possible discrepancies.

You should note that the DataCheck facility will **not** identify data entry errors (e.g. entering the wrong amount or posting to the wrong nominal code). The accuracy of data entry is your responsibility, and you should therefore aim to minimise the number of errors you make by being careful to check your work at all stages.

5.7 Making corrections

Many people are understandably a little nervous when using a computer system for the first time. They worry that they may break the system, or make mistakes that cannot be corrected.

Don't worry: Sage offers a number of easy ways to amend or delete errors. However, a full record of all amended or deleted transactions are maintained for audit trail purposes.

These are covered in a later chapter so don't panic if you do something wrong. You are only practising at this stage, and it is good to make mistakes initially as you will learn how to correct them! You are allowed to amend errors in the AAT computer based test and will not be penalised for doing so. We all know that mistakes happen in the workplace and errors are often rectified.

5.8 Backing up your work

It is important that you save your data regularly to guard against accidental losses which can prove very costly and time-consuming to recover or re-input. Backing up your data should become part of your daily routine.

To back up data:

From the File menu at the top of the screen select 'Backup' (ignore the figures in the screenshot below as they are included for demonstration purposes only).

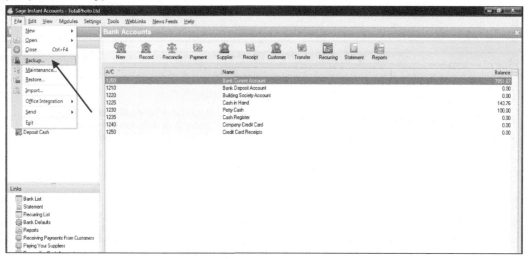

SAGE now asks if you would like to check your data before you run the backup – you should select [Yes]

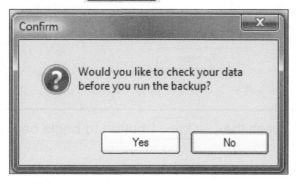

Hopefully there are no problems with your data files and so you will now be able to backup your data.

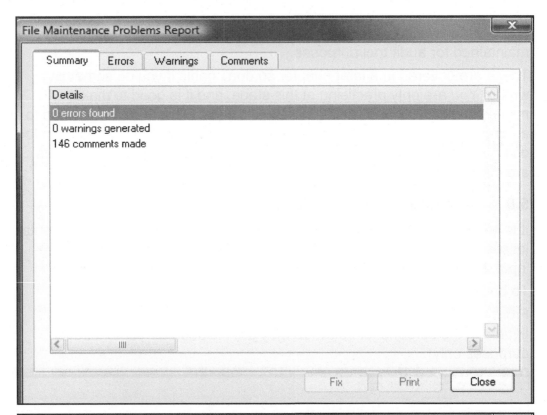

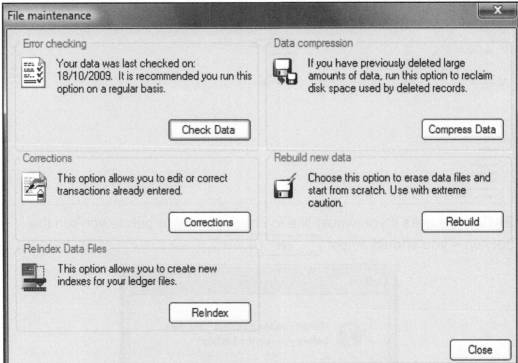

From this screen press the [Close] button to begin backup.

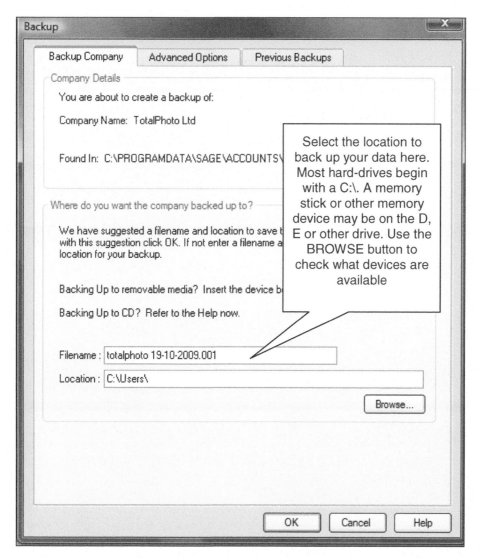

You need to select an appropriate file name – here, the name of our Case Study firm TotalPhoto Ltd has been used. Select **OK** to back up. The screen will now show a "Backup" box which indicates the progress of the backup. Another suggestion for a file name would be to include your name and this would be beneficial in the computer based test as it will help the assessor identity your work.

When this process has finished Sage will tell you that the backup has been successfully completed and you can click **OK**.

You should note as well that Sage invites you to back up your data each time you close the program down – the process is identical to that described above.

The nominal ledger

Introduction

The nominal ledger is probably the most important element of the Sage (or indeed any) accounting system. This chapter focuses on the use of nominal codes and then how to enter and report on the information required.

KNOWLEDGE
1.3 Create new accounts in the nominal ledger
2.3 Enter initial capital
4.1 Produce a trial balance
4.6 Produce nominal ledger account reports

CONTENTS
1   Introduction
2   Entering a nominal code
3   Entering an opening balance
4   Creating a journal for initial capital
5   Printing reports

1 Introduction

1.1 The importance of the nominal ledger

The nominal ledger is probably the most important element of the Sage (or indeed any) accounting system. The key aspect to this is the list of nominal codes. This is simply a series of different accounts which are used each time a transaction is recorded.

Each of these accounts is given a unique four digit code number. To view the list of Nominal Codes go to the **COMPANY** screen, and then **NOMINAL LEDGER.** Then select 'List' from the layout menu.

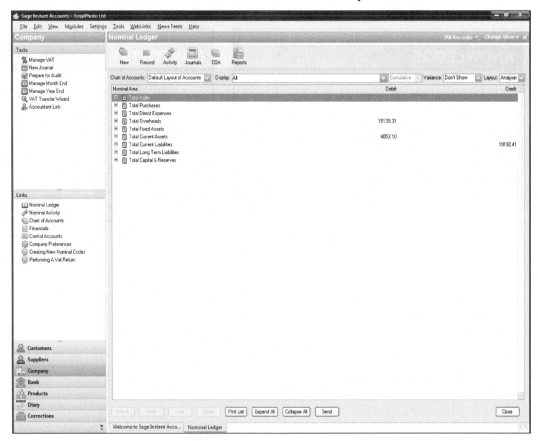

1.2 Nominal codes

This now shows you a list of all of the nominal codes (N/Cs) for the business (ignore any figures shown above as they are for demonstration purposes only).

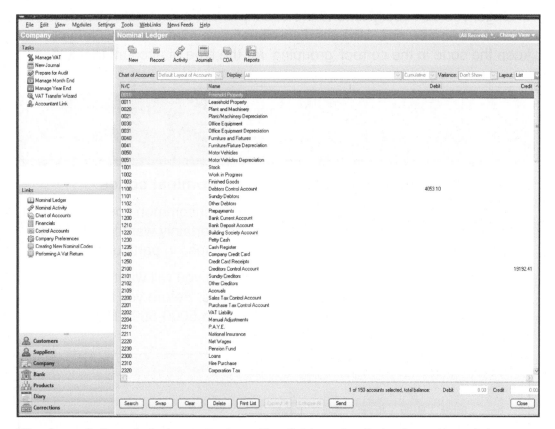

The four-digit code is important, as the list is actually broken down into groups:

0000-0999	Fixed Assets and Depreciation (e.g. Buildings, Equipment)
1000-1999	Current Assets (e.g. Stock, Debtors, Bank)
2000-2999	Liabilities (e.g. Loans, Creditors)
3000-3999	Capital and Reserves
4000-4999	Sales
5000-5999	Purchases
6000-6999	Direct Expenses (e.g. Direct Labour)
7000-7999	Miscellaneous Overheads (e.g. Phone, Rent, Postage)
8000-8999	Bad debts and Depreciation
9000-9999	Suspense and Mispostings

Sage uses these 'groupings' of codes to ensure that items appear in the correct part of the Income Statement or Statement of Financial Position. You may have heard of these financial statements referred to as a 'Profit and Loss Account' or 'Balance Sheet'. Don't worry you will learn how to deal with these as part of your level 2 accounting qualification.

In Sage, you can easily amend the description of a nominal code, or indeed add a new one. However, you must always make sure that you keep the code in the correct 'grouping' for the type of account that it is.

2   Entering a nominal code

2.1   Amending and creating specific nominal codes

The default Chart of Accounts contains the most common codes set up for a general business. However, you will almost certainly want to add to, or amend, these Nominal Codes to suit your business in particular.

For example, in your case study TotalPhoto Ltd you will want to be more specific when recording its sales and purchases. Before you do this, have a look at your listing of Nominal Codes. Find the 5000-5999 Range (remember, these are set aside for Purchases).

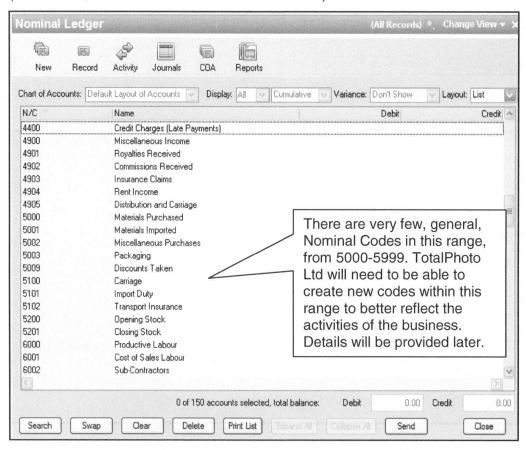

Now, from within the NOMINAL module click on the Record button.

You should now have a blank record screen, as below.

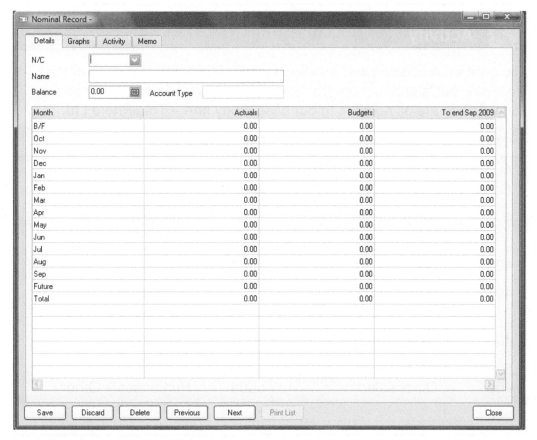

To **AMEND** an existing code:

- Enter the Nominal Code (or select from the pull down menu)

- Type in the new name

To **CREATE** a new code:

- Enter the new Nominal Code (making sure it is in the correct range)

- Type in the new name

There is also the option of using a 'wizard' to set up a new nominal code. It is a very straightforward process and it guides you through the relevant steps. To do this, click on '**Company'** and then '**New**'.

Activity

To practice amending and creating Nominal Codes, enter each of the following N/Cs and names. Do them one by one, and then save each one. These are all relevant to our case study firm – TotalPhoto Ltd.

SALES		PURCHASES	
Nominal Code	*Name*	*Nominal Code*	*Name*
4000	Sales – Individuals & Family	5000	Purchases – Film
4001	Sales – Weddings	5001	Purchases – Paper
4002	Sales – Corporate	5002	Purchases – Cartridges & Toner
4003	Sales – Nurseries & Schools	5003	Purchases – Stationery
4004	Other sales	5004	Purchases – Other Consumables

Once you have created and amended the nominal codes from the previous activity, close down the window and generate the Nominal List report for the range 4000-5999.

 Activity

You should now print out the list of nominal codes. Do this by simply pressing the [Print List] button located towards the bottom of the screen. The full list of default Nominal Codes should now print.

You should now keep this list safe, as you will need to use it when entering transactions in the future.

KAPLAN PUBLISHING

This report should look like this:

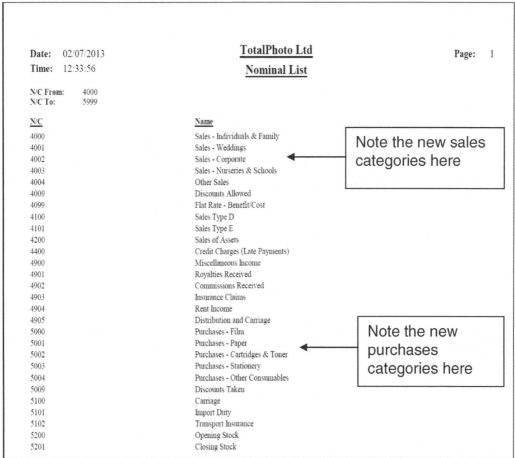

Date:	02/07/2013	**TotalPhoto Ltd**	Page: 1
Time:	12:33:56	**Nominal List**	

N/C From: 4000
N/C To: 5999

N/C	Name
4000	Sales - Individuals & Family
4001	Sales - Weddings
4002	Sales - Corporate
4003	Sales - Nurseries & Schools
4004	Other Sales
4009	Discounts Allowed
4099	Flat Rate - Benefit/Cost
4100	Sales Type D
4101	Sales Type E
4200	Sales of Assets
4400	Credit Charges (Late Payments)
4900	Miscellaneous Income
4901	Royalties Received
4902	Commissions Received
4903	Insurance Claims
4904	Rent Income
4905	Distribution and Carriage
5000	Purchases - Film
5001	Purchases - Paper
5002	Purchases - Cartridges & Toner
5003	Purchases - Stationery
5004	Purchases - Other Consumables
5009	Discounts Taken
5100	Carriage
5101	Import Duty
5102	Transport Insurance
5200	Opening Stock
5201	Closing Stock

Note the new sales categories here

Note the new purchases categories here

Well done! Now you can amend or create new nominal codes. You have also printed a list of nominal account codes.

3 Entering an opening balance

3.1 Entering an opening balance

Activity 1

You now need to enter the opening balances for each of the accounts relating to TotalPhoto Ltd. You need to enter the financial balance on each account for TotalPhoto Ltd. This needs to be the first date you begin using the SAGE system to record financial transactions for the company. Remember for TotalPhoto Ltd this was 30th September 2016. The list of opening balances is shown below.

Detailed guidance on how to enter these balances follows this activity.

Important

1   You will need to create a new Nominal Codes for Photographic Equipment.

2   You should also re-name the following nominal accounts:

- Petty Cash (1230) to 'Cash Account'
- Sales Tax Control Account (2200) to 'VAT on sales'
- Purchase Tax Control Account (2201) to 'VAT on purchases'
- Ordinary Shares (3000) to Capital introduced

3   Be very careful to enter each balance correctly as either a **debit** or a **credit** balance. Take your time to complete this activity as it will prevent errors at this stage.

You will now enter opening balances for some of TotalPhoto Ltd's accounting.

TotalPhoto Ltd

Opening Balances

	Nominal code	Debit	Credit
Bank Current Account	1200	668.80	
Cash Account	1230	252.00	
VAT on sales	2200		369.36
VAT on purchases	2201	382.56	
Capital introduced	3000		1000.00
	5000	1568.9	
Purchases – Film		0	
Purchases - Stationery	5003	343.90	
Sales – Individuals & Families	4000		565.80
Sales – Weddings	4001		328.50
Sales – Corporate	4002		952.50
		3216.16	**3216.16**

Step One - From the main screen click on the '**Company**' button. This will bring up the Nominal Ledger screen.

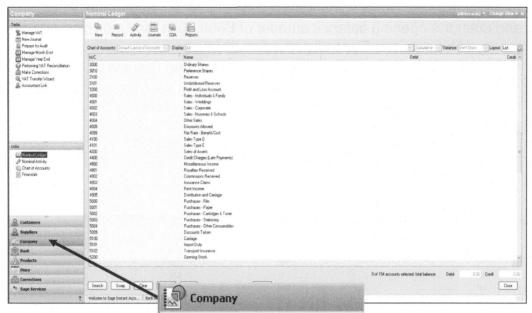

Step Two - Highlight the Nominal Code for which you want to enter an opening balance.

The first amount we need to enter is a debit balance of £668.80 for Bank Current Account (1230). Double-click your mouse on this code.

Now click on the 'Opening Balance (**OB**)' icon.

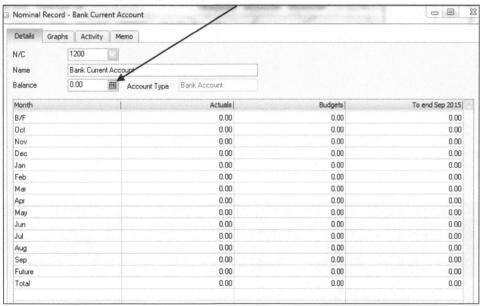

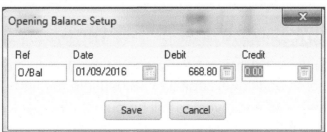

Keep the Ref as "O/Bal". Change the date box to 1st September 2016, and enter the opening balance amount of £668.80 in the Debit box. Leave the credit box at zero. Then click the Save button

Notice how the detail record for Nominal Code 1200 (Bank) has now changed, showing your entry in September. When you return to the Nominal Ledger page you should also see the new balance reflected there.

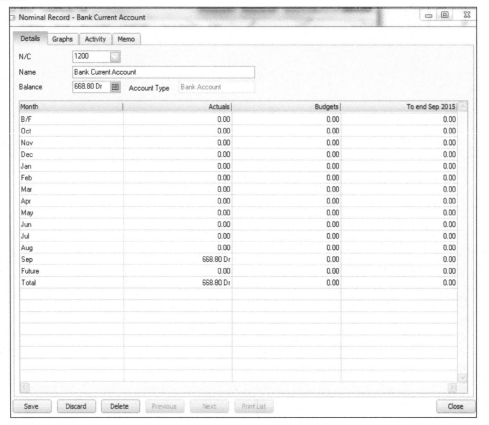

Month	Actuals	Budgets	To end Sep 2015
B/F	0.00	0.00	0.00
Oct	0.00	0.00	0.00
Nov	0.00	0.00	0.00
Dec	0.00	0.00	0.00
Jan	0.00	0.00	0.00
Feb	0.00	0.00	0.00
Mar	0.00	0.00	0.00
Apr	0.00	0.00	0.00
May	0.00	0.00	0.00
Jun	0.00	0.00	0.00
Jul	0.00	0.00	0.00
Aug	0.00	0.00	0.00
Sep	668.80 Dr	0.00	0.00
Future	0.00	0.00	0.00
Total	668.80 Dr	0.00	0.00

You should now enter all the other opening balances for TotalPhoto Ltd.

4 Creating a journal for initial capital

4.1 Creating a journal

 Activity 2

On 15th September, 2016 Matt Evans, one of the directors of TotalPhoto Ltd invested some additional capital of £2,000 into the firm.

The amount that Matt has invested will be put into the bank account, so we need to increase the figure in the bank account and increase the amount of capital invested.

A journal is created to record this transaction in both accounts.

	Debit	**Credit**
Bank current account	2,000.00	
Capital introduced		2,000.00

Detailed guidance on how to enter these balances follows this activity.

Take your time to complete this activity as it will prevent errors at this stage.

4.2 Guidance for Activity 2

Step One - From the main screen click on the '**Company'** button. This will bring up the Nominal Ledger screen.   Then click on the Journal icon in the task bar or task list.

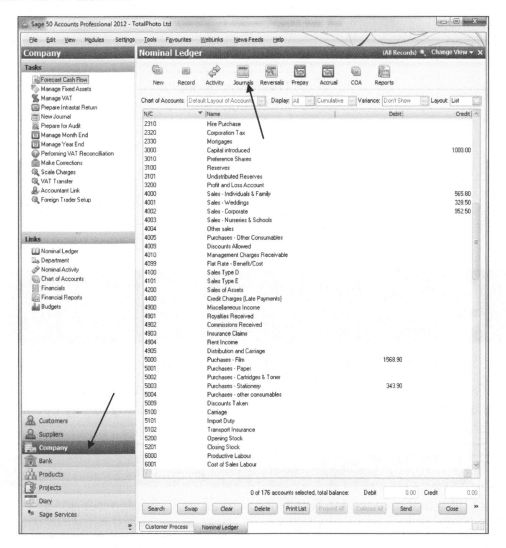

Step Two - In the Journal task screen enter the following details:

- Enter **J001** as the reference to identify this as the first journal transaction that has been processed in the computerised accounts system.

- The Posting date is the date of the transaction: **15/09/16**

- Enter the journal transaction as shown on the following screen. Make sure that you enter a narrative into the Details field so that the reason that this journal transaction was made can be identified at a later stage.

- Check that the total debits and credits should be the same, and the Balance remaining at the top of the screen should be 0.00

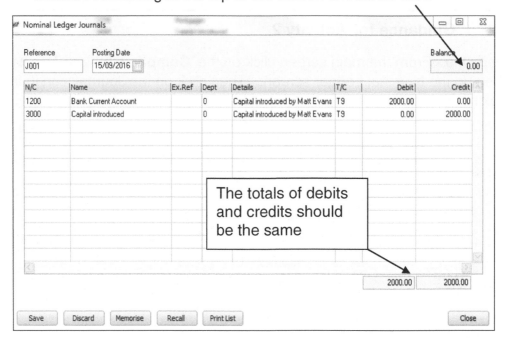

5 Printing reports

5.1 Printing the period trial balance

You should now have entered all the opening balances for TotalPhoto Ltd. You are now ready to begin entering transactions on a day to day basis. Before you do this, you should print off a Trial Balance.

 Activity 3

Print off a trial balance for TotalPhoto Ltd as at 30 September 2016. Guidance on how to do this follows.

KAPLAN PUBLISHING

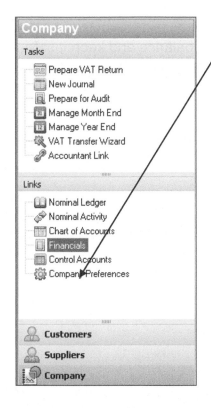

Step One - From the **Company** screen, select "**Financials**" in the links section.

This will create a new screen, from which you can quickly produce a series of the most useful reports in SAGE, including the Trial Balance, the Balance Sheet and the Profit and Loss Account.

Step Two - Double-click on 'Financials' to show this screen.

Step Three - From the toolbar at the top of the Financials screen, select the Trial icon

Step Four - You are now asked to select how you want to print the report.

For now, you will just preview the report (i.e. view it on screen). Highlight this and the press the

`Run` button.

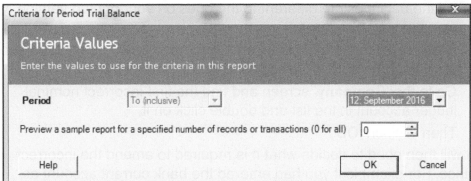

Step Five – As you want to view the trial balance as at September 2016, to see the opening balances you have entered, make sure you amend the date box to show September 2016. Leave the next box as 0, and click OK.

Step Six - This should bring up a trial balance showing balances for the period up to September 2016. You may need to maximize the screen to see the whole report on screen – do this by clicking the *maximize* icon in the top right corner of the window (⬜)

If you have entered everything correctly you should see that both columns (debit and credit) balance to £5,216.16 and there should be

no account called 'Suspense' in the list.

Step Seven - You should now print out this trial balance and keep it safe. This shows what your trial balance should look like after entering all of the opening balances.

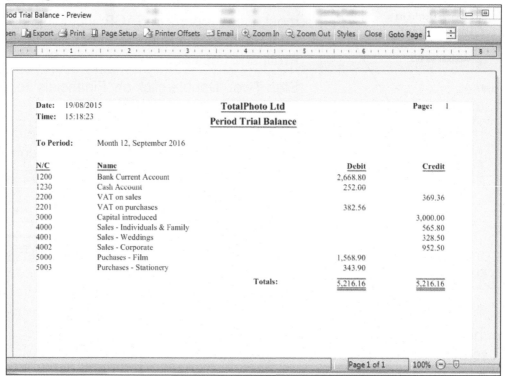

5.2 How to amend an incorrect opening balance

If any of the balances are different to the ones on your printed version, you are able to amend as follows:

- Firstly tick off your trial balance to determine which opening balances have been entered incorrectly and make a note of them.

- Go to the '**Company**' screen and find the first incorrect nominal ledger account in the list and double click on it.

- Then click on '**OB**'.

You will then need to decide what it is required to amend the incorrect balance. For example if you had entered the bank current account as £688.80 Dr as opposed to the correct balance of £668.8.00 Dr, you would need to credit the account with £20.00 to reduce it to the correct figure. If you prefer, you can reverse your original entry by doing the exact opposite of what you did originally. In the example error above, enter an opening balance of £688.80 Cr and that will revert the account back to its original nil balance. You can then repeat the step with the correct figure.

After you have amended and saved any incorrect balances you can print off another Trial Balance to check that it is correct.

Setting up supplier and customer details

Introduction

Business organisations will use computerised accounting systems to keep records of all their suppliers and customers.

The organisation will need to keep very accurate and timely records of all transactions with their suppliers and customers. These transactions will typically include:

1) Invoices and credit notes

2) Payments made to suppliers and monies received from customers.

In addition, it would be very convenient to have all the contact details of each supplier and customer easily to hand.

Fortunately, Sage provides a very comprehensive management system which covers all these requirements (and more). You will see how this works shortly, but firstly you will need to enter your suppliers' and customers' details.

KNOWLEDGE
1.1 Add new accounts to the purchase ledger.
1.2 Add new accounts to the sales ledger.
4.5 Produce customer details reports
4.6 Produce supplier details reports

CONTENTS
1   Supplier details
2   Customer details

1 Supplier details

1.1 Supplier data

We can now start inputting some data on to the computerised system using our case study firm, TotalPhoto Ltd.

 Activity 1

TotalPhoto Ltd has six suppliers, whose details are given below. Enter these onto the computerised system. Guidance on how to enter these records for suppliers follows.

Supplier details

Mackay Films Ltd	**A/c Ref : MF001**
33 West ParadeMiltonby	Tel 01828 827493
Lancashire	Contact: Carl Richardson
LN87 7HD	Credit Terms: **30 days**
	Nominal code: 5000

K2 Films Ltd	**A/c Ref : KF001**
Tokyo House	Tel 0207 867 6599
72-84 Great Milne Street	Contact: Kim Nakajima
London	Credit Terms: **30 days**
WC4 6DD	Nominal code: 5000

The Stationery Cupboard	**A/c Ref : SC003**
21 Potter Way	Tel 01482 417378
Hull	Contact: Alan Pensill
Humberside	Credit Terms: **14 days**
HU87 6YY	Nominal code: 5003

Mills Paper Products	**A/c Ref : MP002**
405 Ream Road	Tel 01726 378918
Bradford	Contact: Mr Shaun Squire
West Yorkshire	Credit Terms: **21 days**
BD5 6QA	Nominal code: 5001

Octopus Inks Ltd	A/c Ref : OI001
Unit 12 Longley Industrial Park	Tel 0191 252 4132
Gateshead	Contact: Sheila Cribbley
Tyne and Wear	Credit Terms: **30 days**
GH77 5TG	Nominal code: 5002

Arthur's Photographic Equipment Ltd	A/c Ref : AP004
77 Overton Lane	Tel 0121 299 0192
Birmingham	Contact: Jennie Reeves
BM97 8YK	Credit Terms: **30 days**

1.2 Entering supplier details

Step One - From the Supplier Process window (below) select the new supplier wizard by clicking on either 'New Supplier' in the Tasks list, or on the New Supplier icon.

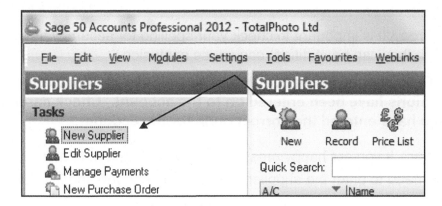

This will bring up the **Supplier Record Wizard**, which will help you to easily enter your suppliers' details.

Refer back to the list of suppliers supplied on the previous pages. The first supplier to enter is Mackay Films Ltd.

Step Two - To complete the first screen of the **New Supplier Wizard** you will need to enter the supplier's name (Mackay Films Ltd) and their unique Account Reference Number (A/C Ref – MF001).

The Account Reference Number is a shorthand way of identifying each of your suppliers. You can use this code on documentation, and also it will appear on reports that you will print out.

It is extremely important that the number you choose is unique and it is useful if it helps to identify the supplier in some way – here MF001 representing **M**ackay **F**ilms.

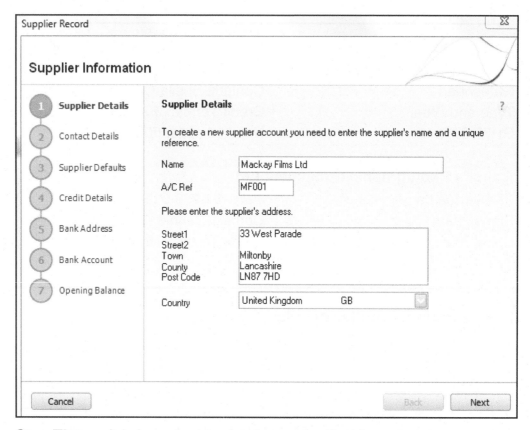

Step Three - It is important to check your spelling for accuracy as errors (although they can be rectified) can cause confusion.

Note: The Account Reference Number cannot be changed after any transactions have been entered on to the account. Check carefully that you have entered the correct code for the account.

Step Four - If you are happy press the [Next] button to move on. You will now need to enter the supplier's address, telephone and fax details.

Again, when you are happy, press the [Next]

Step Five - Now you can enter the firm's contact details. In this case we have not got an e-mail or website address, or the VAT number. Don't worry, though, as these can easily be entered at a later date.

You can enter the telephone number and Carl Richardson's name at this point, though, before pressing the [Next] button.

Step Six - The next screen asks you to enter details of any discount available from this supplier, the nominal code against which purchases from this supplier will be recorded, and also the most common VAT rating for the goods that you buy from them.

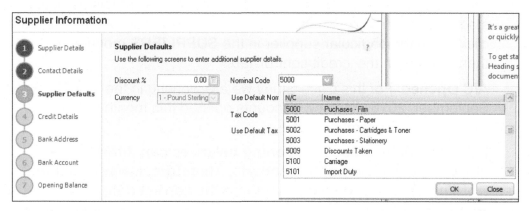

Mackay Films Ltd do not offer any discount, so this can be left at **0.00.**

The firm supplies films to TotalPhoto, so the Nominal Code should be 5000. The VAT code is T1, meaning that the majority of purchases from this supplier will have VAT added at 20%.

Supplier Defaults   ?

Use the following screens to enter additional supplier details.

Discount %	0.00	Nominal Code	5000
Currency	1 - Pound Sterling	Use Default Nominal Code for Purchases ☑	
		Tax Code	T 1 20.00
		Use Default Tax Code for Purchases ☐	

If you are happy with this press the 〔 Next 〕 button.

Step Seven - Now you can enter credit details agreed with this supplier.

- **Credit limit** is the amount of credit allowed by this supplier. In this instance, we have not been given any details so **leave this as zero**.

- **Settlement Due Days and Sett. Disc**% relate to any extra discount allowed by the supplier if the invoice is paid within a certain time. In this instance, no settlement (or cash) discount has been given, so **leave both these boxes as zero.**

- **Payment Due Days** are the credit terms that the supplier offers. Most suppliers will insist on payment within a certain period of time – typically seven to twenty eight days **(the payment due days).** However, some suppliers may also offer a discount for payment within an earlier period **(the settlement due days)**.

  Mackay Films Ltd offer credit terms of **30 days** meaning TotalPhoto Ltd must pay invoices within 30 days after the invoice date.

- **Terms** Enter the terms agreed as text: 30 days.

- **Terms agreed** This box should be ticked as this tells Sage that the details have been confirmed. If you forget to do this at this particular stage, don't worry as you can choose to tick terms agreed by double clicking on the particular supplier in the **SUPPLIERS** module, and then clicking on the 'credit control' tab.

- **A/C Opened** For this Case Study we are working in the month of September, 2016. Any new accounts opened this month will be dated the 1st September, 2016.

  Note: The date to use for opening balances can differ to the 'today's date' given in the scenario. Therefore, always read the wording carefully to ensure you use the correct date.

Step Eight - On the following screen either type the date (30/09/2010) or use SAGE's calendar facility to enter it, as shown below. The date of the **Next Credit Review** can be left blank.

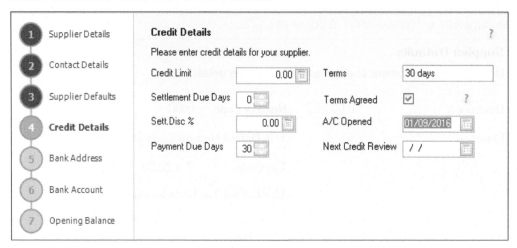

Check that the details you have entered into Sage are the same as the image on this page. If you are happy with this press the [Next] button.

Step Nine - The next two screens ask you to enter the details of your supplier's bank. This is essential if the business is paying their suppliers using methods such as BACS. It is not necessary for you to do this in this example and you will not be required to in your AAT assessment.

Sage now asks if this supplier has an outstanding balance – in other words, if at the time of entering their details you already owe them money. As all the TotalPhoto supplier accounts you are entering are new suppliers, click the option shown below.

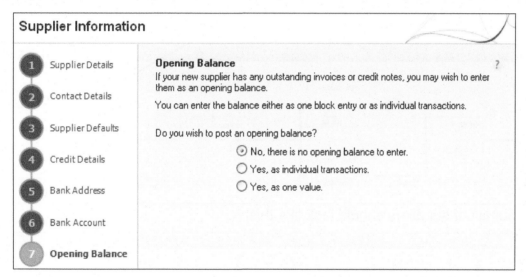

Well done! You have now entered your first supplier details. To recap, you began by entering their company details, such as their address, phone and fax numbers and contact details. Then you entered the credit terms that this supplier makes available.

Step Ten - Sage now confirms that you have successfully entered the supplier's details. The next stage is important – you **must** press the [Finish] button to save the details and to post the opening balance.

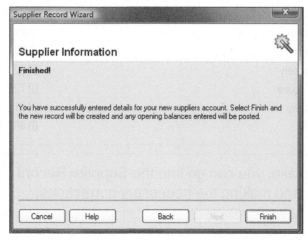

Activity 2

You have already entered one of TotalPhoto Ltd's suppliers (Mackay Films Ltd).

You should now enter the full details for each of the remaining five suppliers, and then save them to Sage.

To see a list of the suppliers you have entered, from the Supplier Process window **Change View** to 'Suppliers'.

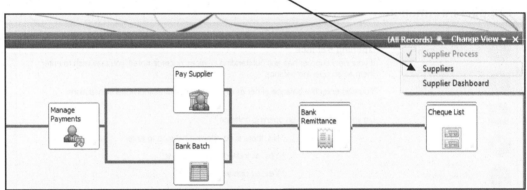

Your list of suppliers should look like this:

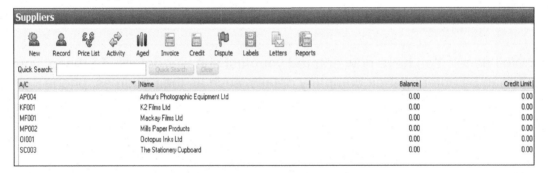

Contact information should have also been completed:

Contact	Telephone
Jennie Reeves	0121 299 0192
Kim Nakajima	0207 8676599
Carl Richardson	01828 827493
Mr Shaun Squire	01726 378918
Sheila Cribbley	0191 252 4132
Alan Pensill	01482 417378

If you spot a mistake, you can go into the Supplier Record by clicking on the Record icon and making the necessary corrections.

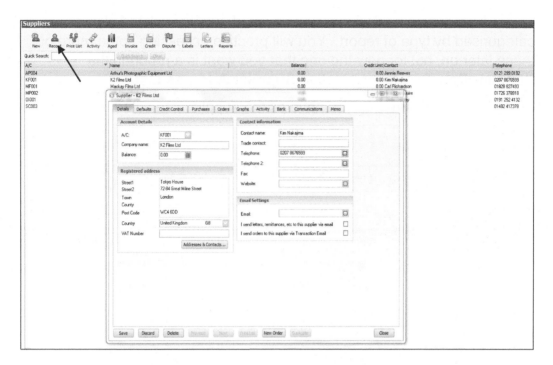

1.3 Printing supplier details reports

You have entered the details of the six suppliers, so let's now check that they are correct by running off a report from SAGE.

The first report to print is the Supplier List.

To do so, from the **Suppliers** window (shown below), click on **Reports** in the **Links** area or the **Reports** icon

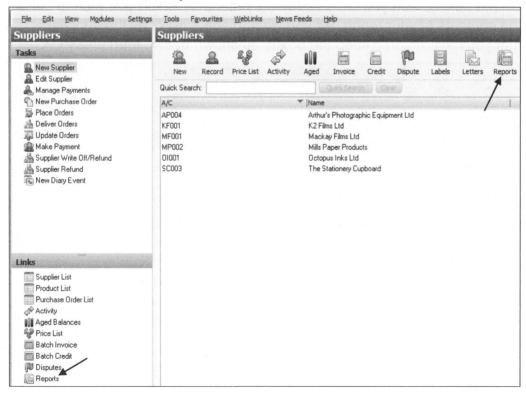

This will produce a new window with a list of supplier-related reports categorised by type of report. You will practice accessing some more of these later on, but for now the one that you want is a report in the **Supplier Details** category entitled **Supplier Address List.**

First of all, make sure that you have all the suppliers selected.

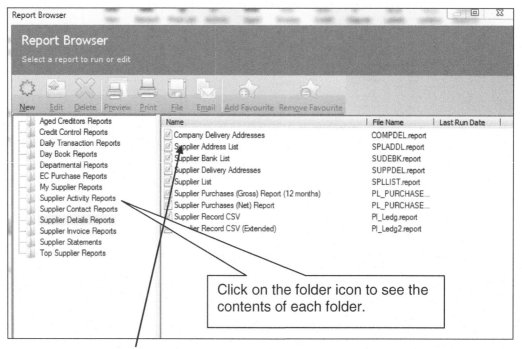

Double click on **Supplier Address List** to produce the report.

On the next screen you can identify the criteria by which you wish to select the contents of your report. As you wish to see a list of all the suppliers that you have entered keep the boxes as shown below, then press OK.

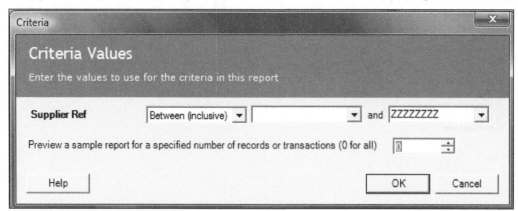

Your report should now show on screen, similar to the one below. Remember, that you might be working on a different version of Sage but the main areas will be the same but possibly with a slightly different presentation.

Date: 02/07/2013   **TotalPhoto Ltd**   **Page:** 1
Time: 11:49:59   **Supplier Address List**

Supplier From:
Supplier To: ZZZZZZZZ

A/C	Name	Contact	Telephone	Fax
AP004	Arthur's Photographic Equipment Ltd 77 Overton Lane Birmingham BM97 8YK	Jennie Reeves	0121 299 0192	
KF001	K2 Films Ltd Tokyo House 72-84 Great Milne Street London WC4 6DD	Kim Nakajima	0207 867 6599	
MF001	Mackay Films Ltd 33 West Parade Miltonby Lancashire LN87 7HD	Carl Richardson	01828 827493	
MP002	Mills Paper Products 405 Ream Road Bradford West Yorkshire BD5 6QA	Mr Shaun Squire	01726 378918	
OI001	Octopus Links Ltd Unit 12 Longley Industrial Park Gateshead Tyne and Wear GH77 5TG	Sheila Cribbley	0191 252 4132	
SC003	The Stationery Cupboard 21 Potter Way Hull Humberside HU87 6YY	Alan Pensill	01482 417378	

There are many other supplier reports available in this section – you should now feel confident enough to access these and to print them out.

The exact list of reports that you will use will depend on your particular requirements, and you will see some of the more common ones later in this manual.

You will feel much more comfortable in generating reports once you have practised, so have a go!

2 Customer details

2.1 Customer data

The process of entering your customers' details is very similar to that of entering supplier information, so you should feel confident doing this now.

Consistent, accurate recording of information is a vital aspect of any credit management system, ensuring that your organisation gets paid as quickly as possible for its sales. This can be the difference between failure and survival for most businesses.

We can now start to look at the 'Customers' process and begin with entering the initial information regarding our case study firm, TotalPhoto Ltd. Again, you will find detailed step by step instructions after this activity.

 Activity 3

TotalPhoto Ltd has six customers with outstanding balances as at 30th September 2010. Their details and guidance on how to enter the customer details into Sage follow.

Customer details

Mr W Haslam	**A/c Ref : HAS004**
22 Brown Street	
Miltonby	
Lancashire LN87 6FD	
Credit terms: Payment in 14 days	

Mrs H Poppy	**A/c Ref : POP002**
120 Forrest Way	
Miltonby	
Lancashire LN87 9YR	
Credit terms: Payment in 14 days	

Mrs T Pashby	**A/c Ref : PAS002**
30A Andrews Street	
Killington	
Lancashire LN85 6TT	
Credit terms: Payment in 14 days	

Campbell & Dunn Ltd	**A/c Ref : CAM004**
12 The Beeches	
Miltonby	
Lancashire LN87 9PP	
Credit terms: 14 days	

Lullabies Nursery	**A/c Ref : LUL002**
104 Victoria Road	
Miltonby	
Lancashire LN87 5PS	
Credit terms: Payment in 14 days	

Miss S Pargenter	**A/c Ref : PAR006**
11 Alexandra Park	
Miltonby	
Lancashire LN87 2WD	
Credit terms: Payment in 14 days	

2.2 Entering customer data

Step One - Go to the Customer Process screen, as below.

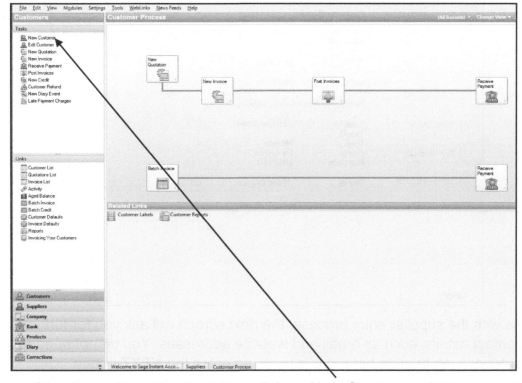

Step Two - From the Task Bar, click on **New Customer**. At the next
screen click NEXT, and you should now be able to enter your first
customer's details, as below.

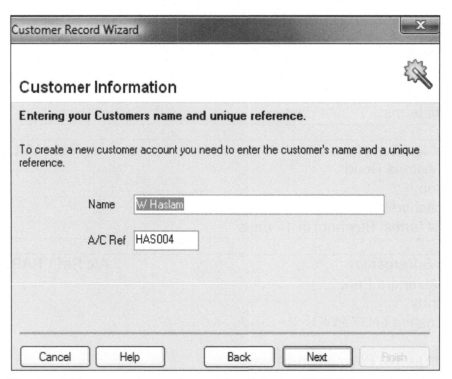

Step Three - When you have done this click the **NEXT** button again, and enter the address details, as below.

As with the supplier entry process, the next screen will ask you for further contact details, such as email and website addresses. You do not need to enter any information here at this point, so press the **NEXT** button.

Step Four - On the Customer Defaults screen, we will keep all the defaults, so you do not need to change anything.

Leave the nominal code as 4000, and the tax code as T1 (20.00), as in the screen above. You will learn more about these shortly.

Step Five - Now you can enter the credit terms. For Mr Haslam we will require payment within fourteen days, and there is no settlement discount for early payment. Mr Haslam opened his account on 01/09/2016.

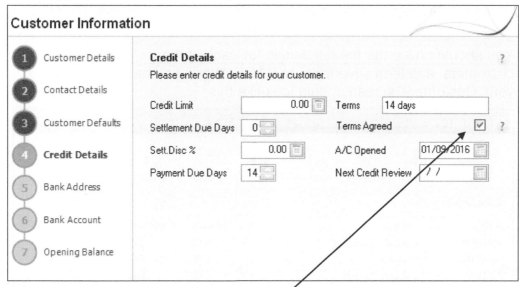

Step Six - Remember to tick the Terms Agreed box.

Be careful to enter all information accurately and correctly at every stage of this process – check that the details you have entered match the source data.

We do not have any bank information for Mr Haslam so we do not need to enter any details on the next two screens.

Step Seven - Sage will now ask if there are any opening balances, and as with the supplier entry screen there is no opening balance as this is a new account.

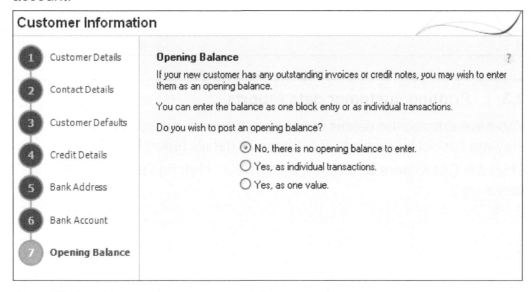

Step Eight - You can now **create** this account.

Step Nine - Click on the '**Finish**' button to complete the process.

Activity 4

You have already entered one of TotalPhoto Ltd's customers (Mr W Haslam).

You should now enter the full details for each of the remaining five customers, and then save them to SAGE. When you have done this, your 'Customers' screen should look like this:

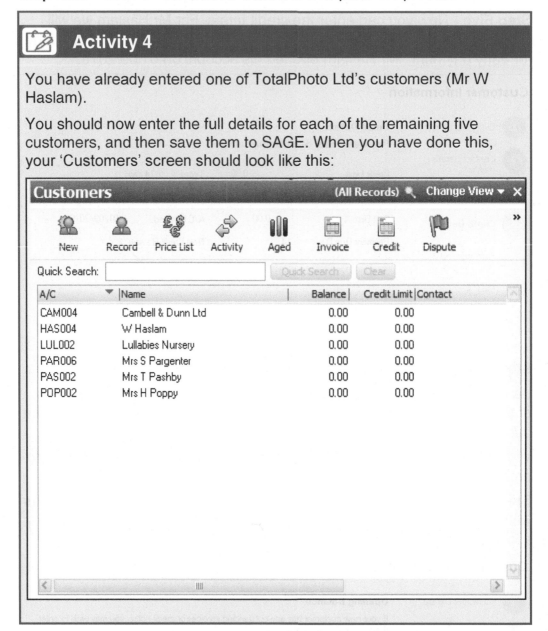

2.3 Printing customer data reports

You have entered the details of the six customers, so let's now check that they are correct by running off a customer details report from SAGE.

From the **Customers** window (shown below), click on **Reports** in the **Links** area.

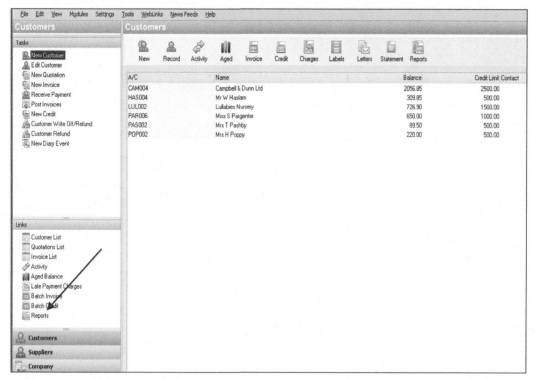

This will produce a new window with a list of customer-related reports that you may want to print and use. You will practice accessing some more of these later on, but for now the one that you want is the report entitled *Customer Address List.*

This is contained within the folder called *Customer Details Reports* – to access the contents of this (or any) folder simply click on the folder icon.

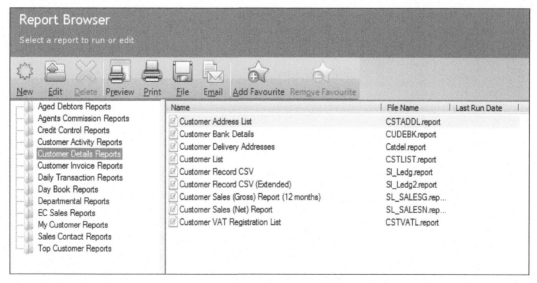

Double click on '*Customer Address List'* to produce the report.

On the next screen you can identify the criteria by which you wish to select the contents of your report. As you wish to see a list of all of the customers that you have entered keep the boxes as shown below, then press OK.

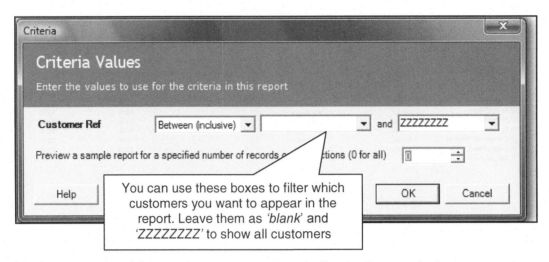

Your report should now show on screen, similar to the one below.

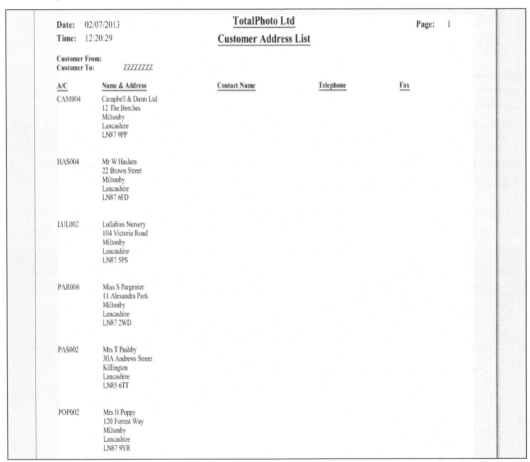

There are many other customer reports available in this section – you should now feel confident enough to access these and to print them out. The exact list of reports that you will use will depend on your particular requirements.

You have now entered account details for six suppliers and six customers of TotalPhoto Ltd. In the next chapter, you will be entering transactions relating to these accounts.

Entering transactions

Introduction

As identified in the previous chapter, a computerised accounting system is required to record business transactions on a daily basis.

Having now set up customer and supplier records, this chapter will focus on the nature of credit transactions and how customer and supplier invoices and credit notes are processed using a computerised system.

.

KNOWLEDGE
2.1 Process information in respect of the sales ledger
2.2 Process information in respect of the purchase ledger
2.4 Process information involving different tax rates
3.1 Calculate batch totals as required
3.2 Reconcile batch totals as required.

CONTENTS
1 Business transactions
2 Credit sales – customer transactions
3 Credit purchases – supplier documents

1 Business transactions

1.1 Cash and credit transactions

Any business will carry out a wide range of transactions every day of the week. The majority of these will fall into one of the following categories:

Credit transactions

*   Purchases of goods and services credit
*   Sales of goods or services on credit
*   Payments made to suppliers (for goods/services bought on credit)
*   Receipts from customers (for goods/services sold on credit)

Cash transactions

*   Purchases made by cash/cheque/card
*   Sales made for cash/cheque/card
*   Payments made to meet other expenses
*   Payment of salaries and wages to staff
*   Petty cash transactions
*   Transactions directly through the bank account (bank charges, interest, direct debits, standing orders)

Each of these transactions will have an effect on two accounts within the Sage system – this is the underlying principle of double-entry bookkeeping. However, Sage simplifies this by carrying out much of the double entry automatically.

Consider the first transactions – purchases and sales made on credit. This means that a legally binding contract is established between the two parties and the goods or services are supplied but payment is not paid until a later date. The key document in this process is the **invoice** – it demands payment and lays down the agreed terms of the transaction.

Hence, entering a credit transaction (whether a purchase or a sale) is a two stage process in Sage:

1   Enter the details of the invoice against the relevant supplier or customer. This will establish the presence and value of the legally binding debt.

2   At a later date, enter the details of the payment of the debt, either the payment sent to the supplier or the receipt received from the customer.

This approach is applicable for both credit sales and credit purchases – you just have to be sure to enter the details in the correct part of Sage.

1.2 Batch control

In order for a transaction to be correctly recorded in a computerised accounting system, the appropriate documentation must first be raised and then the details entered into 'the system'. Rather than enter each document on to the computer as it is received, many organisations use a batch control system.

In a batch control system all similar documents are collected and processed together in one batch. For example, purchase invoices and sales invoices will be sorted into separate batches and each batch will be processed separately. Similarly, documents recording receipts from customers will be separated from those that record payments to suppliers.

A batch control system will save time as the data processer is just focusing one task at a time.

Batch control is also useful to help to check that the entries made on the computer are accurate. First, a manual calculation is made to total each batch of documents. These totals are then checked against the computer system.

 Activity 1

The following six sales invoices now need to be processed.

Date	Invoice No	A/c No	Customer	Nominal Code	Net Amount	VAT	Gross Amount
30/09/2016	4891	POP002	Poppy	4001	£105.00	£21.00	£126.00
30/09/2016	4892	HAS004	Haslam	4000	£24.50	£4.90	£29.40
30/09/2016	4893	PAR006	Pargenter	4000	£12.00	£2.40	£14.40
30/09/2016	4894	LUL002	Lullabies Nursery	4003	£100.00	£20.00	£120.00
30/09/2016	4895	CAM004	Campbell & Dunn	4002	£45.00	£9.00	£54.00
30/09/2016	4896	HAS004	Haslam	4000	£12.00	£2.40	£14.40

Calculate batch totals and record them on the following batch control sheet:

Batch Control Sheet – Sales Invoices

Sales invoice batch totals 30th June 2016	Total net amounts £	Total VAT amounts £	Total gross amounts £
Totals			

You will now input these invoices on to Sage.

2 Credit sales – customer transactions

2.1 Entering customer invoices

 Activity 2

Enter each transaction onto the computer, making sure that the computer generated batch totals agree with the totals on the batch control sheet.

The easiest way to do this is to input all the invoices at the same time. To do this you will use the **Batch Customer Invoices** screen.

To enter a batch of customer (sales) invoices go to the '**CUSTOMERS**' module and then press the '**INVOICE**' button.

You can then insert data into the next screen as follows:

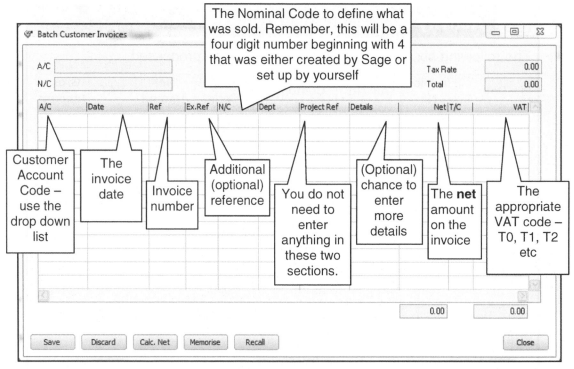

Once you have entered all invoices in the batch you should then review them to ensure you have entered them correctly, and then [Save] them. This will post the invoices to Sage and update the system accordingly.

Activity 3

Enter the six invoices for TotalPhoto Ltd using the batch invoicing method.

Enter the details in the batch customer invoices screen as detailed below. You can choose suitable wording for the 'details' tab and a suggestion has been given for each.

When you have entered all six invoices, your screen should look like this.

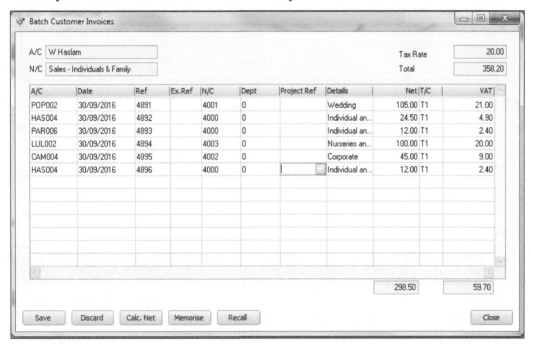

Check that the Total Net figure, the Total VAT figure and the Total figure at the top of the screen all match the totals you wrote down on the Batch Control Sheet. If the totals don't match check that the entries you made on the computer are accurate.

When you are happy press the [Save] button.

 Activity 4

Print out another trial balance for September 2010. Compare the two reports and identify the changes that have occurred.

Here is a copy of how the Trial Balance should now look:

```
Date:    19/08/2015              TotalPhoto Ltd                    Page:    1
Time:    15:48:59
                                Period Trial Balance

To Period:      Month 12, September 2016

N/C       Name                                    Debit           Credit
1100      Debtors Control Account                 358.20
1200      Bank Current Account                  2,668.80
1230      Cash Account                            252.00
2200      VAT on sales                                            429.06
2201      VAT on purchases                        382.56
3000      Capital introduced                                    3,000.00
4000      Sales - Individuals & Family                            614.30
4001      Sales - Weddings                                        433.50
4002      Sales - Corporate                                       997.50
4003      Sales - Nurseries & Schools                             100.00
5000      Puchases - Film                       1,568.90
5003      Purchases - Stationery                  343.90
                                      Totals:    5,574.36         5,574.36
```

2.2   Entering customer credit notes

A credit note is essentially a 'negative invoice' and is produced and sent to customers when a refund is needed. The most likely time this will happen is when goods that the organisation has sold to a customer have been returned as faulty. However, they can also be used to correct errors.

Producing a credit note in SAGE is straightforward and effectively mirrors the process for producing an invoice.

 Activity 5

Let us suppose that the sale of a 6" × 4" colour print made by TotalPhoto Ltd to Mrs Poppy for £12.00 (plus VAT) is returned as faulty. It is necessary to issue a credit note so that this debt is effectively 'removed' from Miss Pargenter's account. The Credit Note No is 25 and the Nominal code to use is 4000

Guidance on how to enter the credit note on Sage follows.

Step One – Complete the batch control sheet

Add up the figures in the Net Amount column, the VAT column and the Gross Amount column and enter the totals onto the batch control sheet:

Sales invoice batch totals 30th June 2016	Total net amounts (£)	Total VAT amounts (£)	Total gross amounts (£)
Totals			

Step Two – Process the customer credit note

From the **CUSTOMER** module select **CUSTOMER LIST** and then from the

icons at the top of the screen select the icon.

KAPLAN PUBLISHING

Here you can enter a batch of Credit Notes (just as you did with the batched invoices). **Sage shows your entries in RED to make it obvious that this is a Credit Note.**

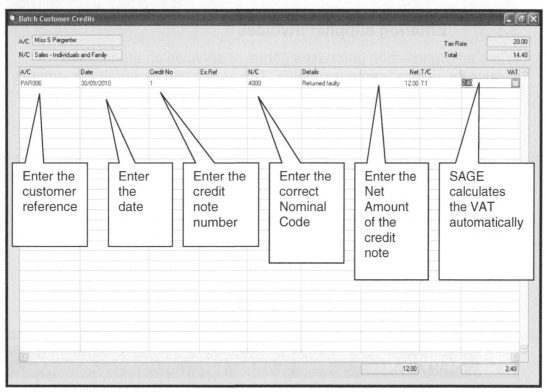

When you have entered all Credit Note(s) in the batch check the totals are the same as the batch control sheet then **SAVE** them to ensure that Sage can process them.

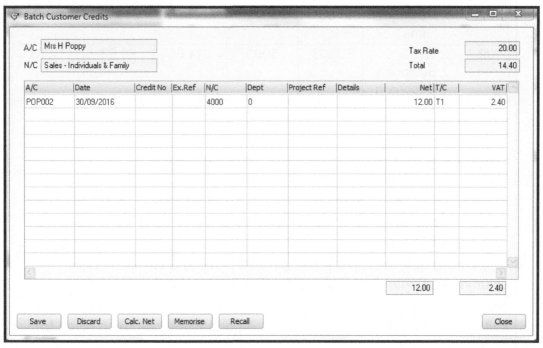

3 Credit purchases – supplier documents

3.1 Entering supplier invoices

When an organisation purchases goods or services on credit, it will receive an invoice from the supplier. These must be recorded immediately in SAGE, even though they may not be paid for some time. We know this is when the business has purchased on credit, i.e. to pay later.

The most common way to process supplier invoices is to **batch** them (in much the same way as you did with the invoices to customers). This way, a number of invoices can be processed at the same time.

The process for entering batches of supplier statements is very similar to that for entering batches of customer invoices – except it is accessed via the **SUPPLIERS** module.

You should enter the **SUPPLIERS** module now.

Invoice

Press the icon and enter the invoice details required.

 Activity 6

TotalPhoto Ltd received the following five invoices on 30th September 2016.

Invoice Ref	Supplier	Account	Nominal Code	Net amount	VAT	Gross Amount
1341	Mackay Films	MF001	5000	£208.75	£41.75	250.50
209	The Stationery Cupboard	SC003	5003	£14.65	£2.93	17.58
216	The Stationery Cupboard	SC003	5003	£78.90	£15.78	94.68
2203	Octopus Inks Ltd	OI001	5002	£309.25	£61.85	371.11
10092	Mills Paper Products	MP002	5001	£162.52	£32.50	195.02

You should now add up the Net amount, VAT and Gross amount columns and enter the totals on the Batch Control sheet.

Then enter the above five supplier invoices as a batch. You can choose suitable wording for the 'details' tab - a suggestion has been given for each.

Batch Control Sheet – Purchase Invoices

Purchase invoice batch totals 30th June 2016	Total net amounts (£)	Total VAT amounts (£)	Total gross amounts (£)
Totals			

When you have done the above activity the screen should look like this:

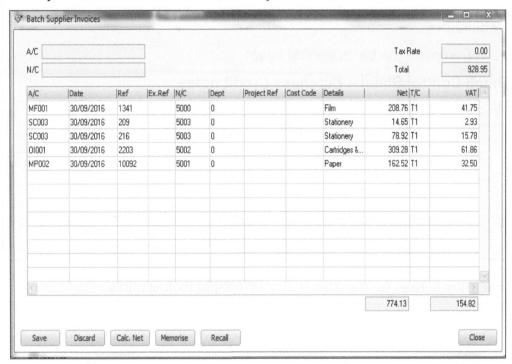

You should verify the entries and then press the '**SAVE**' button to post your entries to Sage.

3.2 Supplier credit notes

These are processed in exactly the same way as you processed credit notes issued to customers. Access the entry screen from the **SUPPLIERS** module.

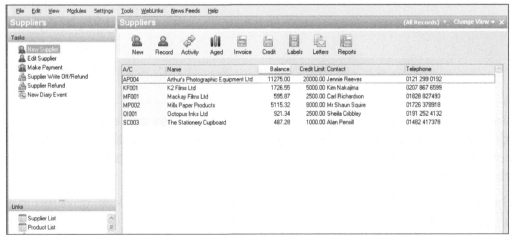

Activity 7

TotalPhoto Ltd receives one credit note. It is from The Stationery Cupboard (Ref SC003) and is a credit for £14.65 (excluding VAT) because the incorrect goods were supplied. The credit note reference is 134C. The Nominal Code for this is 5003 (Stationery).

Required:

a)   Complete the batch control sheet

Batch Control Sheet – Purchase Credit notes

Purchase credit note batch totals 30th June 2016	Total net amounts £	Total VAT amounts £	Total gross amounts £
Totals			

b)   Process the credit note using a suitable narrative for the details section (a suggestion has been shown).

Your entry screen for the above activity should look like this:

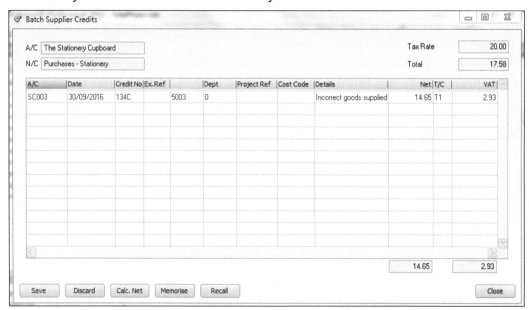

Note: Sage shows your entries in red so that they are easily identifiable as a credit note. When you have checked the accuracy of your entries against the figures you entered in the batch control sheet you should press the 'SAVE' button.

Having completed this, it is important to back up your work as covered in a previous chapter.

Processing payments and receipts

18

Introduction

This chapter looks at a second group of common business transactions, addressing the processing of payments and receipts.

.

KNOWLEDGE
2.1 Process information in respect of the sales ledger
2.2 Process information in respect of the purchase ledger
2.4 Process information involving different tax rates
2.5 Process information in respect of cash and cheque payments and receipts
3.1 Calculate batch totals as required
3.2 Reconcile batch totals as required

CONTENTS
1   Bank transactions
2   Credit payments and receipts
3   Cash payments and receipts
4   Reports

1 Bank transactions

1.1 Common payments and receipts

Businesses deal with a wide range of monetary transactions every day of the week. These include money being paid to the business from customers (receipts) and money being paid by the business to others (payments):

Receipts

- Receipts from cash customers for goods bought by cash/cheque/credit card

- Receipts from customers for goods/services sold on credit

Payments

- Payments made to suppliers (for goods/services bought on credit)

- Payments made to meet other expenses

- Payment of salaries and wages to staff

1.2 Sage bank accounts

To record this, Sage allows you to run a number of 'bank accounts'. These need not necessarily all be held at a Bank Current Account – they could also include cash in hand and recorded in the Cash Account.

The principles for making payments in or out of any of these accounts are the same.

Enter the **Bank** module. You can see that SAGE has already set up a number of different bank accounts, each with its own Nominal Code. You can of course amend these or add to them if you wish.

The most commonly used bank account is Nominal Code 1200 (Bank Current Account). This is the one that you will use in this manual for payments in and out of TotalPhoto Ltd's main current account. You can see that it has a balance at the moment of £2,668.80. You may recall that this relates to the £668.80 opening balance that you entered earlier and the additional capital introduced of £2,000.00

None of the entries that you have made since then have affected the bank balance.

2 Credit payments and receipts

2.1 Recording receipts from credit customers

Businesses will regularly receive monies from customers that have previously bought from them on credit.

 Activity 1

On 30th September TotalPhoto Ltd also received two amounts from customers in respect of their outstanding invoices a **receipts from customers listing** has been completed

Date	Receipt type	Customer	Amount (£)	Details
30/09/16	Cheque	Lullabies Nursery	120.00	Payment of Invoice 4894
30/09/16	Cash	Mrs H Poppy	111.60	Payment of Invoice 4891 and Credit Note 25

Enter these transactions onto a computerised system.

Guidance follows.

To enter the receipt for Lullabies Nursery:

Step One - click the icon from with the **Bank** module.

Step Two - In the top half of the screen in Customer Details search for the correct account, LUL002 enter the date and the Reference.

At this stage do not enter the amount of the receipt

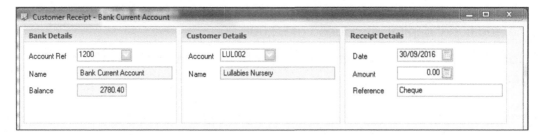

Note how Sage presents you with the outstanding invoices in the bottom half of the screen for the particular supplier. This allows you to decide which outstanding invoices you want to pay.

Step Three - Enter £120.00 in the Receipt column for Invoice 4894 – this is the invoice being paid on this occasion.

Note that SAGE can automatically decide which invoices to pay, or, if you wish to pay **all** outstanding invoices, you can select to Pay in Full

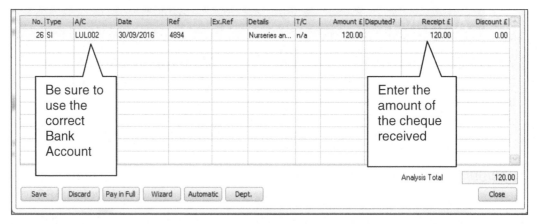

Step Four - Click **Save** to post this entry to Sage.

Now enter the second receipt, from Mrs Poppy for £111.60

This payment is to be allocated to two transactions on Mrs Poppy's account:

Sales invoice (SI) no 4891 for   £120.00

Sales credit note (SC) no 25 for £ 14.40

Total amount outstanding   £111.60

Note: In Sage you should always allocate the credit note first before you allocate the invoice

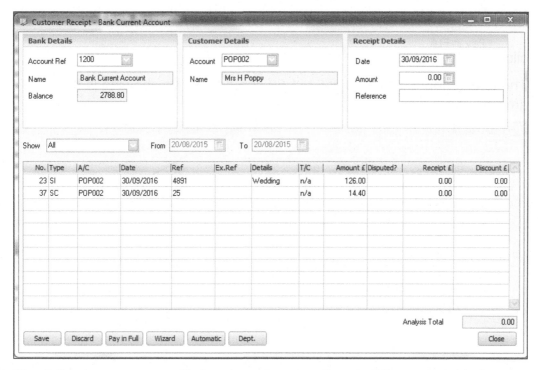

The following screens will show you how to allocate this payment in two stages:

Step One - go to the Credit Note (SC) row then click on the receipt column

and Pay in Full

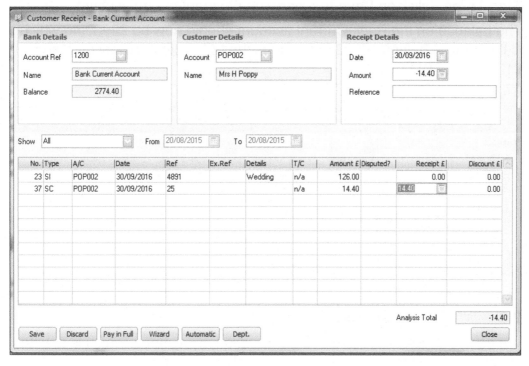

Step Two - go to the Invoice (SI) row then click on the receipt column and

click [Pay in Full]

The total amount allocated of £111.60 should now be showing in the amount box.

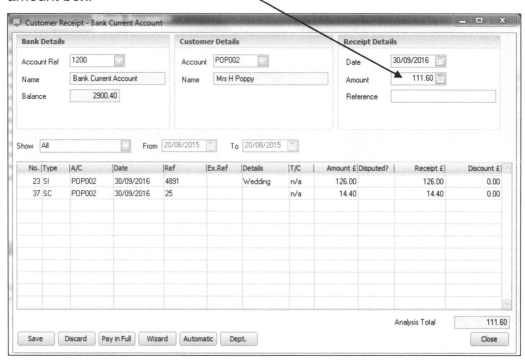

Step Three - click on **Save** to record the payment on the account.

The balance on the Bank Current account should now be £2900.40 which is the original balance of £2688.80 plus the two receipts from customers, £120.00 and £111.60

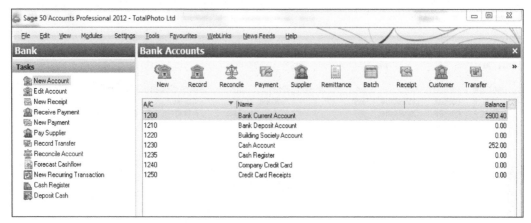

2.2 Paying suppliers

We can now look at the other common area for payments which is paying suppliers when the business has previously bought goods on credit. This is especially common for buying inventory/stock.

Activity 2

TotalPhoto Ltd also decides to pay two outstanding creditors on 30th September, as follows:

A payments to suppliers listing shows details of these payments.

Date	Receipt type	Customer	Amount (£)	Details
30/09/16	Cheque No 3567	MacKay Films Ltd	250.51	Payment of Invoice 1341
30/09/16	BACS transfer	The Stationery Cupboard	94.70	Payment of Invoices 209 and 216 and Credit Note 134C

Enter these supplier payments onto Sage.

Guidance follows.

Step One - To enter these payments onto Sage click the Supplier button.

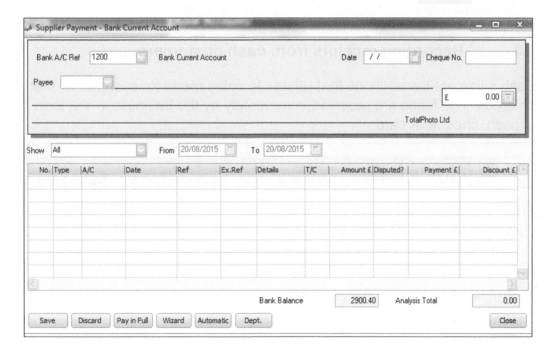

Step Two - Use the drop down menu to select the first supplier to pay (MacKay Films Ltd). Enter the correct date, The cheque number '3567' in the Cheque No box, and the amount being paid £250.51.

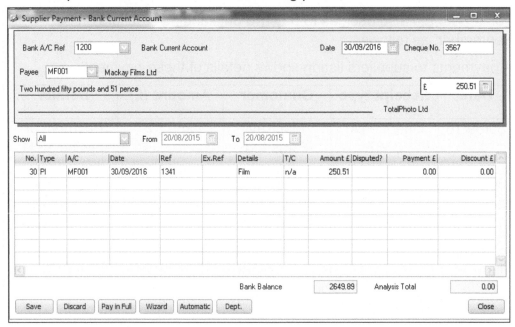

Step Three - You can now enter the payment of £250.51 in the payment column or select [Pay in Full]

Now enter the payment to The Stationery Cupboard.

Note: Remember to allocate the credit note first!

2.3 Recording receipts from cash customers

Cash sales are transactions that relates to sales made for cash rather than on credit. The funds are received immediately by the business in the form of cash, cheque or card.

 Activity 3

TotalPhoto Ltd also sells items to two customers who pay cash on 30th September. The first of these is a 6" × 4" Colour Print for £12.00 plus VAT (use nominal code 4000); the second is for School Photos (Set 2) for £28.00 plus VAT of 20% (nominal code 4003).

Enter these cash sales into the bank current account on Sage.

Detailed guidance follows.

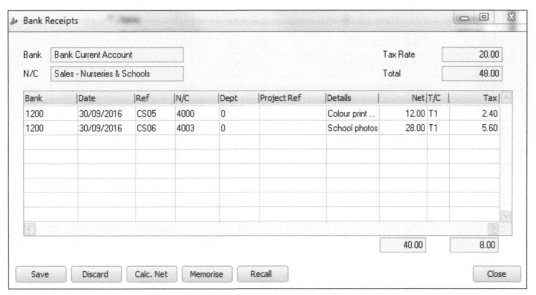

Step One - Click the Receipt button within the 'Bank' screen.

Step Two - Enter each transaction on a separate line. Be careful to make sure you select the appropriate nominal code for the sales, and also the correct VAT rate. Your entries should look like this:

Bank	Date	Ref	N/C	Dept	Project Ref	Details	Net	T/C	Tax
1200	30/09/2016	CS05	4000	0		Colour print ...	12.00	T1	2.40
1200	30/09/2016	CS06	4003	0		School photos	28.00	T1	5.60

Bank: Bank Current Account
N/C: Sales - Nurseries & Schools
Tax Rate: 20.00
Total: 48.00

40.00   8.00

Save   Discard   Calc. Net   Memorise   Recall   Close

Step Three - Click the **SAVE** button to post your entries to SAGE.

3 Cash payments and receipts

3.1 Cash payments

Cash payments are recorded in exactly the same way as any other payments made from a bank account.

Also be sure to enter the correct VAT code for each transaction. Many items commonly paid for out of petty cash are zero-rated or exempt – but not all.

For standard rated items you use the tax code (T/C) T1

For zero-rated items you will use the tax code (T/C) T0

You will be using the Bank Current Account (1200) for these transactions

Activity 5

TotalPhoto Ltd makes the following payments out of petty cash on 30th September 2016.

Voucher No	Description	Amount	VAT?
11762	Window cleaner	£4.00	No
11763	Tea and milk	£2.65	No
11764	Newspapers	£3.00	No
11765	Stamps	£3.60	No
11766	Pens	£1.99	Inclusive at 20.0%
11767	Taxi fare	£8.00	No

Enter the above transactions onto SAGE.

Guidance follows.

Step One - Enter these by clicking on the button within the BANK module.

Step Two - Make sure that the account selected is 1200 – Bank Current account

Enter each of the transactions above.

Your screen should look like this:

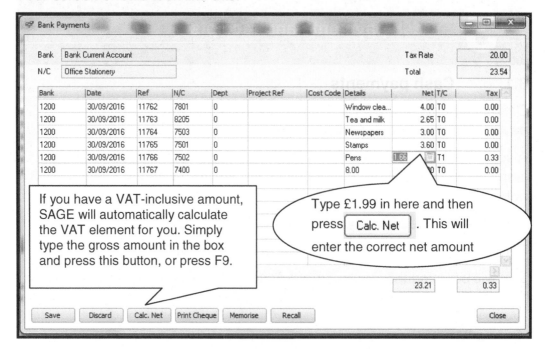

If you have a VAT-inclusive amount, SAGE will automatically calculate the VAT element for you. Simply type the gross amount in the box and press this button, or press F9.

Type £1.99 in here and then press | Calc. Net | . This will enter the correct net amount

Step Three - Once you have verified this click **Save.**

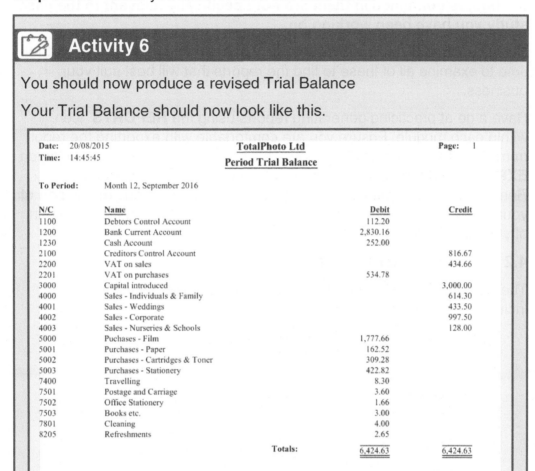

Activity 6

You should now produce a revised Trial Balance

Your Trial Balance should now look like this.

| Date: | 20/08/2015 | **TotalPhoto Ltd** | Page: | 1 |
| Time: | 14:45:45 | **Period Trial Balance** | | |

To Period: Month 12, September 2016

N/C	Name	Debit	Credit
1100	Debtors Control Account	112.20	
1200	Bank Current Account	2,830.16	
1230	Cash Account	252.00	
2100	Creditors Control Account		816.67
2200	VAT on sales		434.66
2201	VAT on purchases	534.78	
3000	Capital introduced		3,000.00
4000	Sales - Individuals & Family		614.30
4001	Sales - Weddings		433.50
4002	Sales - Corporate		997.50
4003	Sales - Nurseries & Schools		128.00
5000	Puchases - Film	1,777.66	
5001	Purchases - Paper	162.52	
5002	Purchases - Cartridges & Toner	309.28	
5003	Purchases - Stationery	422.82	
7400	Travelling	8.30	
7501	Postage and Carriage	3.60	
7502	Office Stationery	1.66	
7503	Books etc.	3.00	
7801	Cleaning	4.00	
8205	Refreshments	2.65	
	Totals:	6,424.63	6,424.63

4 Reports

4.1 Computerised accounting reports

Activity 7

You should now produce customer and supplier activity reports.

Although it is possible to create and produce your own Sage reports, there are a number of extremely useful report layouts already set up within Sage. You have already seen a number of these.

You should now make yourself familiar with these, plus the other reports shown below. **These reports are for demonstration purposes only and the figures contained in them are not specifically relevant to the case study you have been working on.**

Note that there are many other reports within SAGE; you should take the time to examine all of these to find the reports that will best suit your business.

Have a go at practicing generating reports using the **REPORTS** icon within each module. Ensure you are comfortable with exporting the report from Sage to create a **PDF** version. This can easily be done by clicking on **EXPORT** (rather than print) each time you generate a new report. Remember to save the file as a PDF type. This may be required as part of your actual computer based assessment process so it's an essential part of your studies.

4.2 Customer Reports

The Customer Activity Report shows all transactions for customers, including purchases and receipts.

Date: 27/06/2012
Time: 12:20:36

Total Photo Limited
Customer Activity (Detailed)

Page: 1

Date From:	01/01/1980	**Customer From:**	
Date To:	30/09/2010	**Customer To:**	ZZZZZZZZ
Transaction From:	1	**N/C From:**	
Transaction To:	99,999,999	**N/C To:**	99999999
Inc b/fwd transaction:	No	**Dept From:**	0
Exc later payment:	No	**Dept To:**	999

** NOTE: All report values are shown in Base Currency, unless otherwise indicated **

A/C: CAM004 **Name:** Campbell & Dunn **Contact:** **Tel:**

No	Type	Date	Ref	N/C	Details	Dept	T/C	Value	O/S	Debit	Credit	V	B
11	SI	30/09/2010		9998	Opening Balance	0	T9	2,056.85 *	2,056.85	2,056.85		-	-
18	SI	30/09/2010	6	4002		0	T1	54.00 *	54.00	54.00		N	-
					Totals:			2,110.85	2,110.85	2,110.85			

Amount Outstanding	2,110.85
Amount Paid this period	0.00
Credit Limit £	2,500.00
Turnover YTD	2,101.85

A/C: HAS004 **Name:** Mr W Haslam **Contact:** **Tel:**

No	Type	Date	Ref	N/C	Details	Dept	T/C	Value	O/S	Debit	Credit	V	B
7	SI	30/09/2010		9998	Opening Balance	0	T9	309.85 *	309.85	309.85		-	-
14	SI	30/09/2010	2	4000		0	T1	29.40 *	29.40	29.40		N	-
19	SI	30/09/2010	7	4000		0	T1	14.40 *	14.40	14.40		N	-
					Totals:			353.65	353.65	353.65			

Amount Outstanding	353.65
Amount Paid this period	0.00
Credit Limit £	500.00
Turnover YTD	346.35

A/C: LUL002 **Name:** Lullabies Nursery **Contact:** **Tel:**

No	Type	Date	Ref	N/C	Details	Dept	T/C	Value	O/S	Debit	Credit	V	B
12	SI	30/09/2010		9998	Opening Balance	0	T9	726.90		726.90		-	-
17	SI	30/09/2010	5	4003		0	T1	120.00 *	120.00	120.00		N	-
92	SR	30/09/2010		1200	Sales Receipt	0	T9	726.90			726.90	-	N
					Totals:			120.00	120.00	846.90	726.90		

Amount Outstanding	120.00
Amount Paid this period	726.90
Credit Limit £	1,500.00
Turnover YTD	826.90

A/C: PAR006 **Name:** Miss S Pargenter **Contact:** **Tel:**

No	Type	Date	Ref	N/C	Details	Dept	T/C	Value	O/S	Debit	Credit	V	B
9	SI	30/09/2010		9998	Opening Balance	0	T9	650.00 *	650.00	650.00		-	-
15	SI	30/09/2010	3	4000		0	T1	14.40 *	14.40	14.40		N	-
84	SC	30/09/2010	1	4000	Returned faulty	0	T1	14.40 *	-14.40		14.40	N	-
					Totals:			650.00	650.00	664.40	14.40		

Amount Outstanding	650.00
Amount Paid this period	0.00
Credit Limit £	1,000.00
Turnover YTD	650.00

The Customer Address List report shows contact details for customers, including addresses.

Date: 19/10/2009		TotalPhoto Ltd		Page: 1
Time: 20:51:56		Customer Address List		

Customer From:
Customer To: ZZZZZZZZ

A/C	Name & Address	Contact Name	Telephone	Fax
CAM004	Campbell & Dunn 12 The Beeches Miltonby Lancashire LN87 9PP			
HAS004	W Haslam 22 Brown Street Miltonby Lancashire LN87 6FD			
LUL002	Lullabies Nursery 104 Victoria Road Miltonby Lancashire LN87 5PS			
PAR006	S Pargenter 11 Alexandra Park Miltonby Lancashire LN87 2WD			

4.3 Supplier Reports

Likewise, the Supplier Address List report shows a list of all suppliers, with contact details.

Date: 19/10/2009		TotalPhoto Ltd		Page: 1
Time: 20:58:33		Supplier Address List		

Supplier From:
Supplier To: ZZZZZZZZ

A/C	Name	Contact	Telephone	Fax
AF004	Arthur's Photographic Equipment Ltd 77 Overton Lane Birmingham BM97 8YK	Jennie Reeves	0121 299 0192	
KF001	K2 Films Ltd Tokyo House 72-84 Great Milne Street London WC4 6DD	Kim Nakajima	0207 867 6599	
MF001	Mackay Films Ltd 33 West Parade Miltonby Lancashire LN87 7HD	Carl Richardson	01828 827493	
MP002	Mills Paper Products 405 Ream Road Bradford West Yorkshire	Mr Shaun Squire	01726 378918	

The Supplier Activity Report shows all transactions for a single, or range of, suppliers, including purchases, returns and invoices.

Date:	29/06/2012					**Total Photo Limited**						Page:	1
Time:	11:43:25					**Supplier Activity (Detailed)**							

Date From:	01/01/1980								Supplier From:		
Date To:	29/06/2012								Supplier To:	ZZZZZZZZ	
Transaction From:	1								N/C From:		
Transaction To:	99,999,999								N/C To:	99999999	
Inc b/fwd transaction:	No								Dept From:	0	
Exc later payment:	No								Dept To:	999	

** NOTE: All report values are shown in Base Currency, unless otherwise indicated **

A/C:	AP004	Name:	Arthur's Photographic Equipment Ltd		Contact:	Jennie Reeves		Tel:	0121 299 0192	

No	**Type**	**Date**	**Ref**	**N/C**	**Details**	**Dept**	**T/C**	**Value**	**O/S**	**Debit**	**Credit**	**V**	**B**
6	PI	30/09/2010	O/Bal	9998	Opening Balance	0	T9	11,275.00 *	11,275.00		11,275.00	-	-
79	PC	30/09/2010	134C	0022	Returned cameras	0	T1	2,531.99 *	-2,531.99	2,531.99		N	-
					Totals:			8,743.01	8,743.01	2,531.99	11,275.00		

Amount Outstanding	8,743.01
Amount paid this period	0.00
Credit Limit £	20,000.00
Turnover YTD	9,165.01

A/C:	KF001	Name:	K2 Films Ltd		Contact:	Kim Nakajima		Tel:	0207 867 6599	

No	**Type**	**Date**	**Ref**	**N/C**	**Details**	**Dept**	**T/C**	**Value**	**O/S**	**Debit**	**Credit**	**V**	**B**
2	PI	30/09/2010	O/Bal	9998	Opening Balance	0	T9	1,726.55	0.00		1,726.55	-	-
84	PP	30/09/2010	00246	1200	Purchase Payment	0	T9	1,726.55	0.00	1,726.55		-	N
					Totals:			0.00	0.00	1,726.55	1,726.55		

Amount Outstanding	0.00
Amount paid this period	1,726.55
Credit Limit £	5,000.00
Turnover YTD	1,726.55

A/C:	MF001	Name:	Mackay Films Ltd		Contact:	Carl Richardson		Tel:	01828 827493	

No	**Type**	**Date**	**Ref**	**N/C**	**Details**	**Dept**	**T/C**	**Value**	**O/S**	**Debit**	**Credit**	**V**	**B**
1	PI	30/09/2010	O/Bal	9998	Opening Balance	0	T9	345.36 *	345.36		345.36	-	-
74	PI	30/09/2010	1341	5000		0	T1	250.51 *	250.51		250.51	N	-
					Totals:			595.87	595.87	0.00	595.87		

Amount Outstanding	595.87
Amount paid this period	0.00
Credit Limit £	2,500.00
Turnover YTD	554.12

A/C:	MP002	Name:	Mills Paper Products		Contact:	Mr Shaun Squire		Tel:	01726 378918	

No	**Type**	**Date**	**Ref**	**N/C**	**Details**	**Dept**	**T/C**	**Value**	**O/S**	**Debit**	**Credit**	**V**	**B**
4	PI	30/09/2010	O/Bal	9998	Opening Balance	0	T9	4,920.30 *	4,920.30		4,920.30	-	-
78	PI	30/09/2010		5001		0	T1	195.02 *	195.02		195.02	N	-
					Totals:			5,115.32	5,115.32	0.00	5,115.32		

Amount Outstanding	5,115.32
Amount paid this period	0.00
Credit Limit £	8,000.00
Turnover YTD	5,082.82

A/C:	OI001	Name:	Octopus Inks Ltd		Contact:	Sheila Cribbley		Tel:	0191 252 4132	

No	**Type**	**Date**	**Ref**	**N/C**	**Details**	**Dept**	**T/C**	**Value**	**O/S**	**Debit**	**Credit**	**V**	**B**
5	PI	30/09/2010	O/Bal	9998	Opening Balance	0	T9	550.20 *	550.20		550.20	-	-
77	PI	30/09/2010	2203	5002		0	T1	371.14 *	371.14		371.14	N	-
					Totals:			921.34	921.34	0.00	921.34		

Amount Outstanding	921.34
Amount paid this period	0.00
Credit Limit £	2,500.00
Turnover YTD	859.48

4.4 Nominal ledger reports

Nominal Activity – Excluding No Transactions show the activity in all active nominal ledger accounts.

Date:	20/08/2015			Stationery & Computer Mart UK						Page:	1	
Time:	14:54:33			Nominal Activity - Excluding No Transactions								

Date From:	01/01/1980	N/C From:	
Date To:	20/08/2015	N/C To:	99999999

Transaction From:	1
Transaction To:	99,999,999

N/C: 0020   Name: Plant and Machinery   Account Balance: 50,000.00 DR

No	Type	Date	Account	Ref	Details	Dept	T/C	Value	Debit	Credit	V	B
32	JD	31/12/2008	0020	O/BALS	Opening Balance	0	T9	50,000.00	50,000.00		-	-
								Totals:	50,000.00			
								History Balance:	50,000.00			

N/C: 0021   Name: Plant/Machinery Depreciation   Account Balance: 3,485.00 CR

No	Type	Date	Account	Ref	Details	Dept	T/C	Value	Debit	Credit	V	B
33	JC	31/12/2008	0021	O/BALS	Opening Balance	0	T9	4,000.00		4,000.00	-	-
613	PI	29/03/2009	MCN001	125	Goods	0	T1	515.00	515.00		R	-
								Totals:	515.00	4,000.00		
								History Balance:		3,485.00		

N/C: 0040   Name: Furniture and Fixtures   Account Balance: 16,900.00 DR

No	Type	Date	Account	Ref	Details	Dept	T/C	Value	Debit	Credit	V	B
34	JD	31/12/2008	0040	O/BALS	Opening Balance	0	T9	16,900.00	16,900.00		-	-
								Totals:	16,900.00			
								History Balance:	16,900.00			

N/C: 0041   Name: Furniture/Fixture Depreciation   Account Balance: 93.00 CR

No	Type	Date	Account	Ref	Details	Dept	T/C	Value	Debit	Credit	V	B
35	JC	31/12/2008	0041	O/BALS	Opening Balance	0	T9	93.00		93.00	-	-
								Totals:		93.00		
								History Balance:		93.00		

N/C: 0050   Name: Motor Vehicles   Account Balance: 20,300.00 DR

No	Type	Date	Account	Ref	Details	Dept	T/C	Value	Debit	Credit	V	B
36	JD	31/12/2008	0050	O/BALS	Opening Balance	0	T9	20,300.00	20,300.00		-	-
								Totals:	20,300.00			
								History Balance:	20,300.00			

Setting up a computerised payroll system

Introduction

This chapter is the first of two covering the basics of payroll systems and processing.

The chapter focuses on the setting up and use of a computerised payroll system, including checking the legislative parameters for the start of the year, entering current and new employees from data given, calculating gross pay for those employees, and backing up the payroll data.

KNOWLEDGE

Computerised Payroll Administration

1 Be able to set up a computerised payroll system

2.1 Input employee data into payroll software

2.2 Maintain company data and legislative parameters in accordance with company policy

3 Be able to enter details of gross pay into the computerised payroll system

4 Be able to process the payroll

5 Be able to back-up and/or restore payroll data

Payroll processing

1 Be able to determine income tax deducted from gross pay

CONTENTS

1 Employer information
2 Employee records and gross pay
3 Processing pay

1 Employer information

1.1 Introduction

When setting up a computerised payroll system there is a certain amount of information that needs to be collected.

This information can be divided into employer information and employee information.

1.2 Employer information

The information needed regarding the employer is:

*   The name of the organisation

*   Address

*   Tax District/Reference

*   Accounts office reference

*   Processing date

> ### Definition
>
> **Tax District/Reference and Accounts office reference:**
>
> These are used by HMRC to identify the employer, and also the employees. They are used to allocate payments from the employer and employee to the correct accounts

Once these are entered the system is ready for the payroll information.

Task 1

1.3   How to input the employer information

1.   Click first on Company, and then on Settings

Company Settings

2.   The New Company Wizard will appear as follows:

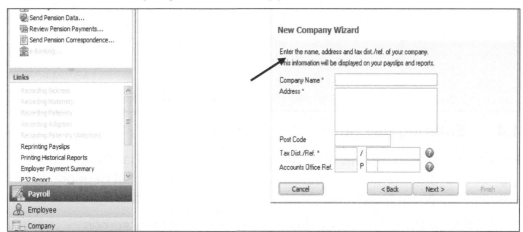

Activity 1

Enter the following details onto the computerised payroll system:

Company Name:	Merry Music Company
Address:	19 Parkside Road Eastnor, Manchester M21 5TT
Telephone:	01973 472987

Email:	merry@music.co.uk
Tax Office:	Shipley
Tax Dist/Ref	101/D75798
Bank details:	Manchester Bank PLC
Address:	74 High Street Eastnor, Manchester M22 7WD
Account Name:	Merry Music Company
Account Number:	33179771
Sort Code:	20-20-14

Once the details have been input the following screen will appear automatically. Change the date as below. This is date that we will use for the payroll run.

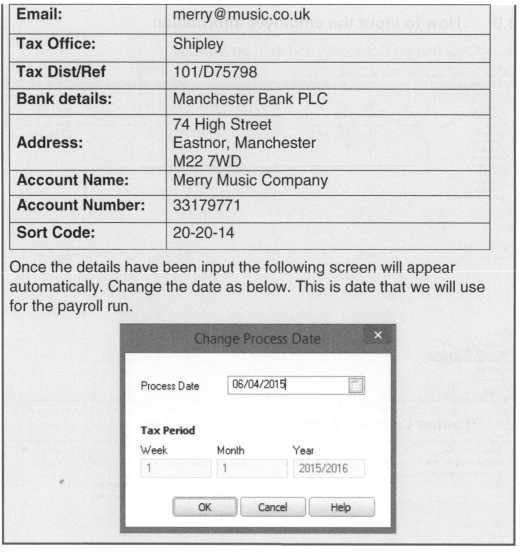

1.4 Entering pay rates

Next to be entered are the standard pay rates. Many organisations have 'pay bands' that are allocated to individual members of staff dependent on the job they do, or the position they hold in the organisation.

1. Click on Pay Elements to access the Pay Elements screen

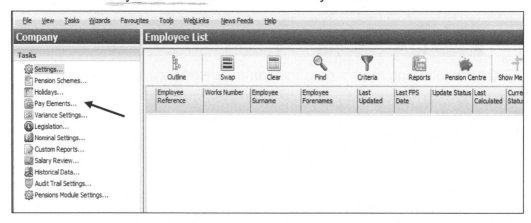

2. To input pay rates for the first time, click on New and enter the data.

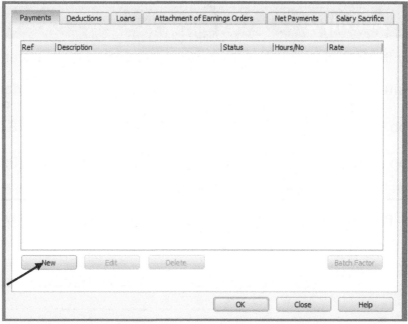

3. In the Description box enter the name of the position, eg, Shop assistant. Leave the Default hours blank, but enter the hourly rate that corresponds to the position.

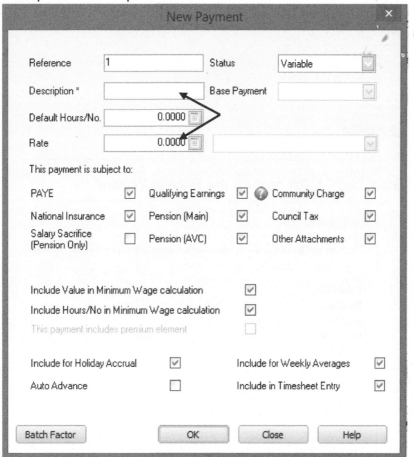

4. Leave all the other boxes as they are, and click on OK.

Activity 2

Enter the following details onto the computerised payroll system:

Position	Hourly rate £	Overtime rate £	Holiday rate £
Shop manager	16.50	24.75	16.50
Shop assistant	13.00	19.50	13.00

5. Before going any further, back up the data as shown below.

- Step One – select Backup

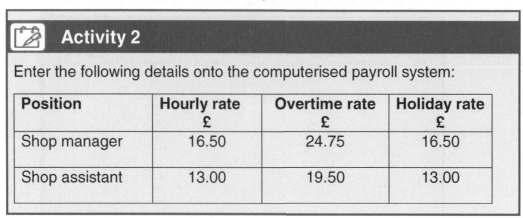

- Step Two – Click next on the Backup Wizard

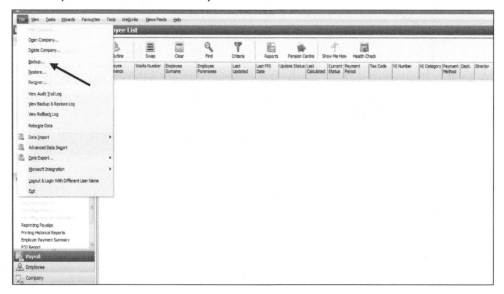

- Step 3 - Name and file your backup (click Browse to see locations to store the file)

- Step 4 - Start the backup by clicking Finish.

- Step Five – Confirm the backup is complete

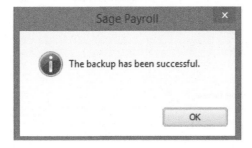

Activity 3

Back up the data calling the file Merry Music Company.

Activity 4

Print out a company details report.

1.5   Legislation

It is important to check the tax and National insurance bands to ensure that the data is in line with current legislation. To do this:

1.   Click on legislation

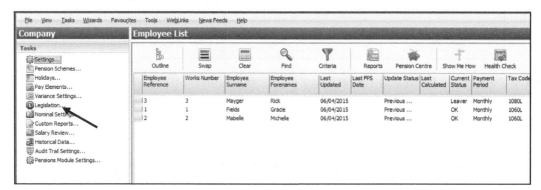

2.   Check the information on the two tabs below, and make any necessary amendments, in these two tabs.

3. To print out reports of these rates use the legislation section in the report generator. Choose the report (or reports) needed from this list.

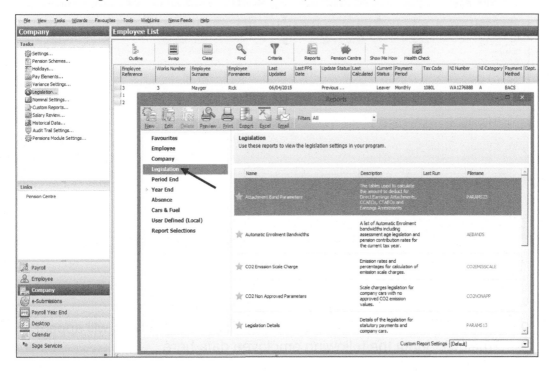

---

2 Employee records and gross pay

2.1 Employee data

This needs to be entered before an employee can be paid.

It must be entered accurately and into the system as below.

1. On the left hand menu select Employee

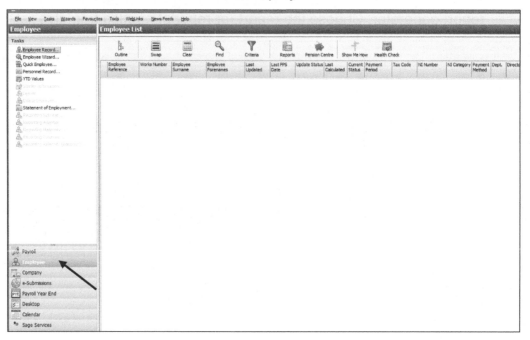

2. Then click on Quick Employee. Immediately a new box will appear (below). Input the following employee data here

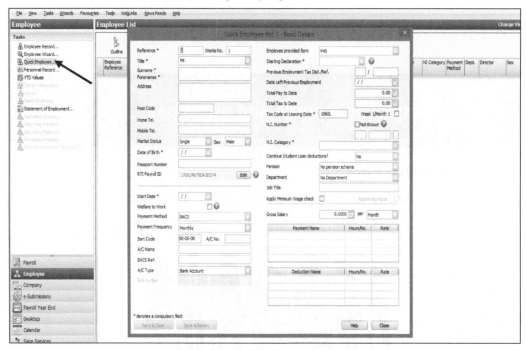

Data to be input will either be of existing employees and will appear in a table, or a new employee.

2.2 New employees

The information will be provided either on a P45 or, more likely on a Starter Checklist. An example of the Starter Checklist is below.

HM Revenue & Customs

Starter Checklist

Employee's personal details

Last name or family name

First name(s)

Are you male or female? ○ Male   ○ Female

Date of birth *eg dd mm yyyy*

Home address

Address line 1

Address line 2

Address line 3

Address line 4

Postcode
(if your address is in the UK)

National Insurance number

Employment start date
eg dd mm yyyy

Payroll ID or works number
(if you have one)

Employee statement

You need to select only **one** of the following statements **A, B** or **C**.

○ **A** - This is my first job since last 6 April and I have not been receiving taxable Jobseeker's Allowance, Employment and Support Allowance, taxable Incapacity Benefit, State or Occupational Pension.

○ **B** - This is now my only job but since last 6 April I have had another job, or received taxable Jobseeker's Allowance, Employment and Support Allowance or taxable Incapacity Benefit. I do not receive a State or Occupational Pension.

○ **C** - As well as my new job, I have another job or receive a State or Occupational Pension.

Do you have a Student Loan which is not fully repaid and all of the following apply:

- You left a course of UK higher education before last 6 April.
- You received your first Student Loan instalment on or after 1 September 1998.

○ No   ○ Yes

Starter checklist 23102012 v1.1

The employee will fill out all the personal details, and tick one of the boxes in the Employee statement section.

The Starter Checklist/P46 categories are:

A.   This is my first job since last 6 April and I have not been receiving taxable Jobseeker's Allowance, Employment and Support Allowance or taxable Incapacity Benefit or a state or occupational pension.

B.   This is now my only job, but since last 6 April I have had another job, or have received taxable Jobseeker's Allowance, Employment and Support Allowance or taxable Incapacity Benefit. I do not receive a state or occupational pension.

C.   Employee declaration unavailable: no tax allowances

The category letter used from the Starter Checklist will dictate the Tax Code that the employee will receive pending HMRC notification, and it is that letter that you will input into the software.

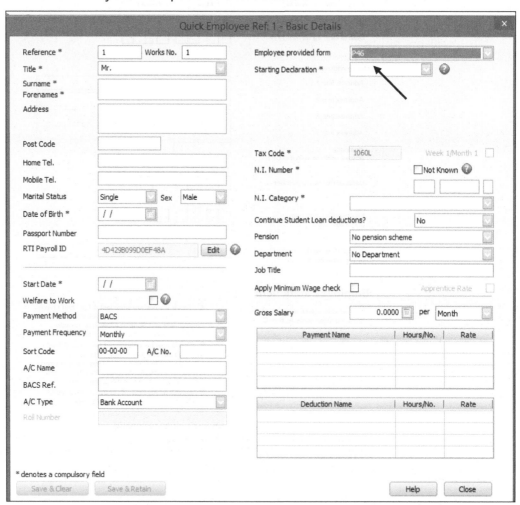

 Activity 5

The following information has been taken from the Starter Checklist.

Set up the new employee on the computerised payroll system.

Name	Rick Mayger
	Male
DOB	15/10/1962
Address	11 Watery Road
	Pondon
	PD6 8WT
NINO*	WA 12 76 88 B

Rick ticked statement A of the Employee Statement

Rick ticked No to the Student Loan question

Rick is single, and employed as a shop assistant. He will be paid by BACS.

Rick provides the following bank details:

Account name: R Mayger ; Account no: 76549182 ; Sort code 11-63-31

*NINO = National Insurance Number

2.3 Existing employees

For existing employees, choose the option as below

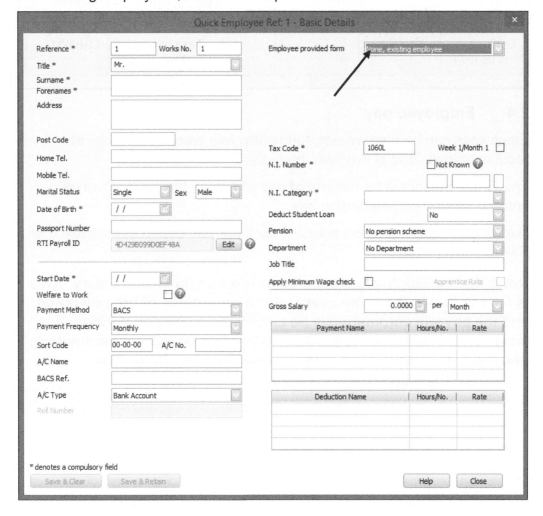

Activity 6

Enter the rest of the employee data into the payroll software system

Employee ref no, name and DOB	Address	Start date	Rate of pay per hour	Job title, NINO and tax codes	Bank account details
Ref 1 Ms Gracie Fields Married DOB 06/07/1965	26 Low Street Manchester M62 3AP	06/04/2013	£16.50	Job: Shop Manager NINO: EB 20 52 76D NI Letter: A Tax code: 1060L	A/c name: G Fields A/c no. 12349876 Sort code: 11-63-31
Ref 2 Mrs Michelle Mabelle Married DOB: 18/12/1971	32 Waverley Road Hartles HG2 4AM	06/04/2014	£13.00	Job: Shop Assistant NINO: CA 15 97 65 B NI Letter: A Tax code: 1060L	A/c name: M Mabelle A/c no. 44228891 Sort code: 11-63-31

2.4 Employee pay

Employees can be paid weekly, fortnightly, four weekly, monthly, at regular intervals and at irregular intervals.

The Gross Salary will be calculated depending on the pay frequency entered into the corresponding box.

For variable pay (where the hours of work per pay period differs) use the Payment Name box.

Note: On the Employee screen there is a box for Gross Salary. This is for pay that is the same every month regardless of hours worked, and the pay will automatically be calculated every pay period. If however, the employee is paid an hourly rate do NOT enter anything into the box, but enter the details in the Payment Name box.

To view employee details either

- double-click on the employee name
- select the employee name and then click Employee Record

At the top of the Employee Record are blue arrows. These are called navigation arrows, and can be used to view other employees' details.

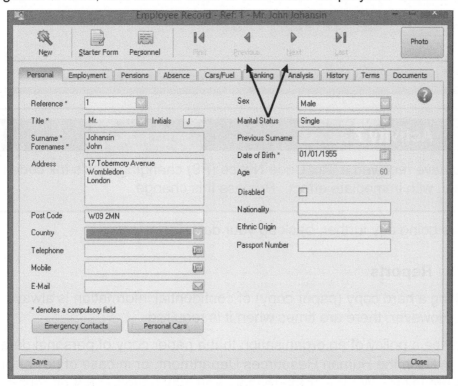

Note: It is on the above screen that the employee's personal and other details can be amended. Don't forget to click on the Save after the amendments have been made.

Below the navigation buttons are the ten tabs, where information can be entered and a history of the employee is retained.

Click on the Employment tab to see the employee's full data, as shown below.

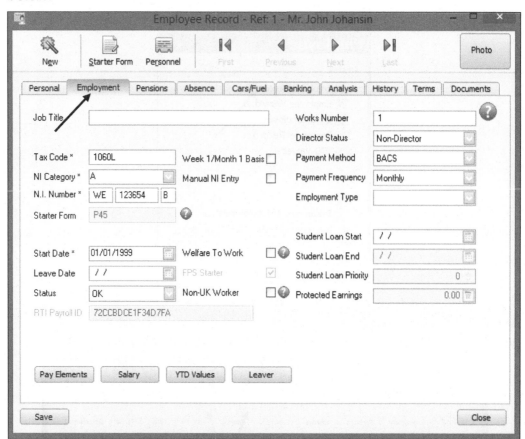

Activity 7

You have received a Tax Code Notice (P9) changing Rick's tax code to 1080L with immediate effect. Process this change.

Before going any further, back up your data.

2.5 Reports

Keeping a hard copy (paper copy) of confidential information is always a risk. However, there are times when it is required.

It may be a policy of an organisation that a paper copy of personal data is kept in file in the Human Resources Department, or in case of power or software failure. Whatever the reason, you may have to print off reports.

To print off a copy of the Employee Details:

1. Click on Reports

To select all employees at once, either

- Click on each employee individually or

- Click on Swap.

(To clear the selection, press Clear. The selected employees will be deselected)

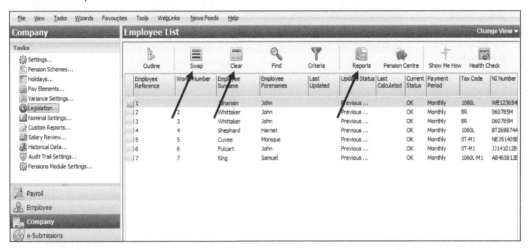

2.   Then go to Employee and scroll down to Employee Details - Personal

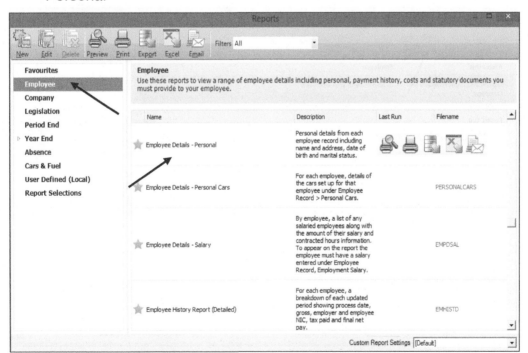

This report is very useful as it shows all personal details for each employee, and worth making a 'Favourite' by clicking on the star next to the name of the report.

Doing this will copy the report into the Favourites, saving time and searching if the report is needed again.

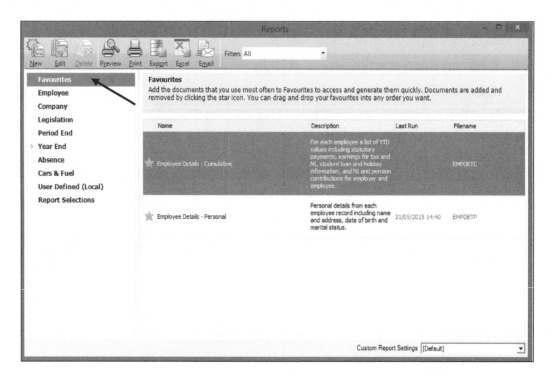

3.   To view or print the report, either click on Preview or Print on the toolbar or place the cursor onto the highlighted name and the same options will appear.

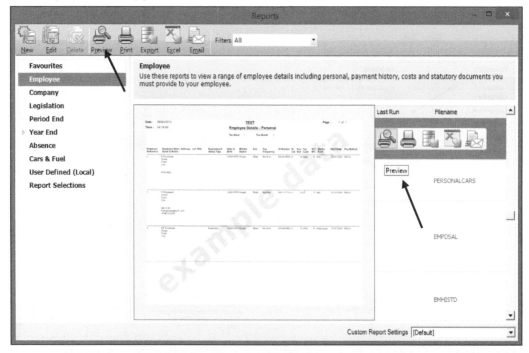

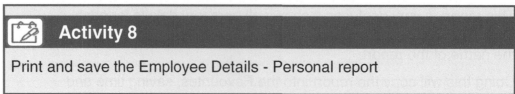

Activity 8

Print and save the Employee Details - Personal report

3 Processing pay

3.1 Checking dates

As this is the first payroll of the fiscal year (the name of the tax year that runs from 6th April one year to 5th April the next), it is worth checking that the software has been updated with the correct tax and National Insurance bands.

1. Click on Company, then on Legislation

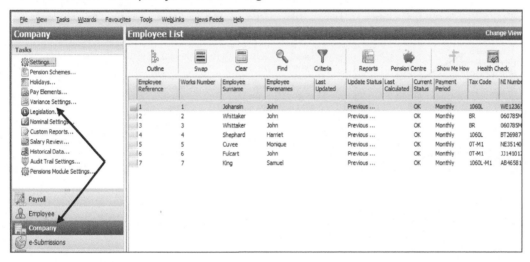

2. A new screen appears. Check the dates against the information given, and amend as necessary.

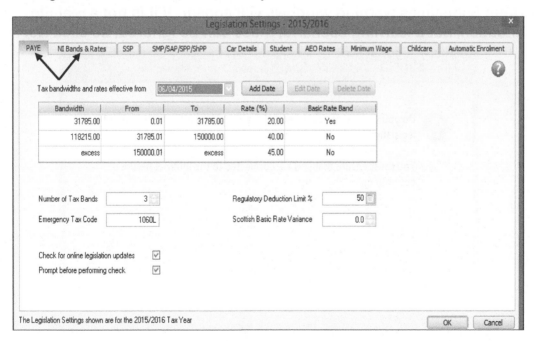

As this is the correct 2015/16 tax and National insurance information, no amendment is necessary

Note: It is more than likely that in the assessment changes will need to be made. Follow the instructions, remembering to click on the OK button afterwards!

3.2 Processing weekly pay

1. Click on Payroll, and then Click on Enter Payments

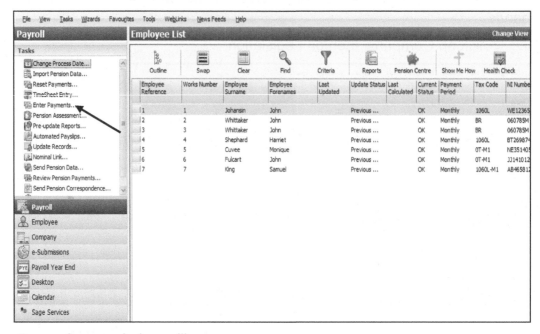

2. A new window will appear.

Note: Sometimes warning windows will appear. If it is not a real-life situation, but a learning scenario, these can be ignored, so click No.

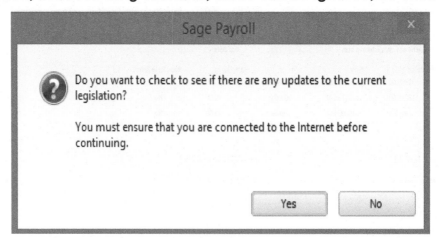

3. Click on Add Payment

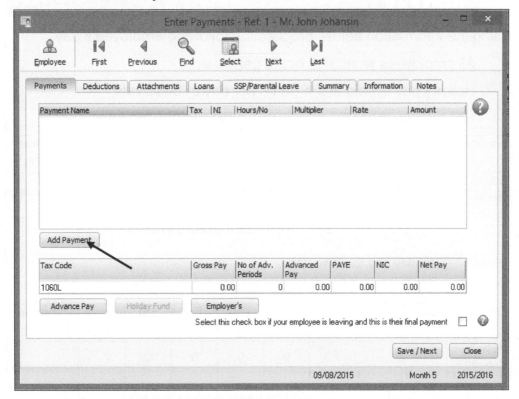

4. A new window appears. It is here that a new payment is entered, or, by clicking on the dropdown box, more payments are added. All new payments should be Pre tax and National Insurance. Do not enter any hours, just the rate and Save.

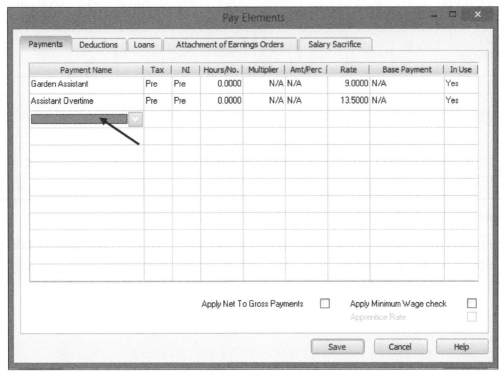

Activity 9

Using the information below, process the following employee's pay

- All employees work 37.5 hours per week.
- Holiday pay is paid at 7.5 hours per day at basic rate.
- Holiday pay **must** be shown as a separate pay element.

Employee	Sun	Mon	Tue	Wed	Thu	Fri	Sat	Basic hours	Overtime hours
Gracie Fields	7.5	7.5	7.5	Holiday	Holiday				
					Total hours worked in week				
Notes	**Holiday pay due two days**								

Employee	Sun	Mon	Tue	Wed	Thu	Fri	Sat	Basic hours	Overtime hours
Michelle Mabelle			7.5	9	9	9	7.5		
					Total hours worked in week				
Notes									

Employee	Sun	Mon	Tue	Wed	Thu	Fri	Sat	Basic hours	Overtime hours
Rick Mayger	7.5	7.5	7.5	Holiday	Holiday				
					Total hours worked in week				
Notes	**Leaving on Saturday Week 1**								

Tick the leaver box on Rick's Enter Payments record screen to ensure that he is processed as leaving.

Notes from Activity 9:

If you have not entered holiday pay as a pay element you can always add it, and any others, through the 'new' option as per the screenshot below.

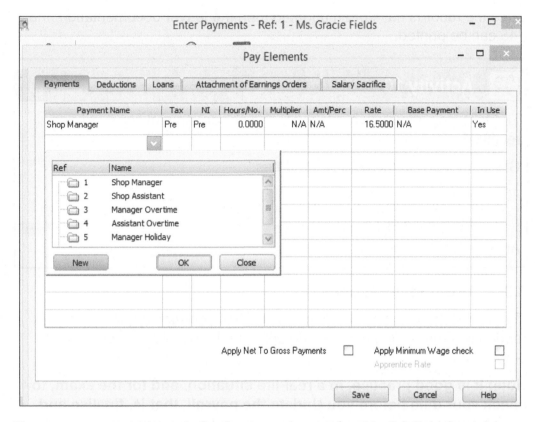

To process an employee's final payment, you should click the check box at the bottom right of the screen. The pay will then be the final payment, and after updating the records, the P45 can be printed.

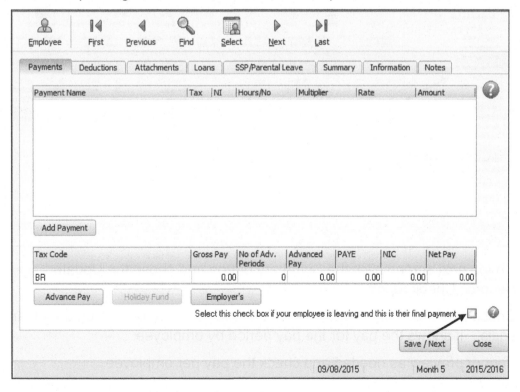

Once the records have been updated then the leaver documentation, the P45 can be printed.

 Activity 10

The following information relating to the current employees has been received:

Gracie Fields has a change of address:

15 Wisteria Close

Manchester MA9 6PQ

Amend Gracie's records accordingly.

3.3 Pre-update Reports

The next step in the process is to run the **Pre-update reports.** These reports summarise the payroll, and print out the payslips for the employees.

Note: It is good practice, in a real-life situation, and for the exam, to check your data before you Update the payroll, that is, finalise and pay the employees. Any errors can easily be amended here.

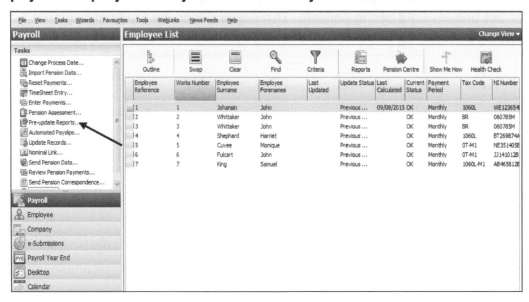

On the next screen click the Summary button and chose the Update Records Check report.

Chose it as one of the favourites, as this report will be printed on a regular basis. It shows the pay for the pay period by employee.

Print or preview as needed and check the pay per employee.

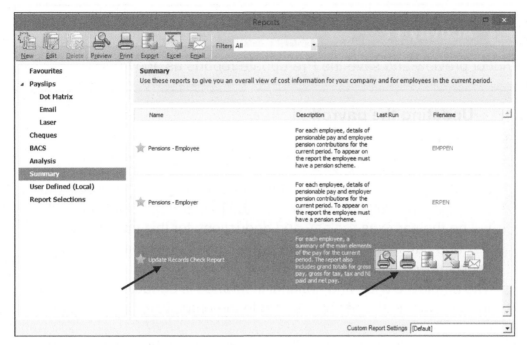

If the pay is correct then proceed to the Payslips, choosing the Laser (2 per A4 sheet) and preview, print and save as required.

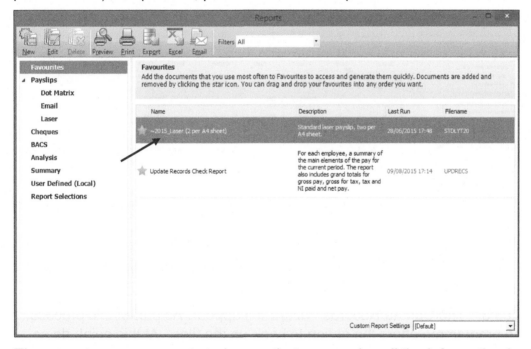

There are two more reports to be run that summarise all the information in the payroll. They are

- Payment Summary part 1 (landscape)
- Payment Summary part 2 (landscape)

If all data is correct, then the payroll can be updated.

Activity 11

Print or preview and save the Pre-update reports as above.

3.4 Updating the payroll

During this process

- All the pay and deductions (tax and national insurance) from this pay period is added to the previous pay and deductions. As this is the first pay period of the new tax year the pay and deductions to date will be the same as the pay and deductions for this pay period.
- Tax and national insurance are added together so that the employer knows how much to pay HMRC.
- The employee's tax and national insurance is deducted from the pay this period and the net pay is paid to the employee.

Step 1 - Choose all employees. This can be done by highlighting them individually, or by clicking on Swap.

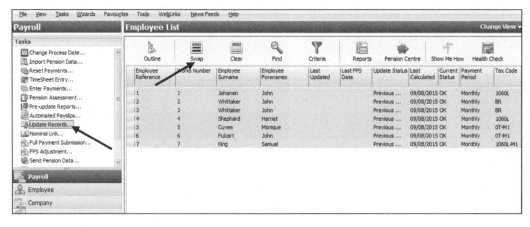

Step 2 - Click on Update Records for the next screen.

A warning will appear as a reminder to print Pre-update reports. As these have already been done, click Yes to continue.

Step 3 – The Update Records Wizard will appear. As part of this process, the programme offers the option to back-up the files. At this point, do so, either naming the file a specific name, or allowing the programme to choose. It will use the company name, and payroll period to distinguish it from earlier backups.

Step 4 - The next screen shows how many employees will be updated.

Step 5 - Continue to the next screen which shows how many employees' records will be updated. If this is correct, then click Finish.

Activity 12

Update Records for Merry Music Company employees.

3.5 Leaver documentation

Now that the pay period has been updated, it is time to print out the leaver documentation.

Go to the employee's record, click on the Employment tab, and then on Leaver.

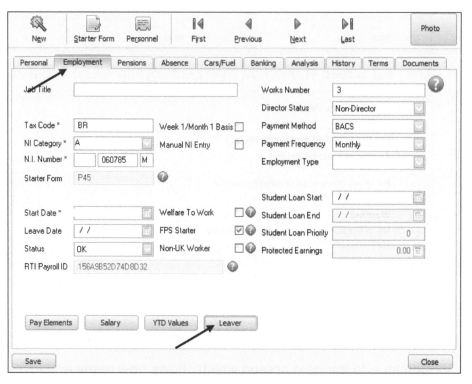

Work through the Leaver Wizard entering the leaving date as directed (in this case Saturday 11 April).

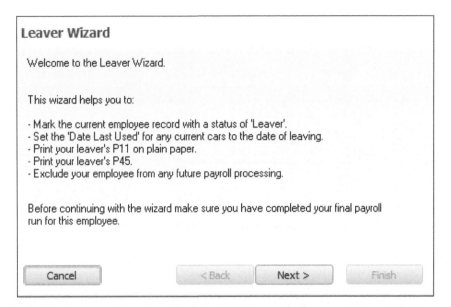

Leaver Wizard

Welcome to the Leaver Wizard.

This wizard helps you to:

- Mark the current employee record with a status of 'Leaver'.
- Set the 'Date Last Used' for any current cars to the date of leaving.
- Print your leaver's P11 on plain paper.
- Print your leaver's P45.
- Exclude your employee from any future payroll processing.

Before continuing with the wizard make sure you have completed your final payroll run for this employee.

Cancel | < Back | Next > | Finish

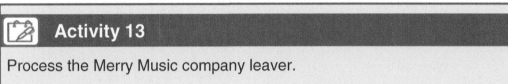

Activity 13

Process the Merry Music company leaver.

3.6 Restore

Occasionally data may need to be restored. This process reloads a selected data file, thus restoring data from a previous pay period. The data will overwrite the current pay data, so the restore function must be used very carefully and only when no alternative action can be taken.

4 Summary

So far you have set up a new business, checked the legislative parameters, entered the employees and calculated the gross pay.

In the next chapter you will be processing the employee pay, and paying them in either cash, cheque or BACS. You will have then completed a payroll cycle that many payroll clerks perform regularly throughout the country.

Preparing and submitting payroll data

Introduction

This section covers the processing of payroll.

It addresses the rules and regulations regarding the authorising, processing, and payment of payroll to HMRC (Her Majesty's Revenue and Customs) and the employee.

It also describes the documentation that needs to be produced for payroll purposes, both employee documentation and employer documentation and considers how payments are made.

KNOWLEDGE
Computerised payroll administration
6 Understand statutory requirements for submitting information
Payroll processing
2 Be able to determine National Insurance Contributions to be deducted from gross pay.
3 Be able to reconcile the payroll and make payments to employees.

CONTENTS
1 Employer responsibilities
2 Payroll documentation

1 Employer responsibilities

1.1 RTI

> **Definition**
>
> **Real Time Information (RTI)** is the name of the electronic system by which employers have to pay HMRC.

There were two main reasons for bringing in RTI.

1. When PAYE (Pay As You Earn) was introduced nearly 70 years ago, employees stayed in a job for most of their life, making record keeping of PAYE and National Insurance contributions fairly easy. With the more fluid job market and employees either changing jobs more frequently, or having multiple employments, HMRC was struggling to keep up.

2. With the advent of the Universal Tax credit system information needed to be up to date and accurate to avoid people being under- or over-paid tax credit.

Now, HMRC can access the information needed every time an individual is paid. It has also stream-lined the whole process of payroll administration.

1.2 Release of information

Within the payroll function a lot of very confidential information relating to an employee is held. Information such as:

*   Name
*   Address
*   Age
*   Ethnicity
*   Bank details
*   Medical history

The **only** time this information can be revealed without an employee's consent is where there is a statutory (legal) duty.

Otherwise an employee has a right to think that this data is held securely, and will not be revealed to other sources without written consent. The payroll clerk must be clear on who can, and cannot have access to the information.

Activity 1

You have had a request from a double-glazing company who are considering a finance option that would enable an employee to buy the windows.

Select the most appropriate answer form the choices below. Choose **ONE** option.

	Tick
Tell the double-glazing company to contact the employee direct as you cannot give out the required information	
Give out the information	
Ask for more information, and then give the double-glazing company the information they want	

 Activity 2

Below is a list of organisations who may request information about an employee. Tick the box you think most likely to apply.

Options	Permission needed from employee	Permission not needed from employee
Mortgage company	✓	
Partner of employee		
HMRC		
Police, if they have a warrant from the courts authorising release of information		
Police, if they do not have a warrant from the courts authorising release of information		
New employer		

1.3 Amendments to information

An employee's personal circumstances can sometimes change. Some changes, such as a change of address or change of name, are known by the employee and the employee should notify the payroll in writing of any amendments.

Pay rises, bonuses and other additions to pay have to be authorised by a senior manager before changes can be made.

An employee's timesheet must be authorised by the employee's direct supervisor or manager who has authority to assign the work to the employee. Annual leave, and permission to take a day off should also be authorised by the immediate manager or supervisor as it is that person who has to manage the workload of the team.

Other employee information, such as tax code, can only be amended on written notification by HMRC.

 Activity 3

Below is a list of amendments and the different people who can authorise the changes. Select who would typically be responsible for each amendment.

Amendments	Employee	Payroll manager	Senior manager	HMRC
Change of name				
Pay rate change				
Bonus				
Change of marital status				
Tax code change				✓
Annual leave of payroll clerk				
Authorise payroll clerk's timesheet				

1.4 Processing payroll – employee information

There is a minimum amount of employee personal data required in order to process the payroll:

- National insurance number (NINO)
- Full name
- Date of birth
- Gender
- Address
- UK postcode
- Payroll number (if applicable)

This is needed to identify the employee and ensure that all the deductions made (PAYE and NIC) are allocated against the employee who paid them.

The following employee pay details will also be needed:

- Taxable pay
- Deductions
- Net pay

The above should be for the pay period **and** totals for the tax year.

1.5 Processing payroll – employer information

Employer information that must be submitted to HMRC in order to process the payroll is:

- Accounts Office reference number
- All payments and deductions made
- Current tax year.
- Employer PAYE reference
- HMRC office number

All the above information has to be submitted to HMRC on a FPS (Full Payment Submission) every time your payroll process is run and deductions made from employee's pay.

 Definition

Full Payment Submission is an electronic report that contains all the PAYE, NI contributions and student loan contributions paid by the employees and employer, and notifies HMRC of the total tax liability.

The FPS also notifies HMRC of any employees joining and leaving the organisation.

The FPS is sent on or before the employees' pay day.

 Activity 4

Below is a list of employee information, some of which it is a legal requirement to appear on the FPS.

Tick the items that will appear on the FPS.

	Tick
PAYE deducted this pay period	
Driving license number	
Address	
Taxable pay	
Next of kin	

Activity 5

Below is a list of employer information, some of which it is a legal requirement to appear on the FPS.

Tick the items that will appear on the FPS.

	Tick
Total payments and deductions made to each employee's pay	
Number of employees in the organisation	
Name of managing director	
Accounts Office reference number	
Employer PAYE reference	

1.6 Submitting the payroll data

As mentioned earlier in this chapter, the FPS must be sent to HMRC before or on the date the employee is paid. All information must be accurate, as, in some cases inaccurate information can cause delay to the payroll. It may also cause the FPS to be rejected, and this can have consequences for the employer – they may receive a warning or a fine from HMRC.

Payment of the amounts due to HMRC (of all the deductions made) must be made no later than 19th of the following month if paying by cheque, or 22nd of the following month if paying electronically.

For the employees, inaccurate or delayed payments can have an impact on their personal lives. So be aware that the payroll information and process must be complete, accurate and timely. It must also be paid according to the company pay policy and timescales.

 Activity 6

Payroll data should be complete, accurate and timely and staff should follow company and legislative policy.

Select the ONE most likely outcome for each scenario.

	HMRC will issue a fine or warning	The payroll may be delayed or inaccurate	No affect
There has been a power cut and the staff could not be paid on time.			
Though the staff have been paid the FPS has not been submitted to HMRC.			

Timesheets could not be signed as the Supervisor was ill			
The FPS is always submitted early			
Payroll software has the prior tax year tax and national insurance rates.			

Activity 7

Tick the True or False box according to whether the statement is correct or not.

Statement	True	False
Pay date was 31 March. HMRC is paid by cheque. The cheque must be received by 22 April		
Pay date was 31 October. HMRC is paid by cheque. The cheque must be received by 19 November		
Pay date was 30 September. HMRC is paid electronically Payment must be received by 22 October		
All electronic payroll payments to HMRC must be received by 22nd of the preceding month		
All electronic payroll payments to HMRC must be received by 22nd of the following month		

Activity 8

Staff are paid monthly. Basic pay is paid at the end of the month, overtime is paid one month in arrears (the month after the month in which the overtime is done).

Tick the box for the statements you think are correct.

Basic pay for June is received in June	
Overtime pay for June is received in June	
August pay includes basic pay for June and overtime pay for July	
August pay includes basic pay for August and overtime pay for July	
Overtime pay for November is received in December	

2 Payroll documentation

2.1 Employee documentation – the P45

When an employee leaves a place of work, they are issued with a P45 form – "Details of Employee Leaving Work". The P45 is a record of the employee's pay to date and the tax that has been deducted so far in the tax year. The P45 is given to the next employer so that the correct tax can be deducted from the employee.

On the P45 is the following information:

- The employer's PAYE reference.

- The employee's name and national insurance number.

- The date of leaving.

- Whether student loan deductions are being made and should be made by the new employer.

- The tax code at the date of leaving, and whether it operates on a week 1 or month 1 basis.

- The last entries for total pay to date and total tax due to date, and the tax week or month in which the entries were made. If the code was being operated on a week 1 or month 1 basis this should be left blank.

- Details of total pay in this employment and total tax in this employment. This should only be completed if it is different to the previous entry. (This will apply if the employee had joined this employer during the tax year, bringing with him a form P45.)

- The employee's branch and works or payroll number (if applicable).

- The employee's address.

- The employer's name, address, declaration that all the details are correct, and the date.

You should hand the P45 to the employee, retaining the part that historically was sent to HMRC (part 1). You will notify HMRC through the FPS. You do not need to send a copy of the P45 to HMRC.

Example

Here is an example of a P45:

A new employee may not be able to hand in a P45. In which case, the new employee should complete The Starter Checklist/P46 as covered in the previous chapter.

The category letter used from both P45 and Starter Checklist will dictate the Tax Code that the employee will receive pending HMRC notification.

If in any doubt ask your supervisor or manager as to which options to use.

To ensure correct up to date information, it is always good policy to ask each new employee to complete a Starter Checklist and inform HMRC of the answers on the next Full Payment Submission (FPS) cycle.

How to input these documents is covered in chapter 14.

2.2 Employee documentation – the payslip

Another important document for the employee is the payslip.

Every time an employee is paid they must be given a payslip showing the calculation of gross pay and the deductions made.

The payslip will show as a minimum the following details:

- Employer's name*
- Employer's PAYE reference
- Employee's name*
- Employee's address
- Employee's NI number
- Employee's payroll number
- Date of payment*
- Payment method (if the pay is paid in several ways the method for each payment must be disclosed)
- PAYE code
- Gross pay and how it is calculated*
- Gross pay this period for tax purposes
- Total gross pay to date for tax purposes
- Tax deducted or refunded this period*
- Total tax deducted to date
- Employee's NI contributions this period*
- Total employee's NI contributions to date
- Student loan deductions*
- Other deductions*
- Net pay*.

* Compulsory information

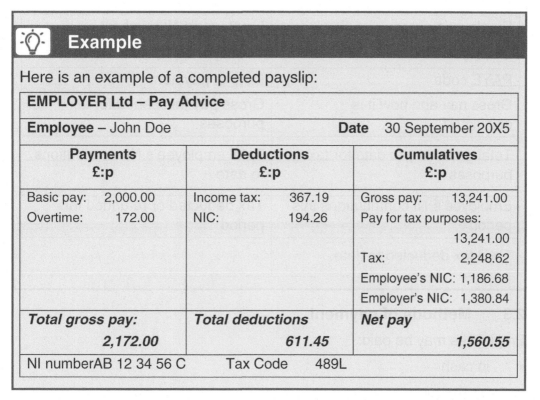

Example

Here is an example of a completed payslip:

EMPLOYER Ltd – Pay Advice		
Employee – John Doe		**Date** 30 September 20X5
Payments **£:p**	**Deductions** **£:p**	**Cumulatives** **£:p**
Basic pay: 2,000.00 Overtime: 172.00	Income tax: 367.19 NIC: 194.26	Gross pay: 13,241.00 Pay for tax purposes: 13,241.00 Tax: 2,248.62 Employee's NIC: 1,186.68 Employer's NIC: 1,380.84

Total gross pay:
          2,172.00
	Total deductions
	              611.45
		Net pay
		              1,560.55

NI numberAB 12 34 56 C	Tax Code 489L	

The payslip will normally be generated by the computer as one of the output documents.

Payslips are confidential documents and should always be distributed in sealed envelopes. Most computer systems use specially prepared stationery where the payslip is automatically sealed.

Your employer will have set procedures for distributing payslips, and this must always be followed. It may involve handing payslips to employees individually or posting them to the employee's home address. The procedure will vary with the size and type of the organisation.

It is important to ensure that payslips are always distributed within the timescale set by the organisation.

Activity 9

List five items that are legally required to appear on the payslip (not all compulsory items are here!)

1	
2	
3	
4	
5	

Employer's name	Employee's NI number
Employee's address	Employee's payroll number
PAYE code	Date of payment
Gross pay and how it is calculated	Gross pay this period for tax purposes
Total gross pay to date for tax purposes	Total employee's NI contributions to date
Employee's NI contributions this period	Tax deducted or refunded this period
Total tax deducted to date	

2.3 Methods of payment

Employees may be paid:

- in cash
- by cheque
- by bank giro credit
- by BACS, the Bankers Automated Clearing System

Where employees are paid in cash, the exact money is required. A cash analysis sheet should be used to calculate the notes and coins required for each employee, and in total.

Example

An employer pays five employees in cash. On 12 June 20X5 their net pay was:

	£
A Jones	171.65
B Smith	202.89
C Brown	52.63
D Flowers	106.34
E Davies	199.71

Show the make up of each employee's pay packet.

Solution

EMPLOYER Ltd		CASH ANALYSIS										12 June 20X5
Employee	Net pay	£20	£10	£5	£2	£1	50p	20p	10p	5p	2p	1p
A Jones	171.65	8	1	-	-	1	1	-	1	1	-	-
B Smith	202.89	10	-	-	1	-	1	1	1	1	2	-
C Brown	52.63	2	1	-	1	-	1	-	1	-	1	1
D Flowers	106.34	5	-	1	-	1	-	1	1	-	2	-
E Davies	199.71	9	1	1	2	-	1	1	-	-	-	1
Total		34	3	2	4	2	4	3	4	2	5	2
Value	733.22	680.0	30.0	10.0	8.0	2.0	2.0	.60	.40	.10	.10	.02

Some employers pay their employees by cheque. Employees should collect their pay cheques in person, or they should be sent to the employee's home address.

The cheques should always be crossed for security. This means that they can only be paid into the employee's bank account.

Even where the employer normally pays employees by bank giro credit or BACS, cheque payments may sometimes be necessary. For example an employee who leaves may receive his last payment by cheque, or an employee who joins late in a pay period may receive the first payment by cheque.

Bank giro credit payments are an easier and more secure means of payment. Employees must have bank accounts, and must provide details of their account to the payroll department.

A list of the payments to be made is sent to the bank, together with one cheque or debit authorisation for the total amount of the payments.

A BACS or bank transfer is even more secure than paying by bank giro credit because the transfers are made electronically. It is sometimes known as 'EFT' – electronic funds transfer.

The transfer may be carried out via an agency, or the employer may itself submit the data electronically to the bank (provided the appropriate computer and security systems are in place).

A further advantage is that the funds are guaranteed to arrive in the employees' bank account on the day next but one following the day on which the list of payments is despatched to the bank. The funds are cleared funds, and so are available to the employees immediately on receipt.

Activity 10

One of your employees, Edward Elgar, has requested that he be paid by cheque. This has been approved by the Payroll Manager.

Prepare the cheque. Enter the information below. Assume that it is correct.

Net pay	£1,587
Gross pay	£2,000
Income tax	£233
National insurance	£180

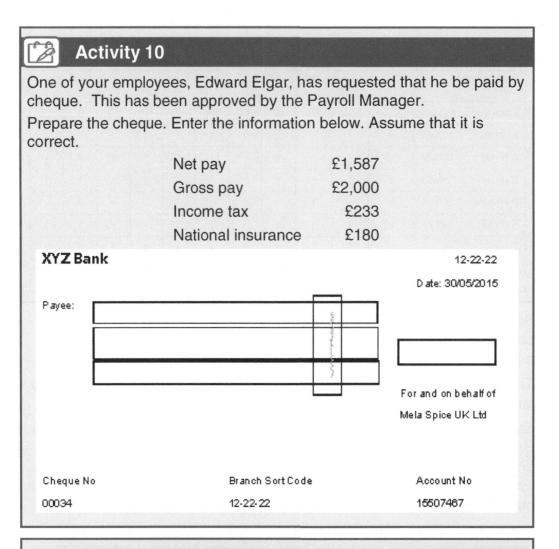

XYZ Bank 12-22-22

Date: 30/05/2015

Payee:

For and on behalf of

Mela Spice UK Ltd

Cheque No	Branch Sort Code	Account No
00034	12-22-22	15507467

Activity 10

Employer Ltd pays its employees in cash.

On 12 June 20X5 their net pay was:

F Jones   £171.65

B Davies   £202.89

Show the make up of each employee's pay packet.

EMPLOYER Ltd			CASH ANALYSIS								12 June 20x5	
Employee	Net pay	£20	£10	£5	£2	£1	50p	20p	10p	5p	2p	1p
Frankie Jones												
Benny Davies												
Total												
Value												

2.4 Employer documentation

The employer, at varying times, will receive from HMRC notification of tax code change (P9). It is on this notice that the employees tax code is held, and the employer must enter that tax code into the employee's pay details as soon as possible.

All these have a specific meaning, and when input into the payroll software will inform the system how, and how much tax to deduct.

The most common tax codes are made up as follows:

L	Entitled to
BR	All income is taxed at the basic rate. There is no personal allowance
P	For individuals between state retirement age and 74 years. They have the basic personal allowance for that age group.
T	HMRC is reviewing the tax position of the individual.
NT	No tax to be deducted.

Tax is deducted from cumulative pay. However, if the tax code is followed by **Week 1/Month 1 (also written Wk1/M/)** then, for the time being, the tax is deducted from pay this period only.

You do not need to remember what the codes mean, just where to input them.

2.5 National insurance contributions

National insurance contributions (NICs) are compulsory contributions that every employee has to make. The contributions go towards many benefits. For the employee the main benefit in which they will be interested is that of the state retirement pension. Every contribution made by an employee will contribute to the amount of pension they will receive when they retire.

The computerised payroll system computes the amount of national insurance contributions each employee makes. The contribution is a percentage of gross pay and is based on how much the employee earns in any given period. This is then deducted from gross pay (as is income tax), and the employee received the net pay.

Since the payroll system performs the calculations there is no need to go into depth as to how this is done. However, the general facts and figures around national insurance contributions that are relevant to this course are as follows:

Letter		Contribution %
A	For all employees under state retirement age	12
C	For all employees over state retirement age (they are receiving their pension, and so do NOT contribute to it.	0

For this course you are not required to make any manual calculations of NI contributions.

2.6 Employer reports

An employer needs to keep records of how much the payroll has cost the organisation, how much to pay HMRC and how much to pay each employee. There are various reports which show this, and they must be produced.

How to print these reports is shown when referring to processing pay. However, a description of what the report shows is below.

Report	Description
Update records check report	For each employee, a summary of the main elements of the pay for the current period. The report also includes grand totals for gross pay, gross for tax, tax and NI paid and net pay
Payment summary (part 1) Landscape	A detailed breakdown of pay for the current period from gross to net. The report included totals per payment period
Payment summary (part 2) Landscape	A detailed breakdown of employer's and employee's NI contributions for the current period. The report includes totals per payment period.
P11 deduction card	A detailed breakdown of the employee total pay, total tax deducted, total NI deducted.

All this information must be kept for at least three years after the end of the tax year to which they are relevant.

Answers to chapter activities

📝 Activity 1

Tell the double-glazing company to contact the employee direct as you cannot give out the required information	✓
Give out the information	
Ask for more information, and then give the double-glazing company the information they want	

📝 Activity 2

Options	Permission needed	Permission not needed
Mortgage company	✓	
Partner of employee	✓	
HMRC		✓
Police, if they have a warrant from the courts authorising release of information		✓
Police, if they do not have a warrant from the courts authorising release of information	✓	
New employer	✓	

📝 Activity 3

Amendments	Employee	Payroll manager	Senior manager	HMRC
Change of name	✓			
Pay rate change			✓	
Bonus			✓	
Change of marital status	✓			
Tax code change				✓
Annual leave of payroll clerk		✓		
Authorise payroll clerk's timesheet		✓		

Activity 4

PAYE deducted this pay period	✔
Driving license number	
Address	✔
Taxable pay	✔
Next of kin	

Activity 5

Total payments and deductions made to each employee's pay	✔
Number of employees in the organisation	
Name of managing director	
Accounts Office reference number	✔
Employer PAYE reference	✔

Activity 6

	HMRC will issue a fine or warning	The payroll may be delayed or inaccurate	Neither consequence
There has been a power cut and the staff could not be paid on time.		✔	
Though the staff have been paid the FPS has not been submitted to HMRC.	✔		
Timesheets could not be signed as the Supervisor was ill		✔	
The FPS is always submitted early			✔
Payroll software has the prior tax year tax and national insurance rates		✔	

Activity 7

Statement	True	False
Pay date was 31 March. HMRC is paid by cheque. The cheque must be received by 22 April		✓
Pay date was 31 October. HMRC is paid by cheque. The cheque must be received by 19 November	✓	
Pay date was 30 September. HMRC is paid electronically Payment must be received by 22 October	✓	
All electronic payroll payments to HMRC must be received by 22nd of the preceding month		✓
All electronic payroll payments to HMRC must be received by 22nd of the following month	✓	

Activity 8

Basic pay for June is received in June	✓
Overtime pay for June is received in June	
August pay includes basic pay for June and overtime pay for July	
August pay includes basic pay for August and overtime pay for July	✓
Overtime pay for November is received in December	✓

Activity 9

1	Employer's name
2	Date of payment
3	Gross pay and how it is calculated
4	Tax deducted or refunded this period
5	Employee's NI contributions this period

Activity 10

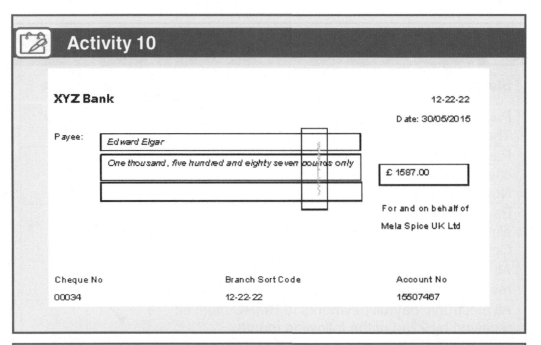

XYZ Bank		12-22-22
		Date: 30/05/2015

Payee:

Edward Elgar

One thousand, five hundred and eighty seven pounds only

£ 1587.00

For and on behalf of

Mela Spice UK Ltd

Cheque No	Branch Sort Code	Account No
00034	12-22-22	15507467

Activity 11

EMPLOYER Ltd	CASH ANALYSIS										12 June 20X5
Employee	Net pay	£20	£10	£5	£2	£1	50p	20p	10p	5p	2p	1p
Frankie Jones	171.65	8	1	-	-	1	1	-	1	1	-	-
Benny Davies	199.71	9	1	1	2	-	1	1	-	-	-	1
Total		17	2	1	2	1	2	1	1	1		1
Value	371.36	340.00	20.00	5.00	4.00	1.00	1.00	.20	.10	.05		.01

KAPLAN PUBLISHING

Spreadsheet Software

Introduction

Assessment of the unit is through a computer based project. Learners will be assessed against a set grid of marks that rewards them in line with the three learning outcomes identified below.

The following chapter provides full detail on all that students are required to do for this assessment including full coverage of the basics of setting up, formatting and using workbooks and worksheets. It also covers the Excel functions and calculations required for success at this level.

KNOWLEDGE
1 Use a spreadsheet to enter, edit and organise numerical and other data
2 Use appropriate formulas and tools to summarise spreadsheet information
3 Select and use appropriate tools and techniques to present spreadsheet information effectively

CONTENTS
1 Spreadsheet basics
2 Formatting worksheets
3 Simple calculations
4 Page presentation and printing
5 Excel functions
6 Assessment guidance

1 Spreadsheet basics

1.1 Spreadsheet Software Applications

There are many different spreadsheet applications available. Microsoft Excel is by far the most commonly used, and this Text is written for Microsoft Excel 2010.

1.2 Opening the application

There are numerous ways to open the application and the way that you do it will depend on the version of Excel that you are using and personal preference.

- Click the Windows button in the bottom left of the screen (or the Start Menu)
- Select (left click) 'All Programs'
- Select 'Microsoft Office'
- Select 'Microsoft Excel 2010'

From the bottom left hand corner of the screen:

Excel will open.

1.3 Workbooks and worksheets

> ### 🔍 Definition
>
> A **worksheet** is a single page or sheet in the spreadsheet. A new spreadsheet will have 3 of these by default (called 'Sheet1', 'Sheet2', 'Sheet3'), but this can be changed, and worksheets can be added or deleted or renamed. The term worksheet is often abbreviated to **Sheet**.
>
> A **workbook** is the spreadsheet file, made up of one or more worksheets. The default blank workbook is made up of 3 worksheets. The workbook name is the filename of the spreadsheet.

When Excel opens, a new, blank spreadsheet will be shown.

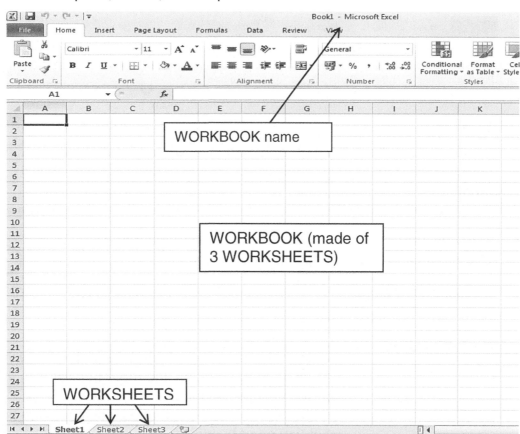

1.4 The Ribbon

The 'Ribbon' is Excel's menu system. It is made up of various tabs and buttons, allowing you access to all of Excel's features. There are many, many options within the Ribbon – the good news is that most people only use a few of them. This guide will concentrate on the key features only.

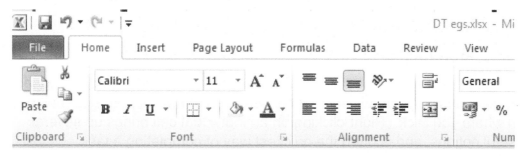

Tabs

There are usually 8 **tabs** across the top of the Ribbon – File, Home, Insert etc. and clicking on these offers different options. Sometimes more tabs appear depending on context – for example if you are editing a graph, the Chart Tools tabs appear.

Click on the name of the tab to change it, and see the different options.

This is the Insert Tab.

Buttons

The buttons on each tab perform a series of tasks – formatting, spreadsheet appearance, analysis etc. Some of them open up a new menu.

Many buttons have a small down arrow next to the name. Clicking on this opens brings up more options.

Although it seems like a lot to take in, the more you use these menu options, the more familiar with them you will become. Also, due to the way they are grouped with similar commands, you can often find what you need by looking in these menus.

Note that if you are not sure what a particular option does, hover the mouse pointer over it for a second or two and more information will be shown.

1.5 Right-click

Using the right mouse button within Excel (and most other Windows based programs) is very useful. Context-sensitive menus will appear depending on where you click. Right-clicking on an individual cell brings up several useful options, and is often the quickest way of completing a task.

1.6 Undo and Redo

Probably the most frequently used command within Excel. Undo, as the name suggests, cancels the last thing you did. The most useful thing about this is that it means you should not be afraid to experiment – if you are not sure what something does, try it. If it did not do what you wanted, undo.

KAPLAN PUBLISHING

Redo allows you to cancel an undo, if you decide that is what you did want!

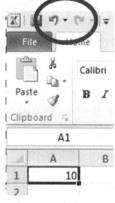

The Undo button (the left arrow) is located in the top-left corner of the file. It is always visible, whichever tab you have clicked on in the ribbon.

The Redo button (the right arrow) is greyed out as there are currently no commands to redo.

Clicking on the blue arrow will undo the last command. Clicking on the small triangle will allow you to undo more than one recent command.

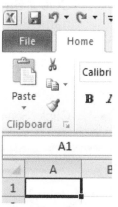

After clicking Undo, the 10 which had been typed in has gone – this has been 'undone'. Note that the redo button has now turned blue – if we click on that, the command (typing 10 into cell A1) will be 'redone'.

Remember, formatting, data entry and formula entry can all be 'undone', so if things start to look wrong, undo what you have done. If you realise you were right, simply redo!

Shortcut

- **Ctrl-z** (hold Ctrl, then press z) will undo the last command
- **Ctrl-y** will redo the last undone command

1.7 Opening a new workbook

If you wish to open a new workbook:

- Select the **File** tab
- Select '**New**'
- Select '**Blank workbook**' from Available Templates.

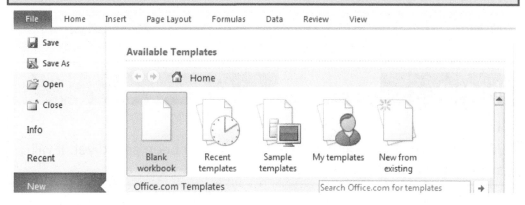

Shortcut

Ctrl-n

Opens a new workbook automatically.

1.8   Saving the workbook

Saving the workbook allows you to give it a more appropriate name, as well as keeping it for future use. To save a file:

- Select the File tab
- Select Save to save the file as it is, or Save As to give it a new name
- The 'Save As' Dialogue Box will open. Navigate to the directory in which you wish to save the file
- Type the name of the spreadsheet in the File name box
- Click 'Save'.

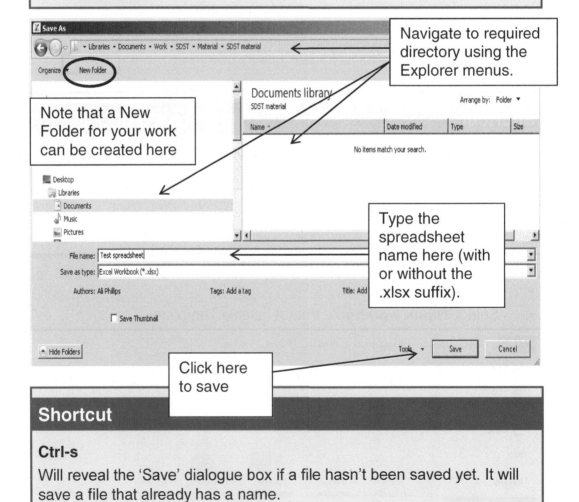

Navigate to required directory using the Explorer menus.

Note that a New Folder for your work can be created here

Type the spreadsheet name here (with or without the .xlsx suffix).

Click here to save

Shortcut

Ctrl-s

Will reveal the 'Save' dialogue box if a file hasn't been saved yet. It will save a file that already has a name.

1.9 Opening an existing workbook

To work on a spreadsheet that has been previously saved, open Excel as before, then:

- Click the 'File' tab in the top left of the screen
- Click the 'Open' button
- Navigate to the file you wish to open
- Click the 'Open' button, or double click on the file.

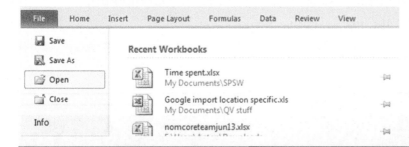

Notice that recently used workbooks can also be selected without having to use the 'Open' button.

Shortcut

Ctrl-o

Will reveal the 'Open' dialogue box.

1.10 Closing the workbook

Having saved your workbook you can then close it. There are 2 options:

1. Click the 'X' in the top right hand corner of the screen – the lower one of the two (the top one closes Excel completely). If you have multiple worksheets open then you get the option to close just the one you are working on.

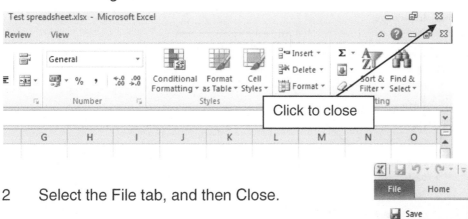

2. Select the File tab, and then Close.

If you haven't already saved the workbook you will be prompted to do so when you click 'Close'. You can then follow the procedure above.

1.11 Renaming the workbook

To 'Rename' your workbook you could:

(a) Save the file using a different name, using Save As (note that this will keep a copy of the original file)

(b) Or with the workbook closed

- Locate the File using Windows Explorer (or My Computer)

- Right Click on the file and select 'Rename'

- Type the new name

- Press Enter.

Shortcut

F2
Renames a file in Windows Explorer.

Shortcut

On your keyboard you have a key with the 'Windows' icon
Press '**Windows-e**' to open Windows Explorer.

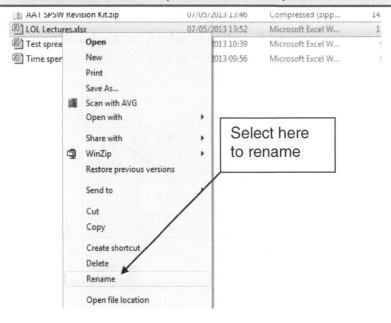

Select here to rename

KAPLAN PUBLISHING

1.12 Renaming a worksheet

To 'Rename' a particular **worksheet** within a **workbook** you should do the following:

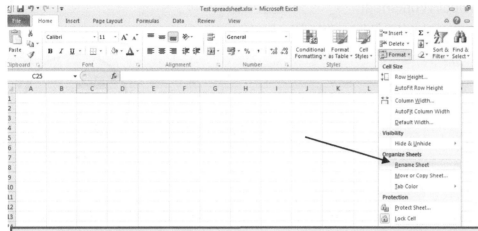

- Select the Home tab
- Select Format
- Select Rename Sheet
- The Sheet name will then be highlighted. Type the new name to overwrite it.

OR

- Right click on the worksheet name at the bottom of the page
- Select rename
- The Sheet name will then be highlighted. Type the new name to overwrite it.

Or

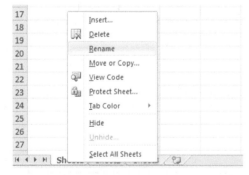

The quickest way is just to **DOUBLE CLICK** on the sheet name to edit it.

1.13 Adding worksheets

There are two ways to achieve this, as with renaming a worksheet:

- Select the Home tab
- Select Insert
- Select Insert Sheet
- A new sheet will be added

OR

- Right click on the worksheet name at the bottom of the page
- Select Insert
- Select Worksheet
- A new sheet will be added

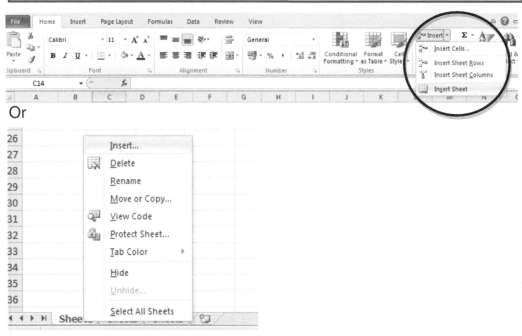

Or

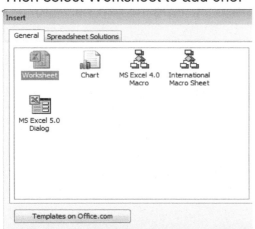

Then select Worksheet to add one.

Shortcut

Shift+F11
Inserts a new worksheet

1.14 Deleting worksheets

Similar method to adding worksheets:

- Select the Home tab
- Select Delete
- Select Delete Sheet
- A warning will show – click Delete
- The current sheet will be deleted.

OR

- Right click on the worksheet name at the bottom of the page
- Select Delete
- A warning will show – click Delete
- The current sheet will be deleted.

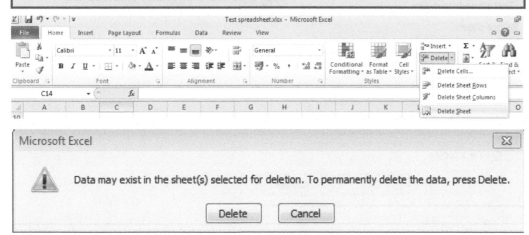

Warning message – take note, once a sheet has been deleted this action **CANNOT** be undone.

1.15 Moving/Copying worksheets

The order of your worksheets can easily be changed in Excel, and you can also quickly copy a sheet to get a duplicate version.

- Select Format on the Home tab
- Select Move or Copy Sheet
- A Dialogue box will open – select where you want the current sheet to be located
- Click OK when complete.

OR

- Right click on the worksheet name at the bottom of the page
- Select Move or Copy
- The same dialogue box will be displayed.

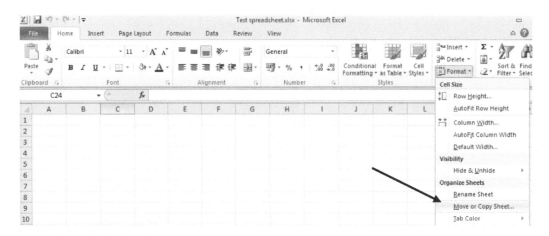

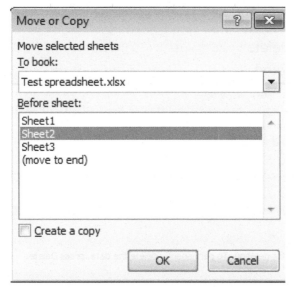

Shortcut

Simply **LEFT CLICK** and **HOLD** the button down while pointing at the sheet name – then **DRAG** the sheet to the position you require

Note that a worksheet can be moved within the existing workbook, or to another workbook you have open. To copy a worksheet, follow exactly the same steps, but tick the 'Create a copy' box before clicking OK.

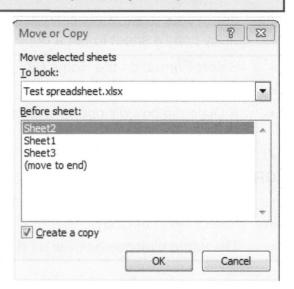

KAPLAN PUBLISHING

Shortcut

If using the **LEFT-CLICK** and **DRAG** approach above, hold down **Ctrl** before releasing the mouse button. A + will appear by the mouse pointer, and a copy made of the worksheet.

1.16   Spreadsheet structure

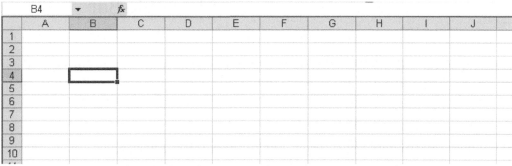

The spreadsheet (worksheet) shown above is made up of 'Rows', 'Columns' and 'Cells:

- The 'Rows' are numbered down the left hand-side from 1 onwards.
- The 'Columns' are lettered along the top from A onwards.
- The 'Cells' are the junction of columns and rows [example cell A1 is the junction of Column A and Row 1].
- The 'Active' cell is where you are be able to enter data and is highlighted with a bold border [See B4 above]. Both the column letter and the row number are also highlighted.

Shortcut

Ctrl-Home takes you to cell A1.

Ctrl-End takes you to the cell furthest into the worksheet that has been active (even if the content has been removed).

1.17   Entering data into your worksheet

Selecting cells

To select a cell, left-click on the cell you wish to select. This is now the Active Cell. The value or formula in the Active Cell will be shown in the Formula Bar, and the Cell Reference will be shown in the Name Box.

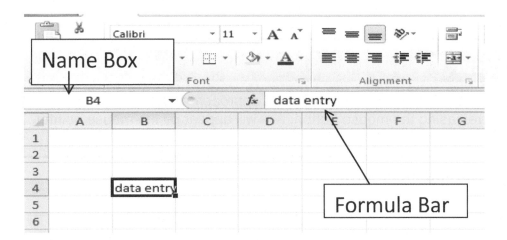

You can also change the selection by using the arrow keys to move the Active Cell Box around the screen until you reach the cell you require, or by typing the cell you require into the Name Box and pressing 'Enter'.

Selecting multiple cells

Selecting several cells at once is easiest using the mouse.

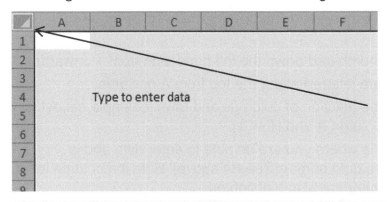

- Using the mouse, **Left-Click** on a cell to select it, but **HOLD DOWN** the mouse button
- **DRAG** the mouse pointer to select neighbouring cells.

If you wish to select non-contiguous (not neighbouring) cells, press the Ctrl key while selecting individual cells.

To select **ALL** cells in a worksheet, click on the box in the top-left of the sheet.

Cell ranges

As we have seen, each cell in Excel has a name (A1, B7 etc). If you select multiple cells, this is a **RANGE** of cells. If you select 2 separate cells, for example C2 and E5, the cells would be separated by a comma, so this would be displayed as **(C2, E5)**. If, as is more common, a **BLOCK** of cells is selected, these are displayed as:

(Top left cell:Bottom right cell)

For example:

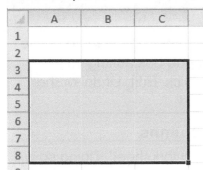

To refer to the cells selected, we would enter **(A3:C8)**.

This notation becomes important when we deal with functions later.

Entering data

To enter data into the active cell, simply type the data required into the cell – either numeric or text. This will overwrite any existing data.

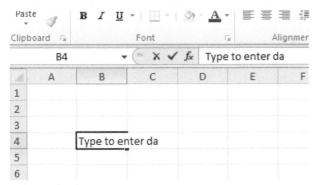

As you type, the data will be displayed on the spreadsheet itself and within the Formula Bar.

1.18   Editing and deleting cell content

Editing existing data

If a cell already contains data and you wish to edit it without overwriting, there are two ways to do this, via the Formula Bar or directly in the cell:

> • **Double Click** on a cell to edit it
>
> Or
>
> • With the cell selected, **Left-click** in the **Formula Bar** to edit its contents.

Shortcut

Press **F2** to edit the Active cell

Deleting data

To **delete** cell content you can do the following

1   Go to the cell you wish to delete. Press the delete key. You can highlight multiple cells and delete in the same way.

2   'Right-Click' in the active cell and then 'Left-Click' **clear contents.** You can highlight multiple adjacent cells and delete in the same way.

CAUTION!!!

If you 'Right-Click' and then click 'delete' Excel thinks you want to delete the cells completely. You will be offered a dialogue box asking you which way you want to shift the cells. You can click 'Edit, Undo' or the undo icon on the toolbar if you change your mind.

1.19   Inserting and deleting rows and columns

You can insert both rows and columns into your 'Worksheet'. Doing so will not increase or decrease the number of rows and columns in your worksheet. Excel will merely insert a blank row(s) or column(s) and shift the other rows or columns down/right. Excel cannot insert if the last row or column are in use. You would need to delete a row or column from elsewhere first.

To add a row to your worksheet

- Select the **'Home'** tab
- Select **'Insert'**
- Select **'Insert Sheet Rows'**

A row will be inserted, and the row with the Active Cell in it will be shifted **DOWN**.

To add a column to your worksheet

- Select the **'Home'** tab
- Select **'Insert'**
- Select **'Insert Sheet Columns'**

A column will be inserted, and the column with the Active Cell in it will be shifted **RIGHT**.

Shortcut

'Right-Click' the row number or column letter where you wish to insert, then click **'Insert'**

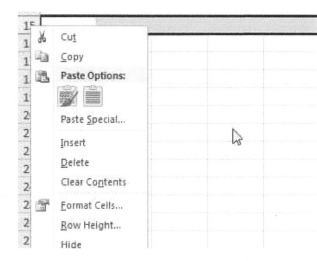

Right clicking on the **'15'** brings up this menu – select Insert to insert a row here.

To delete a row from your worksheet

- Select the **'Home'** tab
- Select **'Delete'**
- Select **'Delete Sheet Rows'**

The data in the row will be deleted, and the rows underneath shifted **UP**

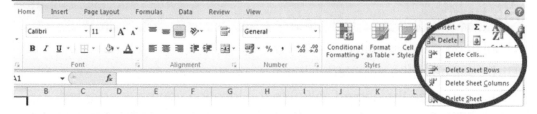

To delete a column from your worksheet

- Select the **'Home'** tab
- Select **'Delete'**
- Select **'Delete Sheet Columns'**

The data in the column will be deleted, and the columns underneath shifted **UP**

Shortcut

'Right-Click' the row number(s) or column letter(s) you wish to delete, then click **'Delete'**

1.20 Copy, Cut, Paste and AutoFill

Copy and paste

Excel allows you to copy data from the 'Active Cell(s)' to other cells.

- Click in the active cell(s)
- Select the **'Home'** tab
- Press the **'Copy'** button
- Select the cell (or cells) where you wish to copy to
- Press the **'Paste'** button

Copy and paste are together on the Ribbon

Shortcut

'**Right-Click**' the 'Active Cell(s)'. Click '**Copy**'.

Select the cell(s) where you wish to copy to.

'**Right-Click**' and then click '**Paste**'.

Shortcut

Highlight the active cells.

Ctrl-c will copy the selected cell(s)

Ctrl-v will paste the copied cell(s) to the location you have selected

Cut and paste

Excel allows you to move data from the 'Active Cell(s)' to other cells.

- Click in the active cell(s)
- Select the **'Home'** tab
- Press the **'Cut'** button
- Select the cell (or cells) where you wish to move to
- Press the **'Paste'** button

Shortcut

'**Right-Click**' the 'Active Cell(s)'. Click '**Cut**'.

Select the cell(s) where you wish to copy to.

'**Right-Click**' and then click '**Paste**'.

Shortcut

Highlight the active cells.

Ctrl-x will copy the selected cell(s)

Ctrl-v will paste the copied cell(s) to the location you have selected

---

AutoFill

The AutoFill tool is an incredibly useful feature within Excel. In the main it is used to quickly copy data into neighbouring cells, but it has several other uses that can save time and effort.

To copy a cell's contents into adjacent cells, hover the mouse pointer over the **bottom right** of the cell. The mouse pointer should change from a fat cross (⊕) to a normal cross.

Once the pointer has changed as shown, **left click** and **drag** the mouse in the direction you wish to copy the information.

Release the mouse button to complete the fill.

Autofill becomes especially useful when copying formulas (see later), and can also be used to save time when typing out common lists, such as days of the week, or repetitive sequences.

Here, 'Jan' has been typed into cell A1. Autofill has been used to 'drag' the cell down for 12 rows. You can see a pop up over B13 there's a box saying 'Dec' – this is telling us that the Autofill is going to put 'Dec' in cell A12 – the last cell in the fill.

The Autofill is complete. Note that if cell A1 was 'January', the other cells would be populated with the full month name too.

Days of the week are another common autofill.

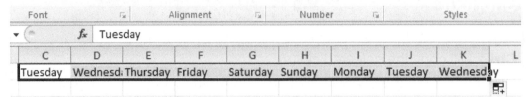

You can also autofill sequences of numbers. To do this you need to have at least the first 2 numbers of the sequence. Highlight both cells and then 'drag' the cells down.

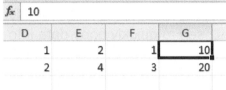

AutoFill completes the sequence.

1.21 Paste Special

There is another function 'Paste Special'. This allows you to paste different aspects of what could be contained in a cell.

> - **Copy** the cell(s) you wish to Paste
> - **Select** the destination cell(s)
> - **Left-click** the down arrow underneath the **Paste** button on the **Home** tab
> - Select **Paste Special**

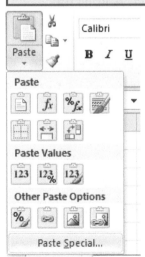

Here you can either select Paste Special, or one of the buttons shown to paste certain features only. Hover over each button to see what they do – a very commonly used one in Paste Values, which removes any formulas and just pastes the cell values.

Shortcut

Ctrl-c to copy the cells
Ctrl-Alt-v to paste special

The Paste Special menu gives all of the options available:

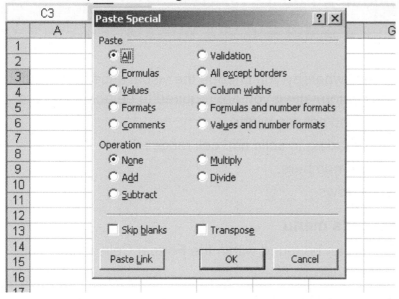

(i)   **'All'** pastes content, formula and formatting but it will not alter column width.

(ii)   **'Formulas'** pastes the formula from the cell(s) to the new location, without affecting the formatting of the destination cell.

(iii)   **'Values'** pastes the value of a cell and not the formula that may have created the value.

(iv)   **'Formats'** pastes any formatting that you might have carried out to the new cell(s). This includes cell shading, borders and number formats, but not column width.

(v)   **'Comments'** pastes any comments that have been entered into a cell to the new location. **'Comments'** allow you to write a note about a particular cell for you – and others – to see.

Once you have written your comment you will be able to delete and/or hide it by 'Right-Clicking' again in the 'Active Cell'.

You will also note that part of the 'Paste-Special' dialogue box allows you to carry out operations. For example the **'add'** operation will add the value of the 'Active Cell' to the value of the cell(s) that you are pasting to. It will add formula outcomes to values and it will also add formulas to formulas.

The last part of the 'Paste-Special' dialogue box allows two other actions

(i)   **'Skip Blanks'** ignores the content –formatting etc – of a cell with no data in it. However, it does maintain the gaps between non-adjacent cells.

(ii)   **'Transpose'** is a useful tool for pasting the content of a column into a row, and vice-versa.

2 Formatting worksheets

2.1   Introduction

Formatting is a process whereby you change the visual aspects of your worksheet. The types of formatting you are required to be able to do are:

1   Adjust row height and column width.

2   Add borders and shading to cells and cell ranges.

3   Formatting text and numbers.

4   Hide columns and rows.

2.2   The format cells menu

Most formatting options can be found within the Format Cells menu. To view the Format Cells menu:

> - Select the cell(s) you wish to format
> - In the **Home** menu, select **Format Cells**
> **OR**
> - **Right-Click** on the cell(s) to format
> - Select Format Cells

Shortcut

Press **Ctrl-1** to bring up the format cells menu.

The **Format Cells** menu has several options, as summarised below:

Number	Changes number formats, for example the number of decimal places, currency type or percentages.
Alignment	Allows adjustment of where data is shown within a cell for example left or right alignment, and merging cells together.
Font	Appearance and size of text, along with special features like bold and underline.
Border	Affects the cell itself, rather than the data within – place lines of varying size and colours around the cell.
Fill	Colour the cell in various shades and patterns.
Protection	Affects whether a cell can be edited (dealt with later).

To Exit the menu, click OK to accept changes, or Cancel to reject them.

2.3 Number formats

Although the name implies that this affects numbers, this option will change the way information within all selected cells will be displayed. Its primary use is to display numeric information in a user-friendly fashion.

General

The default format is 'General', where no special formatting will apply.

50
15.6
1005
-516
text
text and 2432

This sample data shows how Excel displays numbers and text by default – with no special formatting.

Number

This format gives more options on how to display numbers. The options are number of decimal places, whether to separate thousands with a comma, and how to display negative numbers:

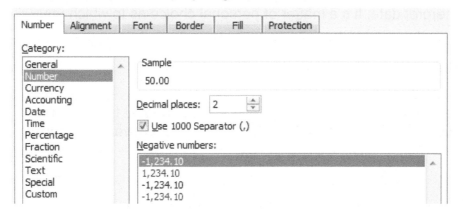

The Sample window shows what the cell will look like with the current options selected. The 1000 separator is an excellent way of making numeric data easier to read. The negative number option can be used to display negative numbers as red, with or without a minus sign.

The same information now formatted as a Number. Note that the text information in the bottom two cells is unchanged – even though there is a number in the final cell, Excel recognises it as text only, and will not format the number separately (this can be done, but is beyond the scope of the syllabus).

50.00
15.60
1,005.00
-516.00
text
text and 2432

Currency

This is very similar to **Number**, with the added option of putting a currency symbol at the front of the number:

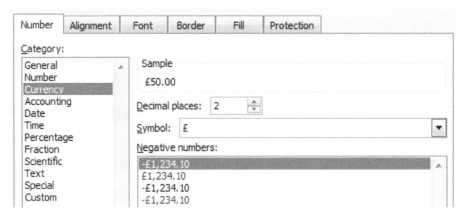

The only difference is the "£" sign at the front of the numbers.

£50.00
£15.60
£1,005.00
-£516.00
text
text and 2432

Accounting

This is very similar to **Currency**, but decimal points and currency symbols will be lined up in a column, potentially making it easier to interpret data. It's a matter of personal choice as to which you prefer.

Percentage

This enables numbers to be displayed with a '%' symbol at the end, and also multiplies the value in the cell by 100 – this will be covered in more detail later.

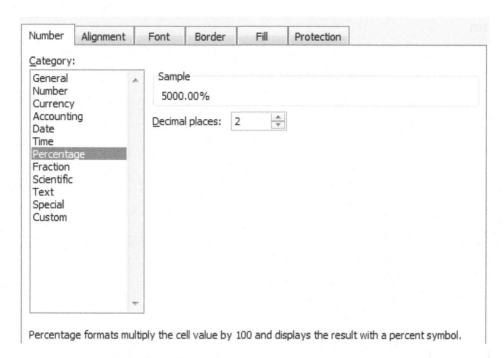

Percentage formats multiply the cell value by 100 and displays the result with a percent symbol.

If 0.1 is typed in a cell and percentage formatting is applied then this will be changed to 10%. 0.5 will be changed to 50%. The % format will come in very useful later on.

0.1
10%
0.5
50%

Date

The **Date** format is used to display dates in various different ways. The best thing to do is type the date in you wish to use, and then select the different options until you find the one you want:

If you type something that looks like a date into Excel, it will convert it to the default date format once Enter is pressed.

23-11-78

Default format is dd/mm/yyyy   23/11/1978

Choosing the appropriate option will display the date as required.

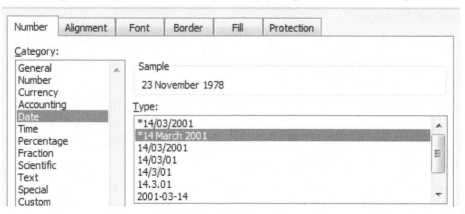

Custom

In the **custom** number list there are a number of formats that can be adapted to create the formatting required.

In the option highlighted above -2345.68 would be (in red):   -2,346

#,##0;[Red]-#,##0, formats numbers to have no decimal places and negative numbers shown in red with a minus sign in front.

You can change this to use brackets instead of the minus sign:

Type:

#,##0;[Red](#,##0

General

The value now looks like: (2,346)

You can also change the colour if required to Black, Green, White, Blue, Magenta, Yellow, or Cyan or keep it as Red, by changing the word in square brackets [ ].

It is possible to use custom number formats to actually hide the content of a cell[s]. For example in the sheet below you can see the salaries of Directors P, Q and R. For the sake of confidentiality it might be considered best to hide individual figures but keep the total visible.

This can be achieved by highlighting the figures you want to hide and then creating the custom number format as below to hide the content.

Three semi-colons ;;; followed by OK will hide the contents of cells

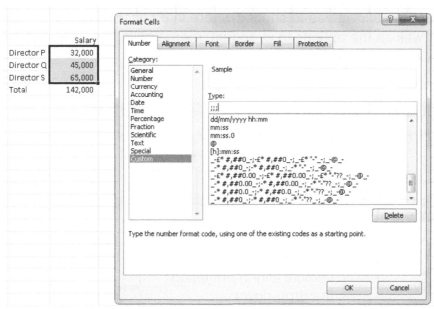

The individual salaries are now hidden from view on the worksheet but if the individual cells are clicked into the values still show in the formula bar.

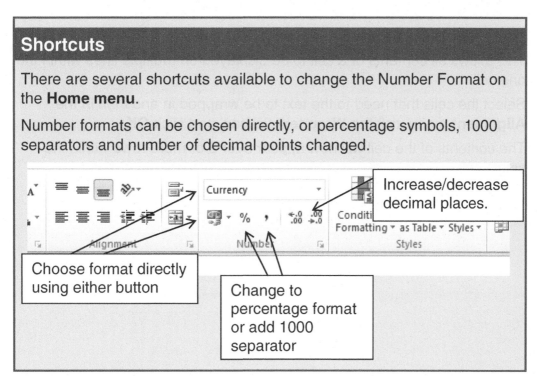

Shortcuts

There are several shortcuts available to change the Number Format on the **Home menu**.

Number formats can be chosen directly, or percentage symbols, 1000 separators and number of decimal points changed.

Increase/decrease decimal places.

Choose format directly using either button

Change to percentage format or add 1000 separator

2.4 Alignment

The **Alignment** tab allows you to choose where in a cell text will be displayed, as well as the options to wrap text, merge cells, shrink text to fit in cells and also adjust orientation of the text in a cell.

Text alignment

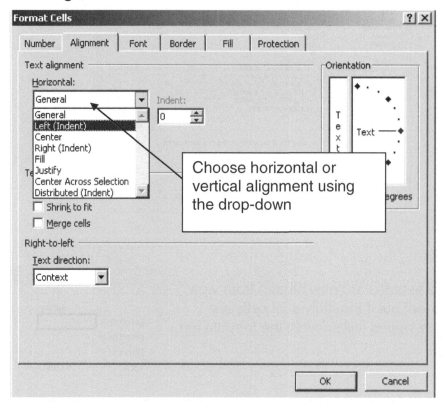

Wrap text

This allows all contents of a cell to be displayed on multiple lines within the one cell.

Select the cells that need to the text to be wrapped in and then in the **Alignment** menu, tick the **Wrap text** tickbox, and click **OK**.

The contents of the cell will now appear over 2 or more rows within the single cell.

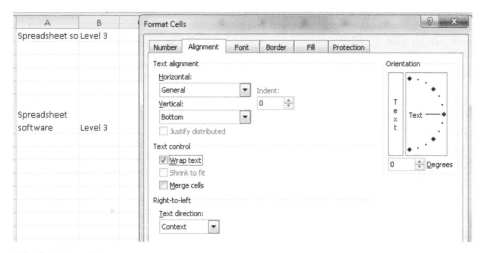

Shrink to fit

An alternative to wrapping the text is to decrease the size of the text to fit in the cell. Again select the cell that needs adjusting and click in the **Shrink to fit** tickbox and click **OK**.

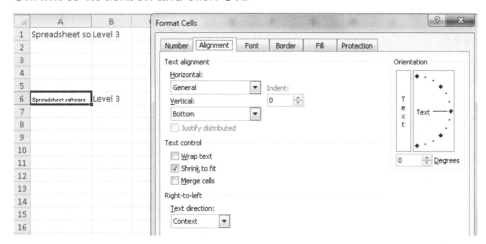

Merge cells

Merging cells joins them together so Excel treats them as one cell. This can be useful for headings that run over more than one column, for example, or if you wish to create a heading across a whole page.

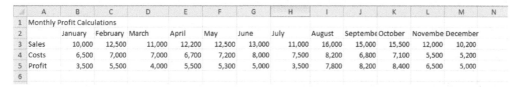

The heading for this data would look nicer if it was centred across the columns. This can be done firstly by merging the cells, then by centering.

First, **select** the **cells** you wish to merge:

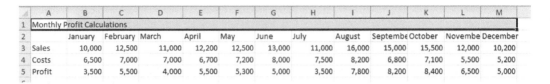

	A	B	C	D	E	F	G	H	I	J	K	L	M
1	Monthly Profit Calculations												
2		January	February	March	April	May	June	July	August	September	October	November	December
3	Sales	10,000	12,500	11,000	12,200	12,500	13,000	11,000	16,000	15,000	15,500	12,000	10,200
4	Costs	6,500	7,000	7,000	6,700	7,200	8,000	7,500	8,200	6,800	7,100	5,500	5,200
5	Profit	3,500	5,500	4,000	5,500	5,300	5,000	3,500	7,800	8,200	8,400	6,500	5,000

In the **Alignment** menu, tick the **Merge Cells** tickbox, and click **OK**. The cells will now be treated as one big cell.

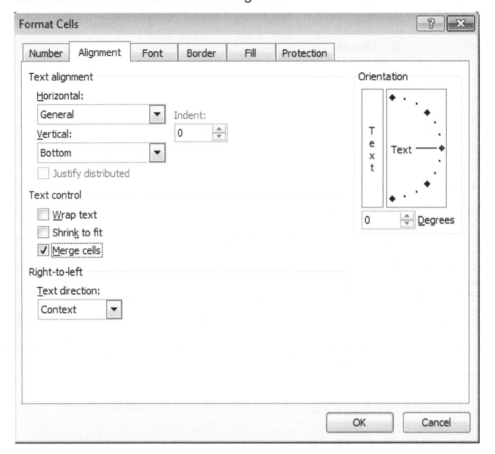

	A	B	C	D	E	F	G	H	I	J	K	L	M
1	Monthly Profit Calculations												
2		January	February	March	April	May	June	July	August	September	October	November	December
3	Sales	10,000	12,500	11,000	12,200	12,500	13,000	11,000	16,000	15,000	15,500	12,000	10,200
4	Costs	6,500	7,000	7,000	6,700	7,200	8,000	7,500	8,200	6,800	7,100	5,500	5,200
5	Profit	3,500	5,500	4,000	5,500	5,300	5,000	3,500	7,800	8,200	8,400	6,500	5,000
6													

In the Alignment menu then select **Horizontal Alignment** as **Center** to show your heading in the centre of the data.

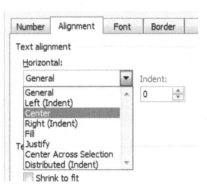

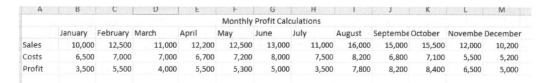

	January	February	March	April	May	June	July	August	Septembe	October	Novembe	December
					Monthly Profit Calculations							
Sales	10,000	12,500	11,000	12,200	12,500	13,000	11,000	16,000	15,000	15,500	12,000	10,200
Costs	6,500	7,000	7,000	6,700	7,200	8,000	7,500	8,200	6,800	7,100	5,500	5,200
Profit	3,500	5,500	4,000	5,500	5,300	5,000	3,500	7,800	8,200	8,400	6,500	5,000

Orientation

Using orientation allows you to rotate the text in a cell to a diagonal angle or vertical orientation. This is often useful for labelling columns that are narrow.

As with the other alignment formatting, highlight the text that needs the orientation changed and choose the degree of angle you require:

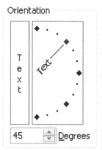

Shortcuts

Home tab, alignment section:

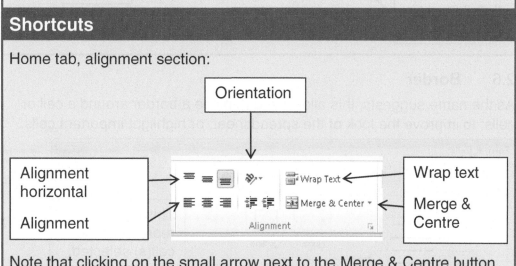

Note that clicking on the small arrow next to the Merge & Centre button also gives you options to merge/unmerge cells without using the Format Cells menu.

2.5 Font

This is used to change the font type, size, and colour and to add effects to the text – the options are fairly self-explanatory:

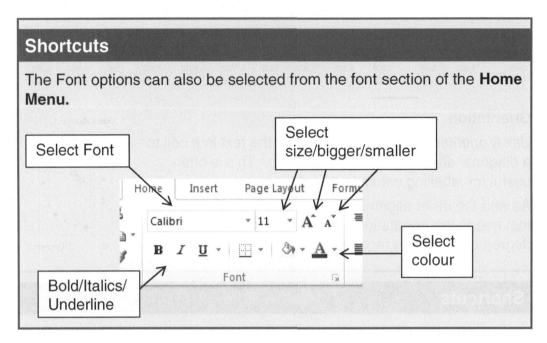

Shortcuts

The Font options can also be selected from the font section of the **Home Menu.**

Select Font

Select size/bigger/smaller

Select colour

Bold/Italics/ Underline

2.6 Border

As the name suggests, this allows you to place a border around a cell or cells, to improve the look of the spreadsheet, or highlight important cells.

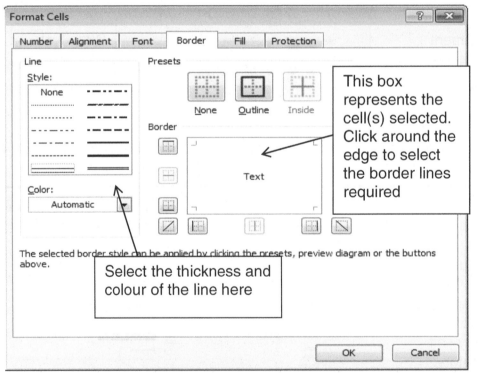

This box represents the cell(s) selected. Click around the edge to select the border lines required

Select the thickness and colour of the line here

If several cells are selected, the same borders will be applied to each:

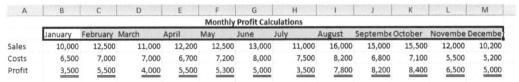

	A	B	C	D	E	F	G	H	I	J	K	L	M
		Monthly Profit Calculations											
		January	February	March	April	May	June	July	August	Septembe	October	Novembe	Decembe
Sales		10,000	12,500	11,000	12,200	12,500	13,000	11,000	16,000	15,000	15,500	12,000	10,200
Costs		6,500	7,000	7,000	6,700	7,200	8,000	7,500	8,200	6,800	7,100	5,500	5,200
Profit		3,500	5,500	4,000	5,500	5,300	5,000	3,500	7,800	8,200	8,400	6,500	5,000

KAPLAN PUBLISHING

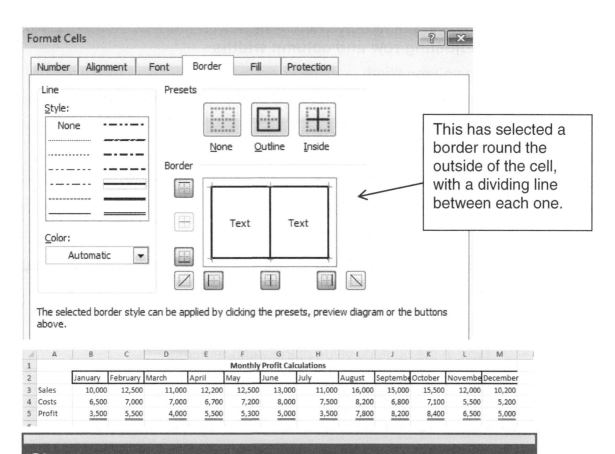

The appropriate border can be selected directly from here.

Shortcut

Borders can be applied directly using the **borders** button in the **Home Menu**

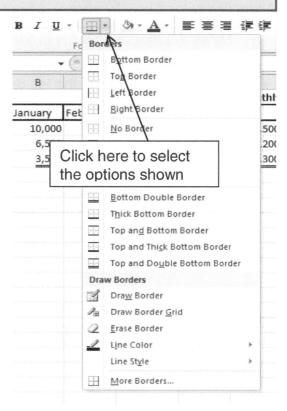

2.7 Adjusting row and column widths

Adjusting column width

You may need to adjust column widths so that all of your data is shown. For example in the screenshot below, columns J, L and M are not wide enough to display the month properly.

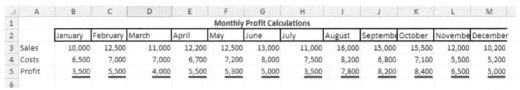

	A	B	C	D	E	F	G	H	I	J	K	L	M
1							Monthly Profit Calculations						
2		January	February	March	April	May	June	July	August	Septembe	October	Novembe	December
3	Sales	10,000	12,500	11,000	12,200	12,500	13,000	11,000	16,000	15,000	15,500	12,000	10,200
4	Costs	6,500	7,000	7,000	6,700	7,200	8,000	7,500	8,200	6,800	7,100	5,500	5,200
5	Profit	3,500	5,500	4,000	5,500	5,300	5,000	3,500	7,800	8,200	8,400	6,500	5,000
6													

There are several ways to adjust the column width.

> - Select the Column or Columns you wish to change the width of
> - In the **'Home Menu'**, select **Format** (in the **Cells** section)
> - Select Column Width
> - Type in the numeric value of the width required.

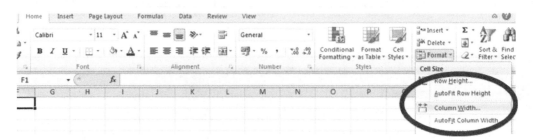

Alternatively (and usually easier), adjust the columns visually as follows:

> - Hover the mouse over the dividing line between two columns. The mouse pointer will change to ✛
> - **Left click** and **drag** to the left or right to adjust the width as required
> - Release the mouse button to accept the new width.

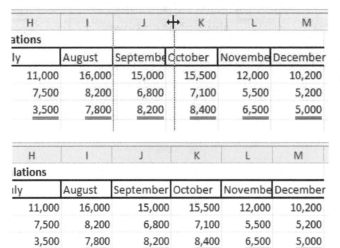

Drag the mouse to the left or right to adjust the column width.

Once the mouse button is released, the column will be the correct width.

KAPLAN PUBLISHING

Adjusting row height

This works in exactly the same way as adjusting column widths.

- Select the Row or Rows you wish to change the height of
- In the **'Home Menu'**, select **Format** (in the **Cells** section)
- Select Row Height
- Type in the numeric value of the width required.

Or

- Hover the mouse over the dividing line between two rows. The mouse pointer will change to ⊹
- **Left click** and **drag** up or down to adjust the height as required
- Release the mouse button to accept the new height.

2.8 Autofit

A very useful feature for setting column widths/row heights is **Autofit**. You may have seen this option when selecting a column width:

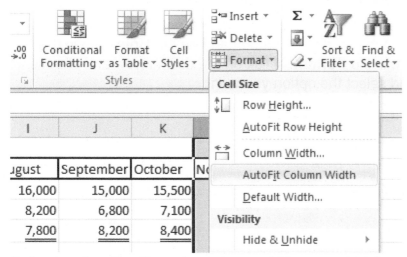

Selecting Autofit will set the column width or row height to match the largest cell in the column. This way you know that all of your data will be visible.

Shortcut

Hover the mouse pointer over the dividing line between two columns/rows and **DOUBLE CLICK** to autofit.

Autofit all rows/columns

After your work is finished, it is sensible to Autofit all rows/columns to ensure that everything is visible.

This is quickly and easily achieved as follows:

- Click the **Select All Cells** button in the top left of the spreadsheet
- Autofit **ANY** column
- Autofit **Any** row

All columns and rows will be correctly adjusted.

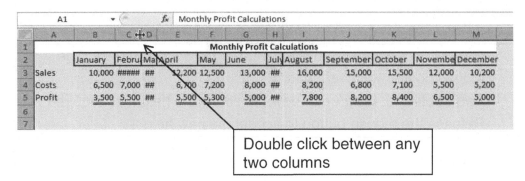

Double click between any two columns

All columns are now wide enough to display their data.

2.9 Hide and unhide columns and rows

It is possible to hide columns or rows on a worksheet. Select the column(s) or row(s) that need to be hidden and on the **Home** tab in the **Cells** section you will find **Format**. Click on the down arrow and choose **Hide & unhide** and select the option you want.

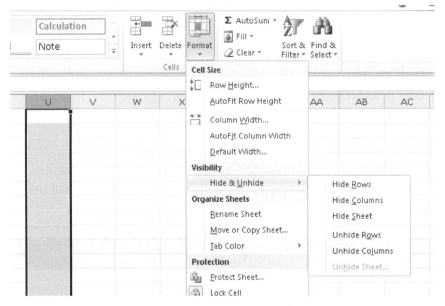

You can see if a column or row is hidden as the letter or number representing the column or row is missing.

Column U is hidden in this example:

.

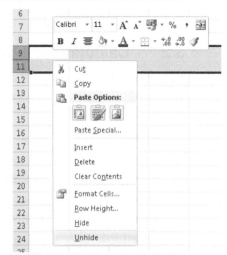

To unhide a row or column highlight the rows or columns on either side of the hidden row or column, right click on the mouse and choose unhide.

You can also unhide by using the Cells section on the home tab and Format.

3 Simple calculations

3.1 Simple calculations

We have already seen how to enter numeric and text information into cells. However, Excel's primary purpose is to manipulate the raw data through calculations and formulas. One of the main things you will use Excel for is simple calculations. The most basic (and most common) calculations are the mathematical functions addition +, subtraction -, multiplication * and divide /.

To use these, you need to tell Excel that you are using a **FUNCTION**. To do this, enter an equals sign, '=', before the calculation you require.

So, to find the answer to 3+5, type in any cell **=3+5** and press **Enter**.

As you type, the formula is displayed above, in the formula bar, as well as on the spreadsheet itself.

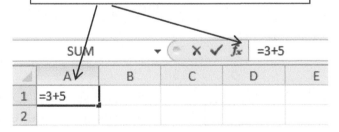

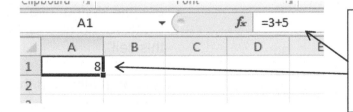

Once enter is pressed, the result of the calculation is shown on the spreadsheet, but the calculation itself is still shown in the formula bar.

Excel can be used in this way as a simple calculator by entering the calculation required, using +, -, * or /.

3.2 Calculations using existing values

Excel is particularly useful when using the values in other cells as part of your calculations. Take the following example:

	A	B	C	D
1	Name	Hourly Rate	Hours Worked	Pay
2	Srnicek	£8.60	30	
3	Watson	£8.60	20	
4	Peacock	£9.00	20	
5	Albert	£11.50	25	
6	Beresford	£10.50	30	
7	Batty	£12.00	40	
8	Lee	£13.00	42	
9	Beardsley	£14.00	35	
10	Ginola	£16.00	15	
11	Shearer	£18.00	35	
12	Ferdinand	£16.00	32	
13				

We need to find each person's pay – as the hourly rate * hours worked. You could simply type each one in, for example **'=8.60*30'** for Srnicek. This is time consuming and not much better than using pen and paper.

We can instead tell Excel to 'take the value in cell B2 and multiply by the value in cell C2'

	A	B	C	D	E
1	Name	Hourly Rate	Hours Worked	Pay	
2	Srnicek	£8.60	30	=b2	
3	Watson	£8.60	20		
4	Peacock	£9.00	20		
5	Albert	£11.50	25		
6	Beresford	£10.50	30		
7	Batty	£12.00	40		
8	Lee	£13.00	42		
9	Beardsley	£14.00	35		
10	Ginola	£16.00	15		
11	Shearer	£18.00	35		
12	Ferdinand	£16.00	32		
13					

Each cell is referred to by its column and row reference. To perform the calculation, start with the **'='** sign to show that you want to perform a calculation. Then type the cell reference of the cell you wish to use. A box will appear around the cell.

	A	B	C	D	E
1	Name	Hourly Rate	Hours Worked	Pay	
2	Srnicek	£8.60	30	=b2*c2	
3	Watson	£8.60	20		
4	Peacock	£9.00	20		
5	Albert	£11.50	25		
6	Beresford	£10.50	30		
7	Batty	£12.00	40		
8	Lee	£13.00	42		
9	Beardsley	£14.00	35		
10	Ginola	£16.00	15		
11	Shearer	£18.00	35		
12	Ferdinand	£16.00	32		
13					

Finish off the calculation as required – the cell references are just saying "use whatever number is in this cell".

Note that although the column letters are always displayed in capitals, if you enter them in lower case it does not matter.

KAPLAN PUBLISHING

	D2	▼	f_x	=B2*C2	
	A	B	C	D	
1	Name	Hourly Rate	Hours Worked	Pay	
2	Srnicek	£8.60	30	£258.00	
3	Watson	£8.60	20		
4	Peacock	£9.00	20		
5	Albert	£11.50	25		
6	Beresford	£10.50	30		
7	Batty	£12.00	40		
8	Lee	£13.00	42		
9	Beardsley	£14.00	35		
10	Ginola	£16.00	15		
11	Shearer	£18.00	35		
12	Ferdinand	£16.00	32		
13					

The result of the calculation is shown – note that the actual calculation being performed is shown in the formula bar above.

Any calculation can be performed using existing information in cells – this allows complex analysis to be undertaken relatively easily.

One huge benefit of this is that if the numbers in the data cells change, then the calculation will be updated to reflect this.

	D2	▼	f_x	=B2*C2	
	A	B	C	D	
1	Name	Hourly Rate	Hours Worked	Pay	
2	Srnicek	£8.60	25	£215.00	
3	Watson	£8.60	20		
4	Peacock	£9.00	20		
5	Albert	£11.50	25		
6	Beresford	£10.50	30		
7	Batty	£12.00	40		
8	Lee	£13.00	42		
9	Beardsley	£14.00	35		
10	Ginola	£16.00	15		
11	Shearer	£18.00	35		
12	Ferdinand	£16.00	32		

Changing the hours worked to 25 has given an updated value in the pay column.

You can use any cell within your formulas, in the same way.

	A	B	C	D	E	F
1	Name	Hourly Rate	Hours Worked	Pay	10% Bonus	
2	Srnicek	£8.60	25	£215.00	=D2*10%	
3	Watson	£8.60	20			
4	Peacock	£9.00	20			
5	Albert	£11.50	25			

Will give

	A	B	C	D	E	F
1	Name	Hourly Rate	Hours Worked	Pay	10% Bonus	
2	Srnicek	£8.60	25	£215.00	£21.50	
3	Watson	£8.60	20			
4	Peacock	£9.00	20			
5	Albert	£11.50	25			

IMPORTANT NOTE – when entering cell references into a formula, rather than typing the reference **'B2'**, you can **LEFT-CLICK** on the cell you wish to use. This way you are less likely to type the wrong cell reference.

3.3   Copying formulas

In the previous example, a formula has been entered into cells D2 and E2. We need to perform the same calculation for the other 10 staff. It would be incredibly time consuming to have to manually enter the calculation into each cell – sometimes spreadsheets can have several thousand rows!

Fortunately Excel deals with this problem very easily. Using the same copy and paste feature seen in chapter 2, we can duplicate formulas used to speed up calculations.

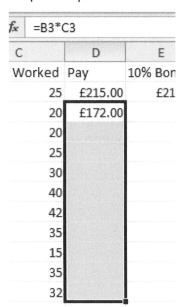

Select all the cells the formula is required in, before pasting (Ctrl-V can be used to paste the formula).

Using Autofill

Another quick way to copy formulas is to use the Autofill function explained in chapter 2. Formulas can be "dragged" up, down, left or right to copy them:

f_x	=D2*10%

C	D	E	F
rs Worked	Pay	10% Bonus	
25	£215.00	£21.50	
20	£172.00		
20	£180.00		
25	£287.50		
30	£315.00		
40	£480.00		
42	£546.00		
35	£490.00		
15	£240.00		
35	£630.00		
32	£512.00		

Hover the mouse over the bottom-right corner of the cell until the cursor changes to a +. Then drag the mouse in the direction you want the formulas copied, and let go of the mouse button.

Shortcut

Instead of dragging the Autofill box down, **DOUBLE CLICK** to automatically copy formulas down to the bottom of a block of cells.

3.4 Operators and the order of precedence

You are going to use simple mathematical functions to analyse your data but in order that you can do this you need to understand the order of priority given to each function. Excel follows the same mathematical rules. Below is a list of the order of precedence (priority). This is not the full list and later on during the course the full order of precedence will be shown.

Operator	Symbol	Order of Precedence
Brackets	()	1
Multiplication	*	2
Division	/	2
Addition	+	3
Subtraction	-	3

The order of precedence determines which operators Excel will use first in its calculations. It can be seen above that Excel will calculate a formula that contains multiplication or division before it calculates and addition or subtraction. By inserting brackets around part of a formula it forces Excel to calculate the content of the brackets first, followed by the remainder of the formula. You can have multiple sets of brackets in a formula as you will see in later chapters when you deal with more complex calculations.

Important

You may have come across the phrase BODMAS during a maths class. This stands for Brackets Off, Divide, Multiply, Add, Subtract – the order of precedence.

Continuing with the same example, we can demonstrate the order of precedence. We need to calculate the tax each person will pay, as 20% of their total pay.

To calculate this using one formula we need to add up two cells, and then multiply the total by 20%. However, due to the order of operations, care must be taken.

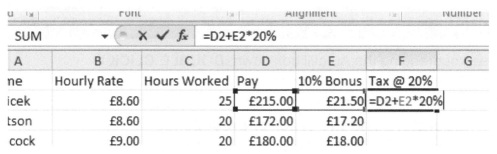

It would be tempting to type the above, as this is what we're trying to do – add up the two cells then multiply by 20%. However, Excel reads this as:

Multiply E2 by 20%, and then add on D2.

So the answer comes out as £219.30

To get round this problem, you must use brackets – put the calculation you want to happen first in brackets, to force the order as required. So:

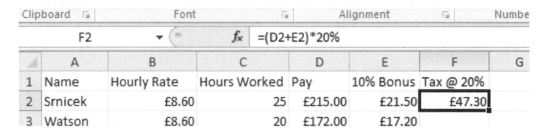

It's often worth sense checking the result of a calculation – a simple typo can give unpredictable results!

3.5 Calculation of percentage

To calculate percentages you can use:

Simple mathematical formula (note formula bar) or format the cells as percentages. The percentage format can be found on the numbers tab of 'Format Cells'.

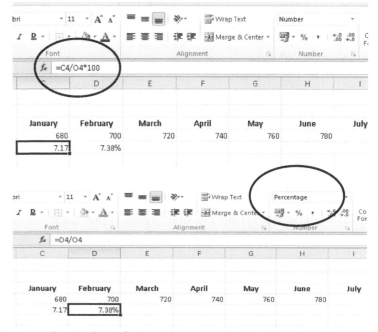

Alternatively it can be found on the format toolbar as a **%** icon.

3.6 Sorting data

Sometimes you will need to change the order of your data so that it is sorted according to your requirements. This can be performed quickly and easily, using the Sort function, located in both the **Home** tab and the **Data** tab.

To sort, select the data you wish to sort, and click on the **Sort** button.

Sort A to Z and Z to A will sort data into either ascending order or descending order. This may not be what you need, so Custom Sort is usually what is required.

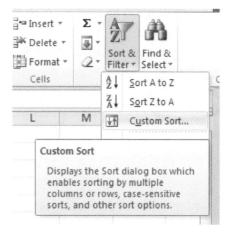

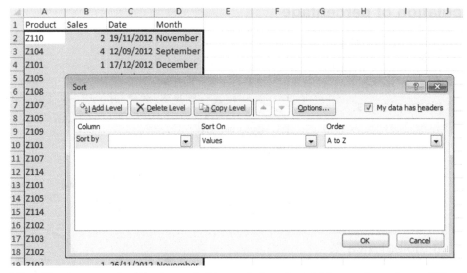

The Sort menu is displayed. Your data should have headers (titles), but if it doesn't, uncheck the check box.

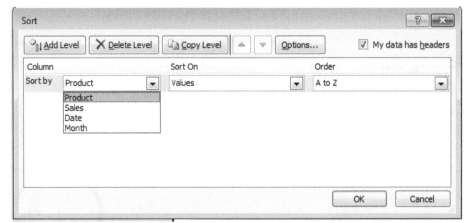

Select the column you wish to sort by, and click OK. The data will be sorted.

You may wish to sort by one column, and then another. For example, with this data set, we might want to have the transactions grouped by product, then by sales volume. This is also done with a custom sort:

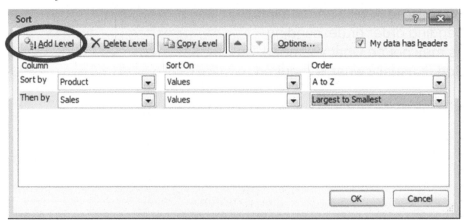

4 Page presentation and printing

4.1 Headers and footers

Headers and Footers are used to provide information in a document such as document titles, data owner, version numbers, page numbers, dates etc. **These are essential** as you may be asked to add headers or footers to your work for your SDST assessment.

To add them, use the **Insert** tab, then **Header & Footer**.

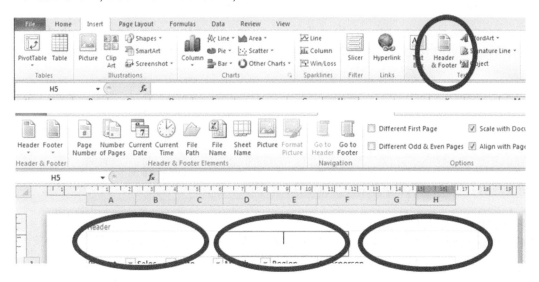

You will be taken to the Header – the page is split into three sections, where you can type in the header required. You can also select from the **Header & Footer Elements** in the Ribbon. These are fairly self-explanatory, but nothing too complicated is required for your assessment.

To edit the **Footer**, either navigate to the bottom of the page and click in the footer, or click the **Go to Footer** button.

4.2 Page Margins, Page Breaks and Orientation

All three of these options can be adjusted from the **Page Layout** tab.

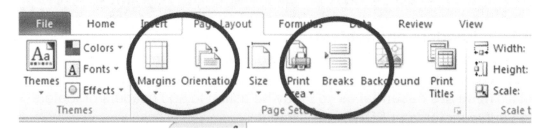

Margins

To prepare documents so that they are visually pleasing – especially for printing – you need to set the page margins. Select the **Margins** button.

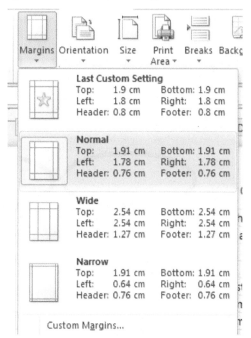

A few standard options are shown.

For more flexibility select the **Custom Margins** option.

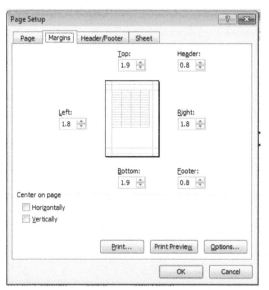

Each individual margin can be adjusted as required.

Once you have selected your margins these will be indicated on your worksheet by broken dashed lines.

Page Breaks

With your margins set, Excel will automatically insert a break in the data so that the right amount of data is displayed on a page. However, you will find that sometimes a natural break in the data is apparent and that you want to insert your own 'Page Break'. Select the **Breaks** button.

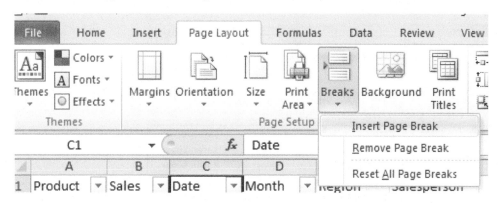

Use this to add or remove breaks as required – select the area on the sheet you would like the new page to start, and **Insert Page Break**. You can also view (and edit) page breaks in **Page Break Preview** mode. In the **View** tab, select **Page Break Preview**.

To return to normal view at any stage, select the **Normal** button just to the left of Page Break Preview.

Orientation

There are 2 ways to orientate your worksheet: Portrait or Landscape.

Excel defaults to 'Portrait', but sometimes it is better to view your document in 'Landscape'. Viewing in this way allows you to view more columns [but fewer rows] on a page.

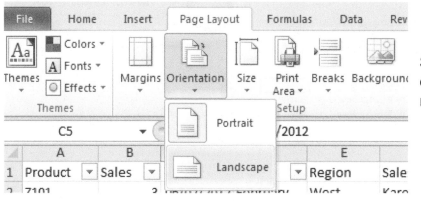

Select the orientation required.

4.3   Set Print Area

Sometimes you may want to print only part of a document. This is quite easy to do. Simply highlight the cells you wish to print, and click the **Set Print Area** button on the **Page Layout** tab.

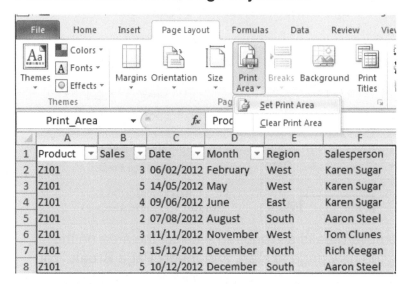

Choose **Clear Print Area** to remove this setting.

4.4   Fitting the data onto one or more sheets

One of the most useful features regarding printing is the ability to specify how many pages you want your data to appear on. Excel will then change the size of the font accordingly. Obviously this has practical limits – if you try and squeeze 1,000 lines of data onto one page, it will be impossible to read! However, it is invaluable for making your work look professional and user-friendly.

One way to do this is using the **Page Setup** menu. This is accessed by clicking on the arrow in the bottom corner of the Page Setup section of the **Page Layout** menu.

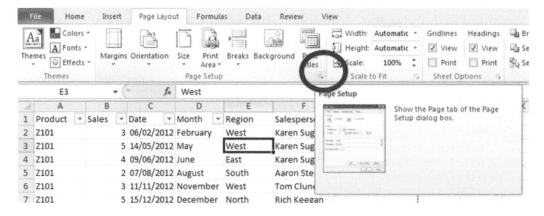

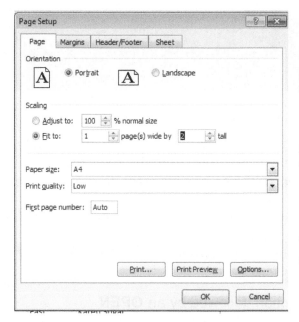

Several of the options already discussed can also be edited in this useful menu.

Use the **Fit to** option to select the number of pages required.

Use Print Preview to check that the final printout will look as desired.

4.5   Print preview and printing

Print preview has changed since Excel 2007. Rather than being a separate window view, Print Preview is found within the **File** tab, by clicking **Print**.

Having made all the adjustments to the data, format etc you will be in a position to print your document. Before you do this you should review it one more time – just to make sure. This is 'Print Preview'. When you are happy that your document is in the condition that you want it to be then you are in a position to 'Print'.

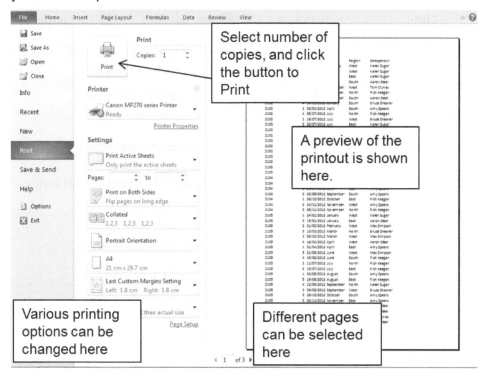

5 Excel functions

5.1 Functions

Functions.are specific words which tell Excel to perform much more than just adding up a couple of cell values. They range from the relatively simple functions like **SUM**, which we shall see in a moment, to more complicated tools.

Using a function

As mentioned at the start of the previous chapter, to enter a function into a cell, always start with an **EQUALS SIGN** first.

You then type the **NAME** of the function, followed by an **OPEN BRACKET** '('.

The **ARGUMENTS** of the function are then required. These tell Excel exactly what to do, and depend on the function required. If more than one argument is needed, they must be separated by a **COMMA**.

The function is ended with a **CLOSE BRACKET** ')'.

5.2 The Insert Function button

A great way of getting used to functions within Excel is the **Insert Function** button f_x located just above the column names.

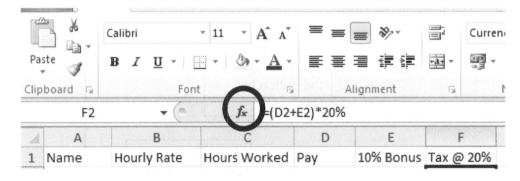

Clicking this button brings up the **Insert Function** menu, which can help work out which function is required.

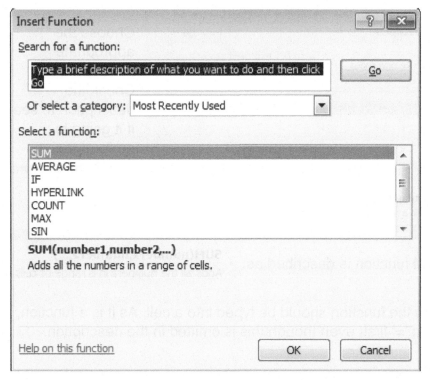

This allows you to type in – in plain English, what you require, and several options will be provided based on your search.

Using **Insert Function** also provides a more user-friendly way of entering the calculation you require, as we shall see.

5.3 SUM

SUM is probably the most commonly used function in Excel. As the name suggests, it is used to add up a selection of numbers. As discussed previously, you could use the **Insert Function** button:

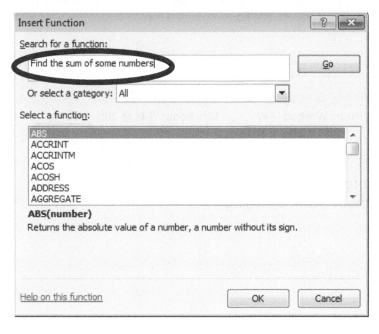

Type in what you require and click the **Go** button.

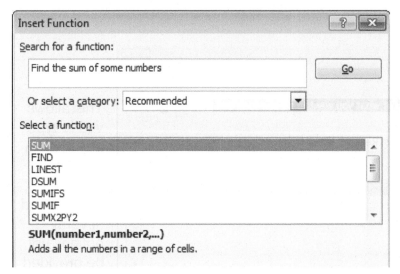

Choose the appropriate formula. Check the description to see if it going to perform the correct function.

To use the **SUM** function is described as:

SUM(number1,number2,...)
Adds all the numbers in a range of cells.

This shows how the function should be typed into a cell. As it is a function, you start with an '=' first, even though this is omitted in the description.

Number1,number2,... are the **ARGUMENTS**. In the case of SUM, these are the numbers (or cells) you wish to add. Each number you wish to add should be separated by a **comma**. For example, typing

=SUM(3,5)

will return the value 8. You can do this for any number of additions, and it is no different to using **+**, as in chapter 4.

Just like using **+**, you can also subtract cell values. In the example below, we want to find Net Pay as the sum of Pay and Bonus, less Tax; this can be done using SUM:

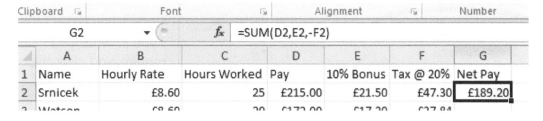

Note the minus sign before the F2 reference to indicate a subtraction. We could have done this without SUM, by typing

=D2+E2-F2

SUM is really useful when you have many numbers to add up – take the following example:

	A	B	C	D	E	F	G
1	Name	Hourly Rate	Hours Worked	Pay	10% Bonus	Tax @ 20%	Net Pay
2	Srnicek	£8.60	25	£215.00	£21.50	£47.30	£189.20
3	Watson	£8.60	20	£172.00	£17.20	£37.84	£151.36
4	Peacock	£9.00	20	£180.00	£18.00	£39.60	£158.40
5	Albert	£11.50	25	£287.50	£28.75	£63.25	£253.00
6	Beresford	£10.50	30	£315.00	£31.50	£69.30	£277.20
7	Batty	£12.00	40	£480.00	£48.00	£105.60	£422.40
8	Lee	£13.00	42	£546.00	£54.60	£120.12	£480.48
9	Beardsley	£14.00	35	£490.00	£49.00	£107.80	£431.20
10	Ginola	£16.00	15	£240.00	£24.00	£52.80	£211.20
11	Shearer	£18.00	35	£630.00	£63.00	£138.60	£554.40
12	Ferdinand	£16.00	32	£512.00	£51.20	£112.64	£450.56
13	Total						
14							

We now wish to put Total figures into columns C, D, E, F and G. Using the methods already discussed, we would either type:

=C2+C3+C4....+C12

Or

=SUM(C2,C3,C4,…,C12)

Neither of which is ideal – nor would it be practical if we had a list of hundreds of numbers to add up. Fortunately, Excel has an easy solution – rather than referring to an individual cell, we can refer to a **RANGE** of cells. We want to add the block of cells from C2 to C12, and would write that as **C2:C12** (the **:** indicating a range). Our **SUM** would be:

=SUM(C2:C12)

However, it is worth looking at how to enter this into a cell.

Direct cell entry

If you know the function required (as we do here), you can just type it in to the cell directly, as follows:

As you type, Excel will suggest possible functions. Note again the equals sign to start the function.

2	Ferdinand	£16.00		32	£512.00	£5
3	Total		=sum(			
4			SUM(**number1**, [number2], ...)			

Open a bracket to enter the arguments. Note that the required format for the function is shown – **number1** is highlighted in bold showing that Excel is expecting you to enter the first number here. This becomes especially useful with more complex functions, as it helps you work out which part of the function you are on.

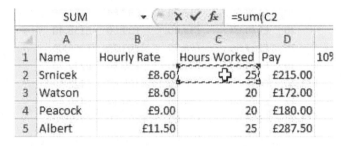

Left-click (and hold) on the first cell you wish to include. Note the formula is updated.

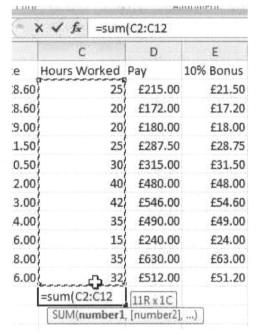

Drag the mouse down to the last cell you wish to include – the formula is automatically updated with the correct syntax. This saves you having to remember how to type the cell reference.

The box around the cells gives a visual display of the cells selected.

Release the mouse button to continue.

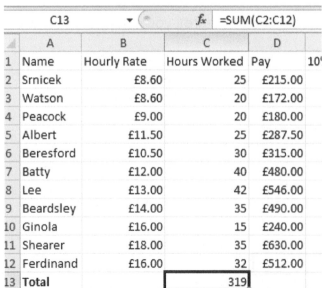

	A	B	C	D	
1	Name	Hourly Rate	Hours Worked	Pay	10
2	Srnicek	£8.60	25	£215.00	
3	Watson	£8.60	20	£172.00	
4	Peacock	£9.00	20	£180.00	
5	Albert	£11.50	25	£287.50	
6	Beresford	£10.50	30	£315.00	
7	Batty	£12.00	40	£480.00	
8	Lee	£13.00	42	£546.00	
9	Beardsley	£14.00	35	£490.00	
10	Ginola	£16.00	15	£240.00	
11	Shearer	£18.00	35	£630.00	
12	Ferdinand	£16.00	32	£512.00	
13	**Total**		319		

Close the bracket and press **Enter** to finish the formula. The correct answer will be shown.

Using Insert Function

Although **SUM** is relatively straightforward to use, it's worth seeing how using **Insert Function** gives a different way of entering formulae.

To enter the sum into cell D13, after selecting the **SUM** function from the **Insert Function** menu:

Number1 has already been populated with the required range – D2:D12. Clicking **OK** would give the required answer. You could also simply type in the numbers or range required into the Number1 box.

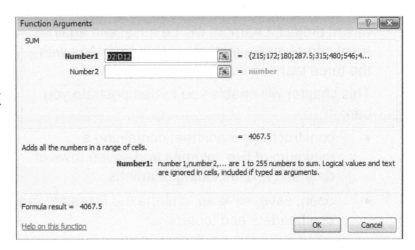

5.4 Autosum

Autosum is a useful shortcut to perform any of the above functions (and a few others) quickly and easily. The **Autosum** button can be found in the top right of the **Home** menu.

Instead of entering the function in the normal way, click in the destination cell and click the autosum button.

Excel will put in a SUM function, and guess at the cells required.

If these are incorrect, you can reselect the cells needed in the normal way.

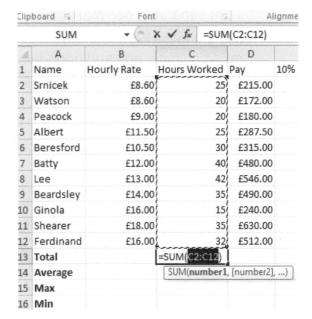

	A	B	C	D	
1	Name	Hourly Rate	Hours Worked	Pay	10%
2	Srnicek	£8.60	25	£215.00	
3	Watson	£8.60	20	£172.00	
4	Peacock	£9.00	20	£180.00	
5	Albert	£11.50	25	£287.50	
6	Beresford	£10.50	30	£315.00	
7	Batty	£12.00	40	£480.00	
8	Lee	£13.00	42	£546.00	
9	Beardsley	£14.00	35	£490.00	
10	Ginola	£16.00	15	£240.00	
11	Shearer	£18.00	35	£630.00	
12	Ferdinand	£16.00	32	£512.00	
13	Total		=SUM(C2:C12)		
14	Average		SUM(**number1**, [number2], ...)		
15	Max				
16	Min				

6 Level 1 assessment requirements

6.1 AAT assessment guidance

Assessment of the unit is through a computer based project. Learners will be assessed against a set grid of marks that rewards them in line with the three learning outcomes identified above.

This chapter will enable you to demonstrate you can:

- construct a spreadsheet containing a minimum of five columns and seven rows of data and text, including headings

- open, save, save as, change the filename, rename a worksheet and use headers and footers

- copy and paste data across different worksheets within the same workbook.

- add, edit, insert and/or delete data, columns and rows

- use the functions confidently to create the required output. These functions and formulas include sum, total, autosum, add, subtract, divide and multiply. Simple percentages may be tested by asking the learner to multiply an increase or decrease in percentage for example 10%, 0.10 or 110%.

- alter the following: font type, font colour, font size, bold, italics, underline, double underline, borders, shading, wrap text, currency, 1000 separator, decimal places, align text and figures

- use the following assumed skills: spell check, add delete rows/columns, edit and undo functions.

- select the most appropriate page layout (for example portrait or landscape), add a header or footer, date and time stamp and be able to change margins, print on one page or scale to fit on one page

- produce readable printouts as part of the assessment in order to be deemed competent.

You are further required to be able to identify, change and format charts and graphs, which will be covered in the following chapter. This includes using colour schemes or pattern fills to ensure discrete representations of data appear distinct from each other when printing in black and white, adding a title, axis titles, legends and scales to line charts or column charts, and add legends and percentages to pie charts, moving and resizing the chart and printing an isolated chart or graph.

Spreadsheet charts and graphs

Introduction

This chapter will guide you on how to create a number of different graphs and how to move and change these charts and graphs within the spreadsheet, therefore meeting the final assessment criteria referenced in the previous chapter. We will be looking at several types of charts and their construction, formatting and location.

In essence there is very little difference between a chart and a graph and the term is interchangeable.

KNOWLEDGE
2 Use appropriate formulas and tools to summarise spreadsheet information
3 Select and use appropriate tools and techniques to present spreadsheet information effectively

CONTENTS
1 Creating charts and graphs

1 Creating charts and graphs

1.1 Excel charts and graphs

Within Excel there are two basic ways to display charts and graphs. There is no right or wrong way, it is down to user preference. It is also a simple matter to switch between the two types.

1   **Chart Sheet** – here the chart or graph becomes the entire worksheet.

2   **Embedded** – here the chart or graph is located on the sheet that contains the data. The chart can be moved around to suit the user.

The easiest way to create a chart in Excel is to **Select** the **Data** you wish to chart, then go to the **Insert** tab, and select the **Chart** you wish to insert.

You can also highlight the data you want in your chart and **press F11**. Excel will create a default (column) chart on a chart sheet.

1.2 Types of charts and graphs

You need to be aware of the following types of graph:

*   Bar and Column charts.

*   Pie and Doughnut charts.

*   Single and double line graphs.

Bar and Column charts

Bar and column charts are used to display and compare the number, frequency or other measure for different discrete categories of data. They are one of the most commonly used types of graph because they are simple to create and very easy to interpret. They are also a flexible chart type and there are several variations of the standard bar chart including component bar charts, and compound bar charts.

Bar charts are useful for displaying data that are classified into categories.

Bar charts are also useful for displaying data that include categories with negative values, because it is possible to position the bars below and above the x-axis.

The chart is constructed such that the lengths of the different bars are proportional to the size of the category they represent. The x-axis represents the different categories and so has no scale. In order to emphasise the fact that the categories are discrete, a gap is left between the bars on the x-axis. The y-axis does have a scale and this indicates the units of measurement.

Single and double line graphs

Line charts are used to plot continuous data and are very useful for showing trends. The more **data series** there are the more lines you can have on your graph.

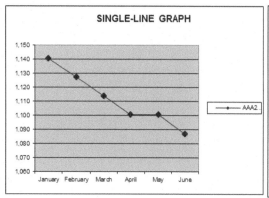

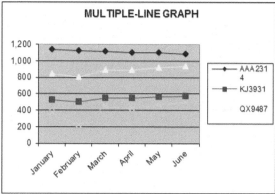

Multiple graph types on one chart

Also known as **Combination Charts** these charts must consist of at least two data series. With this chart type you can have either two graph types on **one** axis or insert a second **value** or 'Y' axis.

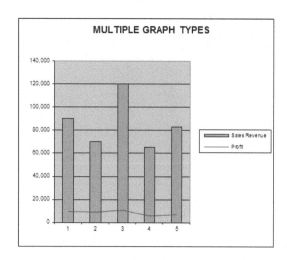

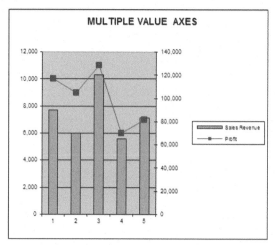

1.3 Creating a chart or graph

Select the data you wish to graph, and on the **Insert** tab, select the chart type you want.

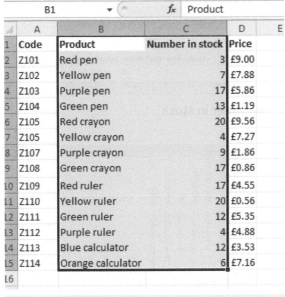

Select the data, then find the chart type you are after.

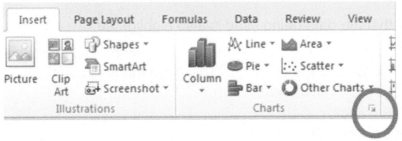

If you cannot see the chart you need, click the little arrow in the corner of the **Charts** menu, and all available charts will be shown.

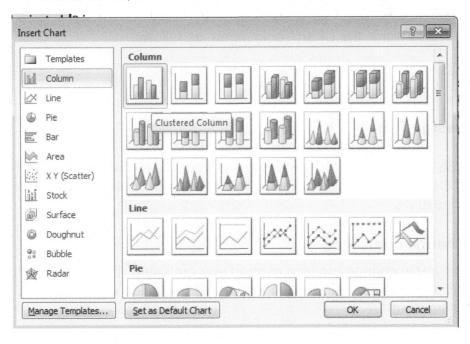

So, if you are asked for a **Clustered Column chart**, and do not know what it is – go into this menu and hover over the options to find what you need. Click **OK** once you have found what you need, and the chart will be shown.

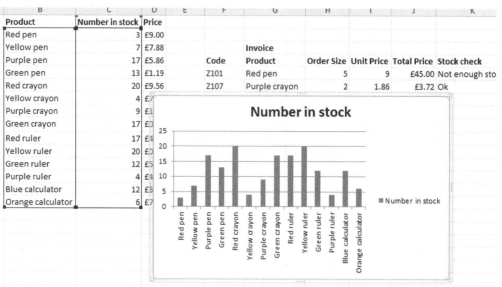

You can also see that the data being used is also highlighted.

As shown, creating a chart is not difficult – what may prove more difficult is getting it to look exactly how you want it to. There are many options available, and these will be dealt with in turn.

1.4 The chart tools tabs

When you create a chart, or have one selected, the chart tools tabs will become available on the Ribbon. These will allow you to change the features of your chart.

There are 3 tabs within the Chart Tools menu, as follows:

1.5 Design Tab

This is to do with the fundamental features of your chart – what sort of chart it is, the data used and where it is shown on your spreadsheet. The main options are:

1.6 Change chart type

This allows you to change the type of chart you are using. The menu showing all available charts is shown, and can be selected in the same way as a new chart.

1.7 Select data

This is a very important menu. It allows you to change the data being used, or add new **Series** (data sets) to the chart.

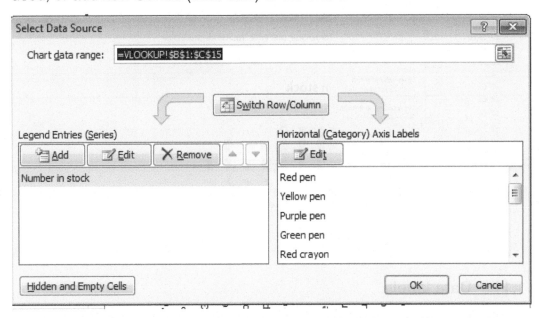

The data range, as shown here, is the original data that was selected to draw the graph. This can be edited if more data is added, or if you wish to add another set of data to the graph.

1.8 Move chart

This allows you to switch between an **embedded** chart and a **Chart Sheet**. Simply click on the **Move Chart** button to change the location of your chart.

1.9 Layout Tab

From the point of view of the SDST assessment, this is probably the most important menu. This is where you can change many of the key visual features of your chart, such as titles and legends.

1.10 Chart title, axis title and Legend

As the name suggests, this allows you to add or remove a main title for your chart (there are also options as to where and how the title is displayed), allows you to add or remove titles for both axes and add, remove or change the location of the Legend. The **Legend** is the 'key' which explains what the different colours or bars on the graph correspond to.

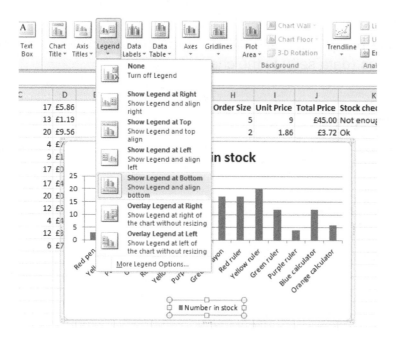

1.11 Data labels

These show the actual values of the data points on the graph. You can turn them on or off, as well as where they appear on the chart.

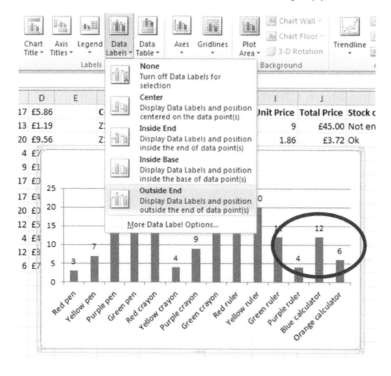

1.12 Data table

A data table shows the actual data points being used to make the chart – like data labels but shown beneath the chart. Use this option to add/remove a data table, with or without a legend (key). The example below shows a data table with a legend key.

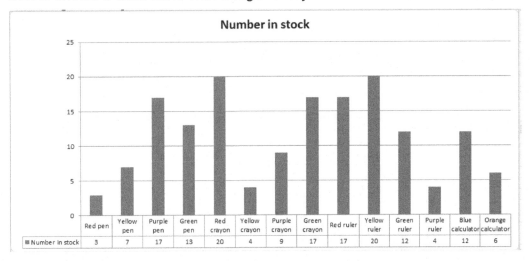

1.13 Format Tab

This tab allows you to change the format of any aspect of your graph – colours, thickness of lines and several other formatting options. Select (left-click on) the area of the graph you need to format and then select the option you need.

1.14 Adding another data set

More data series can be added if you want to show more information on your graph. This is done within the **Select Data** option. Click **Add** to add more data.

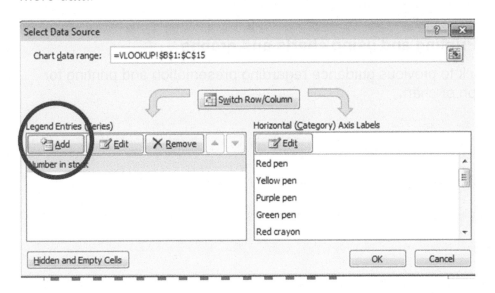

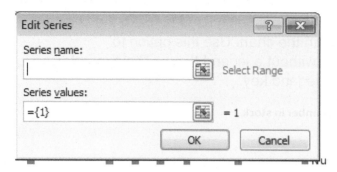

The **Series name** box allows you to select the name for your new data set – this can either be a cell reference or typed value.

The **Series values** represent the actual data points, which can also be selected.

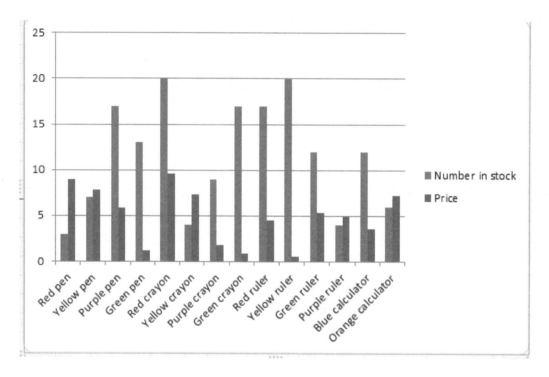

The new data series is shown on the graph.

1.15 Printing and using charts and graphs

Refer back to previous guidance regarding presentation and printing for your graph or chart.

Mock Assessment – Access Award in Accounting

Introduction

The following is a Mock Assessment to be attempted in exam conditions.

You should attempt and aim to complete EVERY task.

Read every task carefully to make sure you understand what is required.

Where the date is relevant, it is given in the task.

Both minus signs and brackets can be used to indicate negative numbers UNLESS task instructions say otherwise.

You must use a full stop to indicate a decimal point.

The assessment is in two sections, the first includes 12 tasks and the second includes 10 tasks.

Time allowed: 90 minutes

1 Mock Assessment Questions

Section 1

Task 1

Organisations have assets, liabilities, income and expenditure.

a) Which of the following statements describes an liability? Place a tick in the appropriate box.

Statement	✓
A liability is something an organisation owns.	
A liability is something an organisation owes.	
A liability is something an organisation earns.	

b) Place a tick in the appropriate column of the table below to show whether each of the items listed is an example of an asset, a liability, income or expenditure.

You should not place more than one tick against each item.

Item	Asset	Liability	Income	Expenditure
Cash sales				
Rent				
Office computers				

Task 2

It is important to understand the terminology used when buying and selling goods for cash and on credit.

Insert an item from the following pick list into the right hand column of the table below to identify the term described. You will not need to use all of the items.

Description	Term described
A person or organisation who is owed money by the company for purchases made.	
A transaction to sell goods when the payment is made one month later.	

Pick list

- A cash sale
- A cash purchase
- A credit sales
- A credit purchase
- A debtor
- A creditor

Task 3

Your organisation purchased 12 packs of printer cartridges at £28.65 per box from MG Stationers.

a)   What is the total cost of the printer paper?

Answer: £ [   ]

MG Stationers have asked for immediate payment.

b)   Is the purchase of the printer paper a cash transaction or a credit transaction?

Tick the correct answer below.

Type of transaction	✓
Cash transaction	
Credit transaction	

Task 4

Organisations issue and receive different documents when buying and selling goods.

Complete the sentences below by inserting the most appropriate option from the following pick list:

- a purchase order
- a receipt
- an invoice
- a statement of account
- a remittance advice
- a credit note

a)   An organisation sends _____ listing items returned to the customer and showing the amount refunded.

b)   An organisation sends _____ to a supplier listing the items it wishes to purchase.

c)   An organisation sends _____ to a supplier along with the payment with details of the transaction included in the payment.

Task 5

You work for Kelly Trading. You are preparing to record some documents in the books of prime entry.

a) Select which ONE of the documents below will be entered in the sales day book.

Document	✓
An invoice sent by a supplier	
A credit note sent by a supplier	
An invoice sent to a customer	

b) Select which ONE of the documents below will be entered in the cash receipts book.

Document	✓
A cheque payments listing	
A cheque received from a customer	
A remittance advice sent to a supplier	

c) Insert an item from the following list into the bottom right hand box of each document to show which book of prime entry that documents will be entered into. You will not need to use all of the items.

Pick list

- Cash payments book
- Cash receipts book
- Purchases day book
- Sales day book
- Sales returns day book
- Purchases returns day book

Kelly Trading		
15 Monmouth Road, Dowton, DT7 9PP		
VAT Registration No. 217 8621 00		
Invoice No. 3897		
To: Lois Tupman 24 High Street, Dowton, TL4 7GD		17 July 20XX
		£
6 lawnmowers @ £410.00 each		2,460.00
VAT @ 20%		492.00
Total		2,952.00
	Book of prime entry:	
Terms: 30 days net		

Doherty & CO **24 High Street, Upton, PE7 4GD** **VAT Registration No. 456 7421 00**	
Credit note No. 49	
To: Kelly Trading 15 Monmouth Road, Dowton, DT7 9PP	24 July 20XX
	£
10 litres of fertilizer @ £5.99 each	59.90
VAT @ 20%	11.98
Total	71.88
Book of prime entry:	
Terms: 30 days net	

Kelly Trading **Cash from customers listing**	
30 July 20XX	
	£
J Shepley & Co	190.00
WB Products	28.90
Total	218.90
Book of prime entry:	

Task 6

Some organisations use coding within the accounting records.

Show whether the following statement is true or false.

Statement	True	False
In an alphanumerical coding system all codes consist of numbers.		

Task 7

Your organisation uses a batch processing system to enter purchases invoices into the accounting records.

Show whether the following statement is true or false.

Statement	True	False
In a batch processing system, it is more likely that errors will not be discovered.		

Task 8

On 24 July 20XX you have been asked to pay the following items into Lewis Ltd's bank account:

- One × £20 notes
- Ten × £10 notes
- Four × £2 coins
- Eight × 5p coins
- One × cheque for £389.50

a) Complete the paying-in slip below:

Date:	**City Bank plc Redport**	£50 notes	
		£20 notes	
		£10 notes	
	Account: Bond Ltd	£5 notes	
		£2 coin	
		£1 coin	
	Paid in by: AAT student	Other coin	
		Total cash	
	30-45-22 10678465	Cheques, POs	
		Total £	

b) Show whether the following statement is true or false.

Statement	True	False
Paying-in slips are a record for the organisation paying in money only.		

Task 9

It is important to ensure cheques sent to suppliers are completed properly.

On 10 July 20XX you are preparing a cheque for £590.40 to send to a supplier, Uddin Electrics.

a)   Which ONE of the following options shows the date as it should be written on the cheque? Tick the correct answer.

Option	✓
10 July	
10 July 20XX	
July 20XX	

b)   Which ONE of the following options shows the payee as it should be written on the cheque? Tick the correct answer.

Option	✓
Mr Uddin	
Uddin Electrics	
Uddin Electrics Organisation	

c)   Which ONE of the following options shows the amount in words as it should be written on the cheque? Tick the correct answer.

Option	✓
Five hundred and ninety pounds and forty pence	
Fifty nine pounds and forty pence	
Nine pounds fifty and forty pence	

d)   Show whether the following statement is true or false.

Statement	True	False
If the amount in words on a cheque is different from the amount in figures the cheque is incorrect.		

Task 10

At the end of every year your organisation calculates the profit or loss for the year.

a) Complete the sentence below by selecting the most appropriate option from the following list:

- equals
- is more than
- is less than

When income _____ expenditure this results in a loss.

Last year your organisation recorded income and expenditure as shown in the table below:

Income and expenditure	£
Sales	192,000
Cost of sales	115,200
Premises expenses	25,920
Heat and light	23,040
Administration and wages	15,808

b) Use the income and expenditure figures to complete the following calculations:

Gross profit £ [   ]

Net profit £ [   ]

c) Use your answer above to calculate gross profit as a percentage of sales. If it is appropriate make sure you give your answer to 2 decimal places.

[   ] %

Task 11

An organisation is reviewing the selling price of some of its products.

The current selling price of product number 689 is £56.00. This is to be increased by 9%.

a) Calculate the increase in selling price for product number 256

Answer: £ [   ]

The current selling price of product number 74 is £208.00. This is to be increased by 1/8 (one eighth).

b) Calculate the increase in selling price for product number 74

Answer: £ [ ]

Task 12

Your organisation keeps detailed records of expenses.

Motor fuel expenses for each of four delivery vehicles are shown in the table below.

a) Complete the table to show the motor fuel expense for Vehicle 1.

Delivery vehicles	Motor fuel expense £
Vehicle 1	
Vehicle 2	241.12
Vehicle 3	221.90
Vehicle 4	259.58
Total	**974.20**

b) Calculate the average motor fuel expense per vehicle.

Answer: £ [ ]

Expenses relating to items of stationery are shown in the table below.

c) Complete the table to show the total stationery expense.

Items	Expense £
Ink cartridges	125.00
Printer paper	119.50
Envelopes	76.80
Pens	53.70
Total	

d) Which of the following is the ratio of the total expense for stationery items to the expense for ink tanks? Tick the correct answer.

Ratio	✓
2:1	
3:1	
4:1	

Section 2

Task 13

There are different types of organisation.

a) Complete the following sentence by selecting the most appropriate option from the list of items below each sentence.

An animal welfare organisation is a _____ organisation.

Pick list

- private sector
- public sector
- charitable

b) Show whether this statement is true or false.

Statement	True	False
The primary aim of an organisation in the private sector is to make a profit.		

Task 14

It is important to understand the role of the accounting department within an organisation.

Show whether the following statements are true or false.

Statement	True	False
Information provided by the accounting department is used by external customers only.		
An example of an internal customer of the accounting department is a close friend of one of the managers of the organisation.		

Task 15

You work for Kazee Krafts and have been asked to send an email to Jude Irving, your manager, to confirm that you have arranged for staff to attend a departmental meeting on 12 July at 9am. You should point out that one member of staff, Janette Bones will not be able to attend as she has a hospital appointment on that day.

Using the items at the bottom of the page, compose an appropriate e-mail in the template below. You will not need to use all of the items.

From:	AATstudent@kazeekrafts.com	
To:		
Subject:		

I am letting you know that most people will be attending the meeting.	Departmental Meeting: Confirmation of attendance	Please accept this email as confirmation that staff have been informed of the departmental meeting at 9am on 12 July. Only one member of staff, Janette Bones, will not be able to attend due to a hospital appointment.	
AAT student	Attendance	Hi Jude	janettebones@kazeekrafts.com
Cheers	Hello Jude	Kind regards,	judeirving@kazeekrafts.com

Task 16

Organisations communicate using different styles and formats.

a)   Show whether the following statements are true or false.

Statement	True	False
Templates are standard documents which do not need to be amended in any way.		
Organisations use a "house style" for documents because it promotes a consistent image		

You have been asked to send to an analysis of the organisation's business to the bank manager.

b)   Select the most appropriate form of communication to accompany the price list.

Option	✓
Letter	
Memo	
Report	

Task 17

It is important to observe confidentiality.

a)   Show whether the following statements are true or false.

Statement	True	False
Information about staff wages should not be held on the computer because it is confidential information.		

b)   Complete the following sentence by selecting the most appropriate option from the pick list below.

The addresses of all staff should be accessible to _____

Pick list

all staff

accounts department staff only

authorised staff only

Task 18

Finance professionals and organisations have a duty to behave in a professional and socially responsible manner.

Complete each sentence in the following table by inserting the most appropriate option from the pick list below. You will not need to use all of the options.

Sentence	Option from pick list
Qualified accounts professionals...	
Behaving professionally means...	
An organisation should adopt socially responsible practices because...	
An example of a socially responsible policy is to ...	

Pick list

- ... do not need to complete any further training.
- ... they should complete sufficient training to maintain professional competence.
- ... acting ethically and being open and honest.
- ... all organisations have a duty to society to behave ethically.
- ... buy paper in bulk.
- ... recycle waste paper.
- ... should continue with further training.

Task 19

Organisations should observe health and safety guidelines.

a) Complete this sentence by choosing the most appropriate option from those provided in bold below.

An organisation should provide a safe environment for [**staff only / visitors only / staff and visitors**].

b) Show whether the following statements are true or false.

Statement	True	False
An employee should deal with all safety hazards themselves immediately.		
A tidy desk will give the impression that you are an organised and professional employee.		

Task 20

It is important to understand the skills and attributes needed by a finance professional.

a)   Complete the sentence by inserting the most appropriate option from the pick list into the boxes provided.

A finance professional should have [   ] and be

[   ] .

Pick list

good artistic skills	good literacy and numeracy skills	careless
organised	no interest in non-financial matters	aggressive

b)   Show whether the following statements are true or false.

Statement	True	False
A finance professional can only acquire knowledge by attending a training course.		
It is important for somebody who is currently training to be a finance professional to meet regularly with their manager to set relevant targets.		

Task 21

It is important to work effectively.

a)   Answer the following questions by selecting the most appropriate option.

It is Thursday and your colleague has just received a report which he doesn't think he will be able to finish before the deadline of Friday afternoon.   You are on schedule with your tasks.

Which ONE of the following actions should you take?

Option	✓
Agree on condition that your colleague buys you a present for helping him.	
Agree to help out after checking that you understand the task and can help to complete it effectively.	
Refuse and tell your colleague that it is nothing to do with you.	

Planning is very important to help you meet your deadlines.

b)   Which ONE of the following documents below is a planning aid?

Document	✓
Organisational guidelines	
Statement of account	
Work schedule	

It is important to use an appropriate form of communication at all times.

c)   Link the description to the appropriate form of communication by drawing a line from each left hand box to the appropriate right hand box.

| An analysis of the financial position of the organisation which is to be presented to the shareholders at the annual general meeting. |

Letter

| A written form of communication that one employee sends to one or more other employees within the same organisation. |

Report

E-mail

| A written form of communication sent to a customer agreeing an increase in their credit terms. |

Task 22

- You work for Evans Motors Ltd
- You have been asked to write a letter to a customer, Geoffrey Holden, at KL Carparts, Lytham Avenue, Marston. ML6 3EP.
- You are to return a cheque received this morning, 18 July 20XX.
- The cheque is in payment of invoice 789 for £585.00
- The words and numbers on the cheque did not match and will have to be returned for a new one to be issued.
- You have a good relationship with KL Carparts who always pay on time.

Using the items below, compose an appropriate letter. You will not need to use all of the items.

18 July 20XX	AAT student Accounts Assistant	Dear Sir
G Holden KL Carparts, Lytham Avenue, Marston. ML6 3EP	Dear Geoffrey	Did you have a nice week-end?
Cheque for £585.00 for invoice 789	Yours faithfully,	Yours sincerely,
You got the cheque wrong and we need another one immediately.	Unfortunately the numbers and the words on the cheque did not match and therefore we would ask that you send a new cheque as soon as possible.	Many thanks for your cheque which we received this morning in payment of invoice 789.
Many thanks for your cooperation.	We received a cheque from you.	KL Carparts Lytham

Answer:

Mock Assessment – Bookkeeping and Accounts

Introduction

The following is a Mock Assessment to be attempted in exam conditions.

You should attempt and aim to complete EVERY task.

Read every task carefully to make sure you understand what is required.

Where the date is relevant, it is given in the task.

Both minus signs and brackets can be used to indicate negative numbers UNLESS task instructions say otherwise.

You must use a full stop to indicate a decimal point.

Time allowed: 2 hours

1 Mock Assessment Questions

Task 1

There are main differences between the roles of bookkeepers and accountants within an organisation.

a) Which of the following statements regarding the differences in these roles are True and which are False? Tick the correct answer.

Statement	True	False
A bookkeeper will be dealing with day to day transactions		
An accountant will be concentrating on the overall financial information		
A bookkeeper, with study and hard work can achieve the role of the accountant		
The bookkeeper position is a job with no career prospects		

b) Show whether the tasks below would be carried out by an accountant or by a bookkeeper in a large organisation.

Link the task with the appropriate job role by drawing a line between the two.

Task	Job role
Authorising a loan to buy a new piece of machinery	
	Bookkeeper
Performing the bank reconciliation	
Reviewing the cash position of the organisation	
	Accountant
Printing off a sales credit note	

KAPLAN PUBLISHING

c) Which of the following is a numerical code? Tick the correct box(es).

Code	Numerical code?
SMITH	
12LG5	
HAGE	
15796	
ALL01	

d) Below is statement about batch control. Is it True or False?

Statement	True	False
Batch control does not save time as items, like sales invoices, are recorded as and when received.		

Task 2

Goods were received by ZDT Ltd on 13 May in accordance with purchase order below.

ZDT Ltd was given a 15% trade discount and a 2% settlement discount for payment within five days.

ZDT Ltd
22 New Ash
Grandy GD1 2PX

Purchase Order No 6866

Be Goods Ltd
179 Alter Way
Darchester
DD17 9LL   13 May 20X5

Please supply 10 boxes of product P21 at £15.00 per box.

---

a) Complete the invoice to be sent to ZDT Ltd by:

- Entering the correct details in the first three columns
- Entering the correct invoice amounts to the final three columns
- Entering the amount of trade discount at the bottom of the invoice

Be Goods Ltd
179 Alter Way
Darchester DD17 9LL

To: ZDT Ltd
178 New Ash
Grandy   13 May 20X5
GD1 2PX   Purchase Order No 6866

SALES INVOICE 256

Quantity of units	Product code	Price per unit £	Total amount after discount	VAT £	Total £

Terms of payment 2% discount for payment within seven days:

This invoice includes a trade discount of: %.

It is important that sales invoices are carefully checked for accuracy before being sent to customers.

b)   Check the sales invoice and identify TWO errors from the list below.

Error	✔
Customer name and address	
Date of invoice	
Purchase order number	
Terms of payment	

ZDT Ltd sent a purchase order to the supplier and after the goods were delivered the supplier sent ZDT Ltd an invoice.

c)   What will be the next action on the part of **ZDT Ltd**?

Action	✔
Send a credit note	
Send Statement of account	
Send a cheque	
Send a bank statement	

Task 3

Three sales credit notes have been partially entered into the sales returns day book.

GGD Ltd	
117 Vinefield Place	
Warminster	
Kent WA1 1BB	
Credit Note 552	**Date:1 June 20XX**
	£
250 products GUP @ £2.00	500.00
VAT @ 20%	100.00
Gross amount refunded	600.00
Terms: Net monthly account	

Day Associates	
2 London Road	
Becksley	
Kent BE7 9MN	
Credit Note 35	**Date:10 June 20XX**
	£
24 products Y12 @ £5.75	138.00
VAT @ 20%	27.60
Gross amount refunded	165.60
Terms: Net monthly account	

Cohen PLC	
25 Main Road	
Rexsome	
Herefordshire HR2 6PS	
Credit Note 1168	**Date:23 June 20XX**
	£
80 products Y12 @ £7.10	568.00
VAT @ 20%	113.60
Gross amount refunded	681.60
Terms: Net monthly account	

Complete the entries in the sales returns day book by inserting the credit note number and the gross, VAT and net amounts for each credit note.

Sales returns day book

Date 20XX	Details	Credit note number	Total £	VAT £	Net £
1 June	GGD Ltd				
10 June	Day Associates				
23 June	Cohen PLC				

Task 4

These are the totals from a sales day book for one month

Date 20XX	Details	Invoice number	Total £	VAT £	Net £
	Totals		2,118.72	353.12	1,765.60

a) What will be the entries in the general ledger? Enter the account name from the list below, enter the amount and tick either debit or credit.

General ledger

Account name	Amount	Debit ✓	Credit ✓

Pick list

Sales	Sales returns	Sales ledger control account
Purchases	Purchase returns	VAT

One of the sales invoices in the sales day book was from L Helps for £72.00 plus VAT of £14.40.

b) What will be the entries in the sales ledger?

Account name	Amount	Debit ✓	Credit ✓

Task 5

The petty cash book below is a book of prime entry, and part of the double entry bookkeeping system.

The imprest amount is £150 and is restored at the beginning of every month. There are two petty cash vouchers to be entered into the petty cash book.

PETTY CASH VOUCHER	
29 June 20XX	**No 521**
	£
Window cleaner	20.00
VAT not applicable	————
Gross amount refunded	20.00

PETTY CASH VOUCHER	
30 June 20XX	**No 522**
	£
Fuel for delivery van	19.20
VAT	3.84
Gross amount refunded	23.04

a) Enter the above transactions into the partially completed petty cash book below.

b) Total the petty cash book and show the balance carried down.

Petty cash book

Details	Amount £	Details	Amount £	VAT £	Motor expenses £	Sundry expenses £
Balance b/d	150.00	Motor fuel	24.00	4.00	20.00	
		Motor oil	23.88	3.98	19.90	
		Window cleaner				
		Motor fuel				
		Balance c/d				

It is important to cross check the totals in the petty cash book to ensure accuracy.

c) Complete the following sentence by removing (putting a line through) one of the highlighted word(s):

When the total expenditure column is subtracted from the balance b/d figure the resulting amount **should/should not** be equal to the amount of money in the petty cash box.

The total of the analysis columns in the petty cash book will be transferred to the general ledger.

d) Will the petty cash expenses be recorded on the debit or credit side of the accounts in the general ledger?

	✓
Debit	
Credit	

At the start of the next month cash was withdrawn from the bank to restore the imprest amount.

e) What was the amount of cash withdrawn from the bank to restore the imprest amount?

Answer: £ [   ]

Task 6

When an organisation receives a bank statement, it is used to update the cashbook.

Referring to the bank statement and the cashbook below:

a) Check the items on the bank statement against the items in the cashbook

b) Enter the ONE lodgement from a credit customer that is in the bank statement but not in the cashbook

c) Enter the ONE cash purchase of £150 plus VAT of £30 that is in the bank statement but not in the cashbook.

d) Total and balance the cashbook

Bank statement

Date 20XX	Details	Paid out £	Paid in £	Balance £
01 Jun	Balance b/d			5,168
03 Jun	Counter credit – R Brown		250	5,418
9 June	Counter credit – A Bate		425	5,843
13 Jun	Cheque – Trafalgar plc	120		5,723
14 Jun	Cheque – P Tuller	138		5,585
19 Jun	Counter credit – R Brown		300	5,885
20 Jun	Cheque – Printer Palace	400		5,485
21 Jun	Cheque - English Electrics	180		5,305
26 Jun	Counter credit – C Beamer		175	5,480
27 Jun	Counter credit – R Giggs		180	5,660

Cash book

Details	Bank	VAT	Cash sales	Sales ledger	Details	Bank	VAT	Cash purchases	Purchase ledger
Balance b/d	5,168				Trafalgar plc	120	20	100	
R Brown	250			250	P Tuller	138	23	115	
A Bate	425	70	355		Printer Palace	400			400
R Brown	300			300	English Electrics				
R Giggs	180	30	150		Balance c/d				
C Beamer									
Totals					Totals				

Task 7

These are the totals from the credit side of the cash book for one month. The cash book is a book of prime entry and part of the double entry bookkeeping system.

There was no opening bank balance at the start of the month.

Cash book – credit side

Details	Bank £	VAT £	Purchase ledger £	Cash purchases £
Totals	14,225	225	6,755	7,245

a) What will be the THREE entries in the general ledger?

Account name	Amount £	Debit ✓	Credit ✓

One of the cash payments was to a credit supplier   BKL Ltd, for £4,876.

b) What will be the entry in the purchase ledger?

Purchase ledger

Account name	Amount £	Debit ✓	Credit ✓

Task 8

It is important to regularly reconcile the bank statement with the cashbook. Returning to the cash book and the bank statement below:

a) Identify the TWO outstanding lodgements that are included in the cashbook but missing from the bank statement.

b) Identify the one unpresented cheque that is included in the cash book but missing from the bank statement.

c) Complete the bank reconciliation statement, do NOT use minus signs or brackets to show negative amounts.

d) Calculate the balance of the cash book and ensure it matches the balance as per cash book you have calculated in the bank reconciliation statement. Do NOT make any entries in the cash book.

Cash book

Date	Details	Bank £	Date	Cheque number	Details	Bank £
01 Aug	Balance b/d	5,776	01 Aug	027651	Franley Ltd	350
05 Aug	M Geyzers	2,150	02 Aug	027652	Moonley Ltd	667
20 Aug	Adison plc	765	03 Aug	027653	English Electrics	1,475
21 Aug	Diamond plc	190	16 Aug	027654	Shore Interiors	3,380
25 Aug	Avril Trading	810	18 Aug	027655	Waterson plc	665
26 Aug	Railing Associates	667	22 Aug	027656	Planters Products	450
26 Aug	Barry Cord	448				

Bank statement

Date	Details	Paid out £	Paid in £	Balance
01 Aug	Balance b/d			5,776
05 Aug	Cheque 027651	350		5,426
08 Aug	Cheque 027653	1,475		3,951
10 Aug	Counter credit – M Geyzers		2,150	6,101
10 Aug	Cheque 027652	667		5,434
20 Aug	Cheque 027654	3,380		2,054
25 Aug	Counter credit – Diamond plc		190	2,244
28 Aug	Counter credit – Avril Trading		810	3,054
29 Aug	Cheque 027656	450		2,604
31 Aug	Counter credit – Barry Cord		448	3,052

Bank reconciliation statement

Balance as per bank statement	£
Add:	
	£
	£
Total to add	£
Less:	
	£
Total to subtract	£
Balance as per cash book	£

Task 9

The following account is in the purchase ledger at the close of day on 31 August:

Billy Buster

Date 20XX	Details	Amount £	Date 20XX	Details	Amount £
03 Aug	Credit note 57	383	01 Aug	Balance b/d	2,556
04 Aug	Bank	209	25 Aug	Purchase invoice 1558	393
27 Aug	Credit note 59	530	28 Aug	Purchase invoice 1582	779
			29 Aug	Purchase invoice 1601	980

a) What will be the balance brought down on 01 September?

Amount £	Debit ✓	Credit ✓

The following account is in the general ledger at the close of day on 31 August.

b) Insert the balance carried down at 31 August together with date and details.

c) Insert the totals.

d) Insert the balance brought down at 1 September together with date and details.

Cash

Date 20XX	Details	Amount £	Date 20XX	Details	Amount £
01 Aug	Balance b/d	1,050	02 Aug	Bank	750
17 Aug	Sales	543	24 Aug	Bank	382

Task 10

Below is a list of balances to be transferred to the trial balance.

Place the figures in the debit or credit columns, as appropriate, and total each column.

Account name	Amount £	Debit £	Credit £
Capital	4,922		
Cash at bank	5,655		
General expenses	1,765		
Petty cash	50		
Purchases	4,334		
Purchase ledger control	1,880		
Sales	7,870		
Sales ledger control	3,326		
Purchase returns	324		
VAT (owing to HM Revenue & Customs)	782		
Totals			

Task 11

Small organisations may use a single entry bookkeeping system to record accounting transactions, while larger organisations will use the double entry system.

a)   Complete the sentences below by circling the correct words

When a double entry bookkeeping system is used **one entry/two entries** will be used per transaction.

A **day book/spreadsheet** may be the record of transactions.

The advantage of keeping records in the double entry bookkeeping system is that the records are **complete/incomplete** but the disadvantage is that it can be **time consuming/quick**.

b)   Show the meaning of each of the accounting terms below by drawing a line between the left hand box and the appropriate right hand box.

Accounting Terms	Meaning
Cash sales	The purchase of goods with payment within an agreed period of time
Cash purchases	A group of contacts from who purchases are made.
Customers	A group of contacts to whom goods are sold.
Suppliers	The purchase of goods with immediate payment.
Credit sales	The sale of goods with immediate effect.
Credit purchases	The sales of goods with payment in an agreed period of time.

Task 12

a) Show the percentage amount for each of the VAT rates by drawing a line between the left hand box and the appropriate right hand box.

VAT rate		%
Zero		5%
Standard rate		0%
Reduced rate		20%

Some organisations have to be VAT registered

b) Choose the correct option below to state when organisations have to register for VAT.

	✓
When the taxable turnover of the business reaches a certain amount	
When the organisation produces their 100th invoice.	

c) What type of business would each of the organisations below be most likely to trade as?

Tick the correct box to give the best description for each.

Organisation	Sole Trader	Partnership	Public limited company
A plumber			
Shop owned by two sisters			
A bus company			
Large business trading in many different areas			

Task 13

It is important to understand accounting terms

a)   Are the following statements true or false? Tick the appropriate box.

Statement	True	False
When a business pays the electricity bill the payment is known as expenditure.		
When a business receives revenue from sales the receipt is known as expenditure		
When a supplier receives a cheque from a customer the supplier will call it a payment		
When a customer sends a cheque to a supplier the customer will call it a payment		

It is important to understand the need for authorisation

b)   State whether the following statements regarding authorisation are True or False.

Statement	True	False
Before a cheque is issued for the purchase of goods it should be authorised by the sales manager		
Before a sales credit note is sent to a customer it should be authorised by the accountant		

Security of confidential information is the responsibility of all who work in the accounting role.

c)   Show whether the following actions should be allowed or not allowed.

Action	Allowed	NOT allowed
Give the company accountant details of amounts owed to suppliers		
Give suppliers details of other supplier's confidential information		
Give customers details of the amounts owed by other customers		
Give HM Revenue and Customers details of payments due to them		

Mock Assessment – Computerised Accounts

Introduction

The following is a Mock Assessment to be attempted in exam conditions.

You should attempt and aim to complete EVERY task.

Read every task carefully to make sure you understand what is required.

Where the date is relevant, it is given in the task.

Both minus signs and brackets can be used to indicate negative numbers UNLESS task instructions say otherwise.

You must use a full stop to indicate a decimal point.

Time allowed: 90 minutes.

Background information

This practice assessment is based on a new business, O'Mara Crafts, an organisation that sells craft kits in a retail shop and online. The owner of the business is Miranda O'Mara who operates as a sole trader.

At the start of the business Miranda operated a manual bookkeeping system but has now decided that from 1 May 20XX the accounting system will become computerised.

You are employed as an accounts assistant.

You can assume that all transactions have been checked for accuracy and authorised by Miranda O'Mara.

Cash and credit sales are to be analysed in two ways:

- Shop sales
- Online sales

Some nominal ledger accounts have already been allocated account codes. You may need to amend or create other account codes.

The business is registered for VAT. The rate of VAT charged on all goods sold by O'Mara Crafts is 20%.

All expenditure should be analysed as you feel appropriate.

Before you start the assessment you should:

- Set the system software date as 31 May of the current year
- Set the financial year to start on 1 May of the current year.
- Set up the company details by entering the name AF computers.

1 Mock Assessment Questions

Task 1

Refer to the list of nominal ledger accounts below.

a) Set up nominal ledger records for each account, entering opening balances at 1 May 20XX and making sure you select, amend or create appropriate nominal ledger account codes.

b) Generate a trial balance, check the accuracy of the trial balance and, if necessary, correct any errors. You do not need to print the trial balance.

List of nominal ledger accounts as at **1 May 20XX**:

Account Name	Debit Balance £	Credit Balance £
Bank current account	535.04	
Cash account	201.60	
VAT on sales		295.49
VAT on purchases	306.05	
Capital from owner		800.00
Shop sales		1135.36
Online sales		342.08
Purchases – goods for re-sale	1,530.24	

Task 2

Refer to the customer listing below.

Set up customer records to open sales ledger accounts for each customer at **1 May 20XX**. There are no opening balances to enter.

Customer name and address	Customer account code	Payment terms
Shepley Crafts 728 Church Street Richmond RC2 9ST	SHE001	30 days
Kazee Korner Faraday Way Orpington OP6 8LY	KAZ001	30 days

Task 3

Refer to the supplier listing below.

Set up customer records to open purchases ledger accounts for each supplier at **1 May 20XX**. There are no opening balances to enter.

Supplier name and address	Supplier account code	Payment terms
Tupman Trading 728 Oulton Close Springhill SP8 4HG	TUP001	30 days
Clancy Cards Wellington Road Middleham MD6 4LY	CLA001	30 days

Task 4

Refer to the e-mail below.

Enter this transaction into the computer.

Email
From: Miranda O'Mara **To:** Accounts assistant **Date:** 2 May 20XX **Subject:** Capital introduced
Hello I have today paid £6,400 from my personal funds into the business bank account. Please record this transaction as capital introduced into the business. VAT is not applicable. Thanks, *Miranda*

Task 5

Refer to the sales invoices provided below.

a) Calculate batch totals and record them on the batch control sheet below.

b) Enter these transactions into the computer, making sure that the computer generated batch totals agree with the totals you calculated in part (a). If the totals do not agree, check your work and make the necessary corrections.

Sales Invoices

O'Mara Crafts

58 Main Street	VAT Registration No
Mossley, MS7 8DT	623 8976 31
INVOICE NO 2010	**Date: 04 May 20XX**

Shepley Crafts
728 Church Street
Richmond
RC2 9ST

	£
Shop sales	750.00
VAT @ 20%	150.00
Gross amount for payment	900.00

Terms 30 days

O'Mara Crafts

58 Main Street	VAT Registration No
Mossley, MS7 8DT	623 8976 31
INVOICE NO 2011	**Date: 13 May 20XX**

Kazee Korner
Faraday Way
Orpington
OP6 8LY

	£
Online sales	965.85
VAT @ 20%	193.17
Gross amount for payment	1159.02

Terms 30 days

O'Mara Crafts

58 Main Street	VAT Registration No
Mossley, MS7 8DT	623 8976 31
INVOICE NO 2012	**Date: 19 May 20XX**

Shepley Crafts
728 Church Street
Richmond
RC2 9ST

	£
Shop sales	227.00
VAT @ 20%	45.40
Gross amount for payment	272.40

Terms 30 days

Batch control sheet

Sales invoice batch totals at 31 May 20XX	Total net amounts £	Total VAT amounts £	Total gross amounts £
Totals			

Task 6

Refer to the following purchases invoices, purchases credit note and batch control sheets.

Enter these transactions into the computer, making sure that the computer generated batch totals agree with the totals shown on the batch control sheets. If the totals do not agree, check you work and make the necessary corrections.

Purchases Invoices

Tupman Trading
728 Oulton Close, Springhill, SP8 4HG
VAT Registration No 521 7856 03

INVOICE NO Z895	**Date: 10 May 20XX**
O'Mara Crafts	
58 Main Street,	
Mossley,	
MS7 8DT	
	£
Goods	1,260.00
VAT @ 20%	252.00
Gross amount for payment	1,512.00
Terms 30 days	

Clancy Cards
Wellington Road
Middleham
MD6 4LY

INVOICE NO 9785	**Date: 18 May 20XX**
Clancy Cards	
Wellington Road	
Middleham	
MD6 4LY	
	£
Office stationery	133.60
VAT @ 20%	26.72
Gross amount for payment	160.32
Terms 30 days	

Batch control sheet

Purchases invoice batch totals at 31 May 20XX	Total net amounts £	Total VAT amounts £	Total gross amounts £
Totals			

Purchases Credit Notes

Tupman Trading
728 Oulton Close, Springhill, SP8 4HG
Vat Registration NO 521 7856 03

Credit Note C42   **Date:15 May 20XX**

O'Mara Crafts
58 Main Street,
Mossley,
MS7 8DT

	£
Goods returned.	225.70
VAT @ 20%	45.14
Gross amount refunded	270.84

Batch Control Sheet

Purchases credit notes batch totals at 31 May 20XX	Total net amounts £	Total VAT amounts £	Total gross amounts £
Totals			

Task 7

Refer to the following receipts from customers listing.

a)   Enter these transactions into the computer, making sure that you allocate all amounts correctly as shown in the details column.

Receipts from customers listing:

Date 20XX	Receipt type	Customer	Amount £	Details
20 May	Cheque	Shepley Crafts	900.00	Payment of invoice 2010
26 May	BACS	Kazee Korner	1,159.02	Payment of invoice 2011

Refer to the following payments to suppliers listing.

b)   Enter this transaction into the computer, making sure that you allocate all amounts correctly as shown in the details column.

Date 20XX	Cheque no	Supplier	Amount £	Details
20 May	000568	Tupman Trading	1,241.16	Payment of invoice Z985 including credit note C42

Task 8

Refer to the following cash receipts listing below.

a)   Enter this transaction into the computer.

Date 20XX	Payment method	Details	Amount £
10 May	Cash	Shop sales	144.40 plus VAT

Refer to the following cash payments listing below.

b)   Enter these transactions into the computer.

Date 20XX	Payment method	Details	Amount £
12 May	Cheque	Rent	190.00 – VAT not applicable
25 May	Cash	Refreshments	28.50 plus VAT

Task 9

Print the following reports:

- Customer details list, showing customer names, addresses and account codes

- Sales ledger accounts (customer accounts) showing all transactions within each account

- Supplier details list, showing supplier names, addresses and account codes

- Purchases ledger accounts (supplier accounts) showing all transactions within each account

- Trial balance at 31 May 20XX

- All active nominal ledger accounts showing all transactions within each account.

Please note the accounting package you are using may not use exactly the same report names as those shown above, so some alternative names are shown in brackets.

Before you finish your work:

a)   **Back up your work** to a suitable storage medium and create a screen shot of the back-up screen showing the location of your back up data

b)   Make sure that you have entered the total figures you calculated on to the batch control sheet in Task Five.

c)   Complete the checklist in the assessment platform to make sure that you have printed all reports as specified in Task Nine.

Mock Assessment - Computerised Payroll and Payroll Processing

Introduction

The following is a Mock Assessment to be attempted in exam conditions.

You should attempt and aim to complete EVERY task.

Read every task carefully to make sure you understand what is required.

Where the date is relevant, it is given in the task.

Both minus signs and brackets can be used to indicate negative numbers UNLESS task instructions say otherwise.

You must use a full stop to indicate a decimal point.

Time allowed: 2 hours.

Background Information

This assessment is based on a new business, The Starkiller Ranch.

The Starkiller Ranch has been set up by the owner, Gareth Greenshoot. This company sells grain products harvested from their fields.

You work in the payroll department of the company accountants and are to produce the weekly payroll for the business.

The company employs the following staff:

- Roger Kota – Farm Manager
- Amanda Sturn - Farmhand
- Juliet Eclipse – Farm Supervisor

Although each employee has a designated role within the company, everyone is expected to get involved in all areas of the business.

The business operates out of a farm which also has a shop attached. The shop is open Sunday – Saturday 0900 – 1730 each day and sells the products the farm produces.

Overtime is paid at time-and-a-half for any hours over 37 hours per week.

Payroll is run weekly, and is paid on a Friday in arrears by BACS. This is the first payroll run for the new financial year and, in line with company policy, you are required to check that the new tax year legislative data is correct.

To enable you to set up the new system, you have been provided with the following information from Gareth.

1 Mock Assessment Questions

Task 1

a) Refer to the information below and set up the payroll software with the following basic information for your company

Company name	The Starkiller Ranch
Address:	Plot 9, The Tatty Inn Arkansas Devon EX7 5PH
Telephone:	0207 8286463
Email:	G.Marek@tattyinnranch.co.uk
Tax Office:	Shipley
Tax Dist./Ref:	101/D01138
Bank Details	Devon Bank PLC
Address:	23 Main Street Exeter Devon EX1 10GH
Account Name:	The Starkiller Ranch
Account Number:	04673748
Sort Code:	17-10-12

b) Print the company details report which shows the company address and bank details

Task 2

Set up the following pay elements for the company:

a) Basic Hourly Rate
b) Overtime Rate
c) Holiday Pay

Task 3

a) Open the Legislation screen and check the Government parameters are as follows:

- Tax year 2015/16
- Emergency Tax Code 1060L

b) Having checked the Government parameters, correct any errors

PAYE

Tax Bandwidths

Bandwidth £	From £	To £	Rate %	Basic Rate band
31,785.00	0.01	31,785.00	20.00	Yes
118,215.00	31,785.01	150,000.00	40.00	No
Excess	150,000.01	Excess	45.00	No

NI BANDS AND RATES

Earnings Bands

Earnings Limit	Weekly £	Monthly £	Yearly £
Lower Earnings Limit	112.00	486.00	5824.00
Primary Threshold	155.00	672.00	8060.00
Upper Accrual Point	770.00	3337.00	40040.00
Upper Earnings Limit	815.00	3532.00	42385.00

Rates – A Standard rate contributions

Weekly Earnings £	Monthly Earnings £	Yearly Earnings £	Employer rate £	Employee rate £
112.01 – 155.00	486.01 – 672.00	5824.01 – 8060.00	0.00	0.00
155.01 – 156.00	672.01 – 676.00	8060.01 – 8112.00	0.00	12.00
156.01 – 770.00	676.01 – 3337.00	8112.01 – 40040.00	13.80	12.00
770.01 – 815.00	3337.01 – 3532.00	40040.01 – 42385.00	13.80	12.00
815.01 and over	3532.01 and over	42385.01 and over	13.80	2.00

Rates – C Employer only Contributions

Weekly Earnings £	Monthly Earnings £	Yearly Earnings £	Employer rate £	Employee rate £
112.01 – 155.00	486.01 – 672.00	5824.01 – 8060.00	0.00	0.00
155.01 – 156.00	672.01 – 676.00	8060.01 – 8112.00	0.00	0.00
156.01 – 770.00	676.01 – 3337.00	8112.0 – 40040.00	13.80	0.00
770.01 – 815.00	3337.01 – 3532.00	40040.01 – 42385.00	13.80	0.00
815.01 and over	3532.01 and over	42385.01 and over	13.80	0.00

Note: If your software asks for a Secondary Threshold, use the same figures as for the Primary Threshold.

c) Print the following reports
- Tax Bandwidths and rates
- NI rates report, showing as a minimum the annual bands and rates for NIC's

Task 4

Refer to the following information below and set up employee records for each new employee. No employee has been identified as having deductions other than PAYE and NI. All employees are category A for National Insurance, and are paid weekly be BACS.

All employees have provided a starting declaration A.

Print a report showing the personal details of all employees.

Employee ref no, name and DOB	Address	Start Date	Rate of pay – per hour	Job title, NINO and tax codes	Bank Account Details
1. Mr Roger Kota Single DOB: 15/08/1965	62 Corusca Way Exeter Devon EX4 4SX	06/04/15	£16.50	Farm Manager NINO: JE 26 46 86 D NI Letter: A Tax Code: 1060L	Name: R Kota No: 46825179 Sort Code: 28-48-62
2. Miss Juliet Eclipse Single DOB: 12/02/1963	48 Coral Lee Road Exeter Devon EX5 3JY	06/04/15	£14	Farm Supervisor NINO: CR 48 97 85 B NI Letter: A Tax Code: 1060L	Name: J Eclipse No: 24789224 Sort Code: 47-65-89
3. Mrs Amanda Sturn Married DOB: 03/03/1980	21 Great Tree Road Exeter Devon EX5 7NJ	06/04/15	£13	Farmhand NINO: HE 23 54 41 D NI Letter: A Tax Code: 1060L	Name: A Sturn No: 87235198 Sort Code: 47-63-32

Task 5

a) Juliet has informed you that she has recently moved address. Change her contact details to:

50 Old Ram Road
Exeter
Devon
EX2 3DD

b) You have received a Tax Code Notice (P9), changing Amanda's tax code to 1005L with immediate effect. Process the change

c) Roger is to take two days holiday pay this week. Holiday pay is paid at 7.5 hours per day taken at basic rate. Holiday pay MUST be shown as a separate pay element. Using the information below, process Rogers pay for period 1.

Roger Kota	Sun	Mon	Tue	Wed	Thu	Fri	Sat	Basic Hrs	O'time Hrs
Week 1	Holiday	Holiday	0	0	7.5	7.5	7		

Task 6

a) You have been informed that Amanda is leaving the company, and that Saturday of week 1 is her final day. Process the payroll for week 1 for the remaining employees. Overtime is paid for any hours over 37 hours per week.

Juliet Eclipse	Sun	Mon	Tue	Wed	Thu	Fri	Sat	Basic Hrs	O'time Hrs
Week 1	0	0	7.5	7.5	7.5	7	7.5		
Amanda Sturn	Sun	Mon	Tue	Wed	Thu	Fri	Sat	Basic Hrs	O'time Hrs
Week 1	10	7	6	7	0	0	10		

b) Print reports showing the following:

- Print a payslip for each employee which also shows employee's address
- Print a Payment Summary which shows Employers National Insurance

Task 7

a) Update your records and process Amanda as a leave

- Process Amanda's P45/Leaver's Statement, or P11 for PAYE and NICs if P45 option is not available in software

- Print a screenshot showing the current status of your employees

Task 8

a) Back up your data to a suitable location as directed by your training provider

b) Print a screenshot showing the screen from which you would restore a backup if required. The screenshot MUST show the date and time of the last backup taken.

Task 9

Payroll data should be accurately produced and staff should adhere to company and legislative policy.

a) Select the most likely outcome for each scenario. Tick ONE box for each scenario.

Scenario	HMRC will issue a fine or warning	The payroll may be delayed or inaccurate	Neither consequence
PAYE and NIC payments are always 5 days after the FPS sent			
Staff bonuses declared one month later than expected			
Timesheets destroyed by fire			

b) When a new employee joins your organisation, you must get specific information from them in order to input their details onto the payroll software.

Select TWO documents where this information can be found.

Item	✔
FPS	
Driving license	
Starter Checklist	
Utility bill	
P45	

c) Choose THREE items of information that are included on the FPS

Item	✔
Employer bank account details	
Date of employee leaving	
Dates of employee's summer holidays	
All payments and deductions made to each employee	
Accounts Office reference number	
Which part of the payroll office the employee occupies	

Task 10.1

a) You have been approached by a bank requesting information about one of your employees who is considering a mortgage to buy a house.

Select the ONE most appropriate answer from the choices below.

Options	✓
Release the information as requested	
Request a copy of the authorisation form that the employee would have signed giving permission for release of the information	
Ignore it	

b)   Who would be the most appropriate person within a large organisation to authorise employee bonuses?

Options	✓
Employee	
Managing Director	
Photocopy clerk	

Task 10.2

a)   Select the ONE correct answer to complete the following statement:

If you, (an employee) are paid one month in arrears, and are new to the organisation, this means:

At the end of the 1st month you get 1st month's pay At the end of the 2nd month you get 2nd month's pay At the end of the 3rd month you get 3rd month's pay At the end of the 4th month you get 4th month's pay	
At the end of the 1st month you get no pay At the end of the 2nd month you get 1st month's pay At the end of the 3rd month you get 2nd month's pay At the end of the 4th month you get 3rd month's pay	

b)   Payroll processing must be accurately produced within the given time frame. Identify the payment deadline for the following payment.

If you pay PAYE tax/Class 1 NICs by BACS, your payment must reach HMRC no later than:

	✓
5th of the month following the end of the tax month or quarter to which it relates.	
6th of the month following the end of the tax month or quarter to which it relates.	
19th of the month following the end of the tax month or quarter to which it relates.	
22nd of the month following the end of the tax month or quarter to which it relates.	

Task 10.3

a)   When should you send the information from a Starter Checklist to HMRC?

Options	✓
With the next payroll run	
It doesn't really matter	

b)   How would new employee information be sent to HMRC?

Options	✓
By post	
On (FPS) Full Payment Submission	

Task 10.4

It is important to make backup copies of data.

a)   Complete the sentence below by selecting your answer from the options available.

Restoring data from a backup is done when data has been [restored / lost / current].

Task 10.5

An employee from The Bouncing Ball Company, has requested that his pay be paid by cash. This request has been approved by the Payroll Manager.

a)   You are to request from the bank the amount needed, **ensuring the smallest number notes and coins are given**. No £50 notes are to be requested. Enter the number of notes or coins needed, and total the amount to check for accuracy.

Net pay	£328.66
Gross pay	£400.00
Income tax	£38.25
National insurance	£33.09

Complete the following:

Denominations	No	£	Denominations	No	£
£20 notes			20p		
£10 notes			10p		
£5 notes			5p		
£2			2p		
£1			1p		
50p					

Mock Assessment – Spreadsheet software

Introduction

You have 1 hour 45 minutes plus 15 minutes of reading time to complete this assessment.

In the assessment you will be given extra time if necessary to allow for possible delays such as printer queries and uploading documents.

There are 16 tasks in this assessment and it is important that you attempt all tasks.

1   Mock Assessment Questions

Task 1

Open a blank worksheet Save this file in an appropriate location and rename it as follows: 'your initial_surname_AAT no_dd.mm.yy_CS'.

Create a footer on the worksheet(s) that you use with your name, AAT number and the date.

Task 2

Simply Pretty sells a range of ethnic knitwear.

After a review with your supervisor it has been decided that you will be able to assist the payroll team with their data entry. Your supervisor has suggested that you start by inputting hours worked by the sales team into a spreadsheet. This will be used to calculate the staff bonuses for week 24 of the payroll year.

Open a blank worksheet and in cells A1, B1 and C1 enter the following column headings respectively: Name, Sales target, Sales actual.

Task 3

a) Fill in the spreadsheet using the data displayed below and the column headings you have already entered as part of Task 2. Identify only the relevant data and then input into the appropriate rows and columns.

b) Rename the worksheet **'SP Week 24'.**

Name	Postcode	Sales target	Sales actual
Wind	SW11 5ND	19	28
Sokoloff	SW11 5NS	32	42
Meadows	SE11 2PQ	37	38
Major	SW1 7MN	20	30
Kassam	SW9 3DZ	41	41
Smith	SW8 8LL	44	80
O'Leary	SE20 2DW	48	50

Task 4

a) In the next blank column (column D), use formulas to multiply the amount of sales made in pounds (£) by £25 per item

b) Give column D the title **'Total sales £'.**

Task 5

a) Use a formula to total columns labelled sales target, sales actual and Total sales £ columns.

b) Insert a column between columns B and C and name it Sales target £.

c) Use a formula to calculate the sales target in pounds (£)

d) Use the spell check tool to identify and correct any spelling errors in the worksheet. (Assume that employee names have been spelt correctly.)

Task 6

In the next blank column (column F)

a) Input the heading 'Difference between target and actual sales'

b) Use formulas to subtract the 'Sales actual' in column C from the 'Sales target' in column E

c) Use a formula to total the column

Task 7

In the next blank column (column G)

a) Input the heading '**weekly wage**'.

b) Use formulas to multiply the Sales actual in Column D by the rate of £5.

c) Use a formula to total the column.

Task 8

When Simply Pretty weekly sales reach a certain amount, the management awards their staff a bonus of 25% of their weekly wages.

a) In the next blank column (column H) enter the heading '**Bonus payable**'.

b) Use formulas to multiply the weekly wage figures in column G and multiply by 25% to calculate the bonus payable in column H.

c) Total the Bonus Payable column using a formula.

Task 9

Ensure that the cells containing text are left aligned and cells containing figures are right aligned.

Task 10

Ensure that all data is in Arial font, size 12. Format all figures in columns Weekly Wage and Bonus Payable columns (columns G and H) to show pounds (£) to two decimal places

Task 11

Make changes to the worksheet as follows:

a) Format the text of all column headings with a blue font colour, italics, underlining and a font size of 14.

b) Ensure that all figures and headings are visible by adjusting column widths and heights as necessary. Use wrap text where appropriate.

Task 12

a) Apply a yellow fill and double underlining to all column total cells.

b) Format all data within the column total cells with bold and italics.

Task 13

a) Insert a row above all of the data

b) Enter the heading '**Simply Pretty Week 24 Sales Staff Wages**' into cell A1

c) Change the font type to Verdana and font size 16

d) Format the heading text to be in italics and underlined

Task 14

a) Ensure that the footer contains the following information: '**your name, AAT number and the date**'

b) Add a time stamp to the worksheet within the footer and make sure it is readable

c) Print this worksheet ensuring that the page orientation is landscape and that all data fit onto one page by altering margins or by scaling to fit. Make sure the whole worksheet is readable and ensure that the content of every cell is visible.

Task 15

Your manager has asked you to produce a column chart showing the amount of bonuses to be paid out in week 24 for each member of staff by name.

Create the column chart and ensure that you do the following:

a) Add data labels

b) Add the chart title '**Simply Pretty Week 24 Sales Staff Bonuses**'

c) Add axis labels

d) Move the chart below the data, so that the top border of the chart area sits on row 13

e) Resize the chart so that the chart area stretches from column A to column H

f) Use a blue pattern to fill the data series (Choose any pattern style you wish)

Task 16

a) Create a footer on your chart containing the following information:
'**your name, AAT number and the date**'

b) Print only the chart using portrait page orientation, ensuring it fits on one page by making adjustments to the margin size if appropriate.

Mock Assessment Answers

The answers to the Mock Assessments featured in this Study Text have not been included to enable more testing assessment-style conditions for students.

To access the answers, please either ask your tutor or contact Kaplan Publishing using the following e-mail address: publishing@kaplan.co.uk

KAPLAN PUBLISHING

INDEX

KAPLAN PUBLISHING